JAMES GLEN

JAMES GLEN

From Scottish Provost to
Royal Governor of South Carolina

W. Stitt Robinson

Contributions in American History, Number 165
Jon L. Wakelyn, Series Editor

GREENWOOD PRESS
Westport, Connecticut • London

Library of Congress Cataloging-in-Publication Data

Robinson, Walter Stitt.
    James Glen : from Scottish provost to Royal Governor of South
Carolina / W. Stitt Robinson.
        p.   cm.—(Contributions in American history, ISSN 0084–9219
; 165)
    Includes bibliographical references (p.   ) and index.
    ISBN 0–313–29760–6 (alk. paper)
    1. Glen, James, 1701–1777. 2. Governors—South Carolina—
Biography. 3. South Carolina—History—Colonial period, ca.
1600–1775. I. Title. II. Series.
F272.G55R63   1996
975.7′02′092—dc20
    [B]   95–501

British Library Cataloguing in Publication Data is available.

Library of Congress Catalog Card Number: 95–501
ISBN: 0–313–29760–6
ISSN: 0084–9219

First published in 1996

Greenwood Press, 88 Post Road West, Westport, CT 06881
An imprint of Greenwood Publishing Group, Inc.

Printed in the United States of America

The paper used in this book complies with the
Permanent Paper Standard issued by the National
Information Standards Organization (Z39.48–1984).

10 9 8 7 6 5 4 3 2 1

For Barry, Robert, Walter, Linda, and Trevor

Contents

Photo essay follows page 68.

Preface

This is a study of James Glen, who was appointed royal governor of Colonial South Carolina in 1738 and came to the colony in 1743 to serve until 1756, the longest tenure of any governor during its colonial period. Educated in law at the University of Leiden (Leyden) in the Netherlands, he followed the tradition of his family in becoming the provost of his native Linlithgow, a Scottish burgh on the road between Edinburgh and Sterling. He was the recipient of several other royal appointments in addition to the governorship: keeper of the royal palace of the Stuarts (Stewarts) in Linlithgow where Mary, Queen of Scots, was born and where James VI of Scotland (later James I of England) resided part of the time; keeper of the castle of Blackness; watchman of the salt duty at the port of Bo'ness (Borrowstounness); and inspector for Scotland of seizures of prohibited and uncustomed goods.

Little has been published on the life of Glen, and no previous discussion of his career has placed his early Scottish experience in perspective or his significant familial relationships with John Drayton and his kin. My study of the southern colonial frontier and an earlier research paper on the role of Governor Glen in frontier policies as they related to Colonial Virginia and Governor Robert Dinwiddie revealed the importance of his experience. I have now completed extensive research in Scotland, England, South Carolina, Ann Arbor, Michigan, and other depositories in the United States to conclude this project.

A study of Governor Glen is long overdue. This point was emphasized by M. Eugene Sirmans in the preface to his volume *Colonial South Carolina: A Political History, 1663-1763* (1966). He stated, "In particular, we need a comprehensive analysis of the membership and power structure of the assembly and biographical studies of the leading politicians, notably Governor James Glen" (p. xii). In addition to the need for a discussion of his role as governor, there are several glaring errors that should be corrected, such as the identification of Glen as a Scottish High Sheriff, the description of him as never married, the denial of his status as the eldest son and major heir of his father, and a statement that he died in office in the mid-1750s. This study also corrects some of Sirmans' statements and revises some of his interpretations based on careless use of Glen's correspondence.

The organization of this biography is a thematic one in a chronological framework. Two subjects in particular demand a thematic approach. First, ethnohistorical information for Indian affairs provides a broader perspective for this subject, and the continuing controversy over the Choctaw revolt and Governor Glen needs discussion beyond the actual date of the efforts to win this tribe over to the English. Second, the governor's extraordinary efforts to respond to imperial inquiries transcend the perennial conflicts among governor, Council, and Commons House and deserve examination as a unit in Chapter 5 without reference to the day-to-day activities of the Assembly.

Two major themes are evident in the study of Glen's administration as governor. First, like other royal governors both before and after his time, he had to struggle to protect the royal prerogative and follow the dictates of his commission and his 110 instructions in the face of the persistent challenge from the Assembly for more power over colonial affairs, particularly the Commons House. Second, Governor Glen's role in Indian affairs was a critical one and dominated much of his time and energy. South Carolina was in the most strategic position for Indian trade and diplomacy on the southern colonial frontier; and Glen, unlike a number of governors, had both a keen interest in and a significant aptitude for Indian negotiations. This second theme adds an important dimension to the study of the colonial experience in the British Empire.

Since the British did not adopt the Gregorian reforms of the calendar until 1752, part of Governor Glen's term falls under the Julian calendar. It has, therefore, been necessary to distinguish between Old Style and New Style. The day of the month from original sources has been retained as Old Style, but the date of the year has been changed to reflect New Style, with the New Year beginning on January 1 rather than March 25. No attempt has been made to calculate the changes resulting from the dropping out of eleven days in the transition to the Gregorian calendar by the British.

One other procedural matter should be mentioned. In the original documents there is confusion in money designations. Three currencies were circulating in Colonial South Carolina: British pound sterling, proclamation money, and colonial currency. Proclamation money was valued at the rate of five-to-one for colonial currency, while colonial currency circulated at seven-to-one for sterling. The mark for British sterling, £, is sometimes used for colonial currency without appropriate identification. In an effort at clarification, I have used the £ sign only for British sterling and described other currencies either as proclamation money or colonial currency.

For assistance in providing valuable research materials for this biography, I express my thanks to the staffs of the following institutions in the United States: South Carolina Department of Archives and History in Columbia with special help from Dr. Charles Lesser; South Caroliniana Library of the University of

South Carolina in Columbia with special assistance from Dr. Allen H. Stokes; South Carolina Historical Society in Charleston; Manuscript Division of the Library of Congress in Washington, D.C.; William L. Clements Library, Ann Arbor, Michigan; North Carolina Department of Archives and History, Raleigh; Libraries of the University of North Carolina, Chapel Hill; and Libraries of the University of Kansas, Lawrence. I also appreciate the excellent cooperation of depositories in Scotland and England. In Edinburgh, the Public Record Office of Scotland made available the Dalhousie Muniments about Glen and other documents. References to these records and quotations from them are made with the approval of the Keeper of the Records of Scotland and of Lord Dalhousie. The staff of two other Edinburgh libraries provided additional assistance: National Library of Scotland and University of Edinburgh Library. In London, the British Public Record Office both on Chancery Lane and opposite Kew Gardens provided valuable documents as did the British Museum.

I express my personal thanks to Lord and Lady Dalhousie for hosting my wife and me at their private castle in Brechin to view the portrait of Governor Glen and for permission to reproduce the portrait as well as use the Dalhousie Muniments in the Public Record Office of Scotland.

For financial assistance I express my gratitude for research grants from the American Philosophical Society and the General Research Fund of the University of Kansas, which also awarded sabbatical leaves. Appointment as a Fellow at the Institute for Advanced Studies in the Humanities at the University of Edinburgh in 1983 also assisted my research.

A special word of appreciation to others. To Professor Lynn H. Nelson of the Department of History of the University of Kansas for assistance in translating Latin documents; to the staff of Greenwood Press of the Greenwood Publishing Group with excellent help from Dan Eades as Acquisitions Editor and Liz Leiba as Senior Production Editor; to Paula Courtney and Pam LeRow of the College Word Processing Center of the University of Kansas for their persistent cooperation; and to my wife, Connie, for her assistance in research and proofreading, and for her consistent loving support.

Introduction: The Nature
and Challenges of Biography

The main body of biography still clings to individuality, still seeks to know how one man or woman lived and worked in his or her time, how one life may have influenced many.

Frank E. Vandiver, 1983

The term *biography* has been used loosely, as is evident from scanning the card or microfiche catalogues of libraries. One may find biographies of the earth, the sea, the gods, or a river. There are biographies of a family, a baby, or even of the unborn. Still others focus on economic institutions such as a business, a bank, a foundation, or a labor union. Educational institutions include the story of a high school or a college, while governmental concerns provide a biography of the Constitution. More esoteric challenges come with the biography of an idea, a song, a painting, or biography as theology. One 1799 publication suggests moral guidance in *Biography for Girls; or, Moral and Instructive Examples for Young Ladies*.[1] Even more unusual are the biographies of bulls for Spanish bullfighters, a grizzly bear, or even a buzzard. The concern in this study, however, is with the more traditional and more direct emphasis of biography on human life.

Where does this study of Governor Glen fall in the diverse pattern of emphases for individual lives? Over the years biography has had a prominent role in literary and historical scholarship, even though challenged in recent times by various forms of literary criticism. Before identifying some of the current attitudes toward biography as they relate to this volume, let me briefly review the nature of life-writing over past centuries, with emphasis on developments that have been most influential in English and American biography. From the self-glorification characteristic of much of early Egyptian and Babylonian writing, the Greeks gave greater emphasis to accounts of individuals as measured by ideal behavior and with attention to maturity, sometimes sacrificing accuracy in order to conform to accepted traditions of the ideal form of biography. The spread of Greek culture to the Roman world combined to influence the most outstanding figure in biography in the Ancient World, Plutarch. He has been described as "one of the greatest biographers of all time."[2] Writing in the first and second centuries A.D., he presented his studies in pairs—a Greek and a Roman—with comparisons that gave greater attention to character than career. Consequently, his biographies did not always provide a chronology of historical value. He did exemplify a new point of view in striving to give a balanced account of his subjects based on substantial research. He also stressed his characters in action with skillful use of anecdotes and was extraordinarily successful in sustaining the interest of his readers. Two other contributors to biography in the Ancient World should be included. First, Gaius Suetonius Tranquillus was noted for his *Lives of the Caesars*, including records of their scandals, and for his larger work, *On Illustrious Men*, both studies revealing vivid accounts of his subjects. Suetonius, however, has often been dismissed as primarily a "mere compiler."[3] Next, a more superior biography came from Cornelius Tacitus of his father-in-law entitled *On the Life and the Character of Gnaeus Julius Agricola*, a work that benefited from the author's personal knowledge of his subject.

From the experiences of the Ancient World, we can identify three principal modes of life-writing that have continued to the present time. One may be designated professional biography, exercising the talent and intellectual curiosity of authors such as Plutarch and Suetonius. Next, we perceive biography resulting from the personal knowledge and relationship between the writer and subject as in the case of Tacitus and his father-in-law. Third, there developed life-writing to cater to the requirements of the time as functional biography or, as one writer has termed it, "demand-biography." Emerging from the emperors' desire for self-glorification, this mode became dominant with the growth of Christianity, from the time of Augustine through the Middle Ages, with the laudation of Christian saints and martyrs.[4] Eventually, however, the spotlight passed from "Saints to Sinners." This study of Governor Glen obviously follows the first mode of professional biography.

The Renaissance with its emphasis on humanism and curiosity about human behavior in the fifteenth century failed to produce major works of biography that shaped the course of development in the field. By the sixteenth century in England, there did appear in 1535 the intimate biography by William Roper of his father-in-law, Sir Thomas More, based in part on the author's personal knowledge of the subject.[5] George Cavendish also contributed an important work in the account of another religious figure in the *Life of Cardinal Wolsey*.

It was not until the eighteenth century that biography reached maturity with James Boswell's *Life of Samuel Johnson*. While Johnson himself made significant contributions in his vigorous search for truth and understanding and in his interest in studying not just the elite but all individuals, it is Boswell's account of Johnson that has set the model for biographies in achieving the epitome of centuries of development. Boswell strove to present a faithful delineation of his subject and benefited by his personal acquaintance with Dr. Johnson. In effect, as one writer notes, he "helped to *live* the biography he was ultimately to write."[6] He did give greatest attention to the twenty-one years of the period after he met Johnson, who was then age fifty-four. His work, nonetheless, exemplifies many characteristics of the best biographic method. One scholar concludes: "Boswell's biography always keeps with admirable tenacity to the fundamental purpose of transmitting personality. . . . All the meticulous detail makes for a unity on which Plutarch could hardly improve."[7]

Boswell had the advantage of personal knowledge of his subject, yet this has sometimes been a "mixed blessing."[8] Although personal knowledge does provide valuable insights about character and personality, biographers of living subjects have on occasion found it difficult, if not impossible, to get unbiased reactions from the persons being interviewed. Individuals want accounts of their lives to reflect them in the best light possible and in positive terms. In efforts to cut through the defensive barrier of the interviewee, biographers may well find themselves in an adversarial position with their subject. On the other hand, such a cordial and personal relationship may develop between the writer and his subject that efforts to achieve scholarly objectivity are seriously hampered. Governor Glen was always interested in having a positive evaluation, as is evident in his correspondence, but conclusions about him must be based on written records.

Nineteenth-century trends produced no significant new methodological innovations in life-writing. Romanticism, however, did add interest and possibly an enhancement of the quality of writing with its emphasis on intuition, emotions, freedom, and individualism. Thomas Carlyle in his *Heroes and Hero-Worship* provided that well-known enthusiastic endorsement of life-writing when he stated that "The History of the world is but the Biography of great men."[9] Ralph Waldo Emerson, with whom Carlyle corresponded frequently, echoed these sentiments in his statement that "there is properly no history; only biography."[10] Walt Whitman, however, expressed less confidence in the effectiveness of this genre in his *Leaves of Grass*:

> When I read the book, the biography famous,
> And is this then (said I) what the author calls a man's life?
> And so will some one when I am dead and gone write my life?
> (As if any man really knew aught of my life,
> Why even I myself I often think know little or nothing of my real life,
> Only a few hints, a few diffused faint clews and indirections
> I seek for my own use to trace out here.)[11]

Three English writers in the twentieth century added their caveats to having their own biography written: George Orwell, T. S. Eliot, and W. H. Auden. Orwell stated his objections in the last sentence of his will. Eliot appended a note to his will stating that "I do not wish my executors to facilitate or countenance the writing of a biography of me." Auden requested his executors to express his desire that recipients of his letters destroy them in order to "make a biography impossible."[12] Glen's will, as later examined, had no specific reference or restriction on such a study.

The second half of the nineteenth century witnessed the increasing importance of science, which has been characterized in intellectual history as the naturalistic mind. The assault of determinism in science in the form of Darwinian evolution and Marxist economic materialism challenged the emphasis on biography and the role of the individual. This scientific emphasis was also evident in the ideas of Sigmund Freud in psychology and psychoanalysis and the inclination of the social sciences to search for "laws" of behavior and to identify general social patterns of the group rather than particularize as in biography. Freud even denounced with acid pen the efforts in life-writing: "Anyone who writes a biography is committed to lies, concealments, hypocrisy, flattery and even to hiding his own lack of understanding, for biographical truth does not exist, and if it did we could not use it."[13] Fortunately, such negative assessments have not prevailed in the world of scholarship. The influence of science, however, has continued into the twentieth century.

In biography, the influence of psychology contributed to the advent of the so-called New Biography highlighted by the publication of Lytton Strachey's *Eminent Victorians* in 1917 and his subsequent *Life of Queen Victoria*. Breaking away from the emphasis of the scientific ideal in scholarship on objective facts and documentation, Strachey presented an iconoclastic view of the once proud Victorians. He stressed the search for character without, however, resorting to the extremes of the imaginative creations of the "fictionized biographer." This trend on the American side encouraged debunkers such as W. E. Woodward in the 1920s.[14] Strachey added his own personal unique contribution, described by one scholar as "his devilish wit, his mastery of irony and innuendo, his epigrammatic style."[15] Scientific influences led one writer to add that the "contemporary biographer must be critic, historian, cultural observer, intellectual arbiter, psychiatrist, physician and minister."[16]

The term *New* has also been applied in literature: the *New Criticism* has minimized, if not excluded, the use of biography in the study of literary works. One of the basic assumptions of the *New Critics* was that the text contained everything necessary for its interpretation. Consequently, biographical inform-ation about the author was unnecessary because his or her background, motives, or intentions were not relevant to an interpretation of the written work.

More recent trends in literary criticism have to some extent continued this challenge to the role of biography. While devotees of deconstruction differ on the importance of knowledge about the author,[17] some writers influenced by semiotics, poststructuralism,[18] and postmodernism[19] continue to diminish or exclude the importance of biography. Other literary scholars urge the "mingling of biography and criticism."[20]

It should be noted that there is a difference between a literary subject and an historical one such as this biography of Governor Glen. Noting that the two start from different premises, one scholar demonstrates the contrasts:

With the literary subject, we are thrown immediately into psychological analyses and interpretations, for the chief consideration if we attempt to blend subject and work is internal, analytical. With the non-literary figure, the historical-political-social axes are so compelling that backgrounds, cultural developments, cause and effect help pre-empt stress on individual psychological development: not eliminate it, but dilute its ultimate significance.[21]

Biographical narrators on either literary or historical subjects may be identified in three types in relation to the story and the methodology of discourse. Ira Nadel has described them "as the dramatic/expressive, the objective/academic and the interpretative/analytic." James Boswell is an example of the first with emphasis on participation; John Gibson Lockhart exemplifies the second with emphasis on detachment for the objective narrator; and Lytton Strachey or the more recent Leslie Marchand is an example of the third with greater attention to analysis.[22] The biography in this study relates most closely to the second type, the objective/academic.

Leon Edel, identified as "a master practitioner" for literary subjects, has suggested the characteristics of an ideal biographer that may also apply to historical studies. The biographer is one who

writes a story of the progress of a life; he must allow himself to feel its failures, its obstacles overcome, its human ambiguities, its fallibilities, and the drama of personality and temperament. If he's a good biographer, he knows how to select and use significant detail. He can't allow himself to be too much the critic, lest his critiques of the work impede the march of the story. A critical biography is a contradiction in terms. . . . The beauty of what a biographer does resides in his insights: we discern the complexities of being, without pretending that life's riddles have been answered.[23]

One additional consideration about approaches to biography is in order. Although there has been increasing attention to life-writing by psychobiography, it is not my intention to complete a psychoanalytic study of Governor James Glen. Some of the essential details of personal life, including early childhood, are missing. Furthermore, I have reservations about the effectiveness of some of the efforts in psychobiography. One writer summarized six principal difficulties inherent in the psychobiographical approach as reductionism, inflated expectations, disparagement, application of contemporary psychology to another era, inadequacies of psychological theory, and the problem of analyzing an absent subject.[24]

Let me reiterate my belief in the value and essential role of human biography in the record of the past, and the validity of a humanistic interpretation of the life of an individual, whatever station in society the subject may represent. Although there have been urgent appeals for history from the "bottom up" with less attention to the role of policymakers and the elite,[25] there are still incredible gaps about these influential individuals in the story of the American colonial experience such as the experience of Governor Glen. My concern is with both career and character; and if either has to receive somewhat greater attention, it is career over character because of the need to fill the above gap in our historical record. Evaluations of the subject proceed with full awareness of the admonition enunciated by Edel among his *Principia* for biographies at a symposium on "New Directions in Biography": "No good biography can be written in total love and admiration; and it is even less useful if it is written in hate."[26] I also share the conviction of Frank E. Vandiver, stated at another conference, that "the main body of biography still clings to individuality, still seeks to know how one man or woman lived and worked in his or her time, how one life may have influenced many."[27]

1

Early Years in Scotland

Of all the palaces so fair,
Built for the royal dwelling,
In Scotland, far beyond compare,
Linlithgow is excelling.

Sir Walter Scott in *Marmion*

Linlithgow, royal burgh and site of the royal palace for the Stuarts of Scotland, enjoyed its greatest period of political and economic significance during the fifteenth and sixteenth centuries. Located in West Lothian on the road between Edinburgh and Stirling, it has a beautiful setting on Linlithgow Loch, traditionally called "Lake in the damp hollow." Early Scottish kings exercised jurisdiction over much of the region and bestowed specific areas to favorite supporters or religious groups by granting *feus*, a feudal practice of a duty to a superior for property held. King David I, for example, granted by charter St. Michael's Church and its lands in the burgh of Linlithgow to the priory of St. Andrew in 1139.[1]

England's efforts to control Scotland fluctuated amid the various tenures of feudalism in which Scottish barons sometimes held English fiefs and contributed to the conflict over political jurisdiction of Scotland. Following the death of the last direct heir of the royal house of Scotland in 1290, King Edward I (1272-1307) of England was able through two different conquests to control Scotland. His successor, King Edward II (1307-1327), however, suffered defeat at the famous battle of Bannockburn in 1314 by Robert Bruce and paved the way for the treaty in 1328 by King Edward III (1327-1377) recognizing the independence of Scotland.[2]

Conflict, nonetheless, continued with the potential for border aggression from the north, particularly after England became involved with France in the dynastic and feudal struggle known as the Hundred Years' War (1337-1453). James I of Scotland (not to be confused with James VI who later became James I of England) became a pawn in the tension between England and Scotland as he was captured by English pirates while heir apparent to the Scottish throne. Henry IV (1399-1413) of England initiated his detention which continued for eighteen years as a hostage for the maintenance of peace with Scotland.[3] Upon his return to Scotland following this forced absence, James I of Scotland included among his achievements the building of the royal palace at Linlithgow beginning in 1424. While his successors made some alterations and possible additions,[4] it was this royal palace for which the subject of this biography, James Glen, was appointed keeper as a sinecure at the time that he was taking up his duties as royal governor of the colony of South Carolina.

The Glen family had a prominent role in the economic and political history of Linlithgow. Originally descending from an ancient family of Norman extraction, the immediate ancestors go back to Robert Glen (died 1506) and the lordship of Bar. Alexander Glen, a descendant of the above Robert and father of James Glen, the future governor, acquired Longcroft and adjacent property amounting to 114 acres in Linlithgow and a life rent by royal charter to the estate of Bonnytune (sometimes spelled Bonjtoune).[5]

The political legacy in the administration of Linlithgow extended over several generations in the office of provost as the chief magistrate of a Scottish burgh. James Glen, the great, great grandfather of the governor of South Carolina, was provost from 1624 to 1626, while his son Andrew Glen (great grandfather of the governor) followed in the same office from 1655 to 1662. The governor's father, Alexander, continued the legacy by serving from 1708 to 1715.[6] He, however, ran into the conflict that emerged with the death in 1714 of Queen Anne of England, the last of the Stuart monarchs, and the accession of George I of the House of Hanover that has continued the Hanoverian succession to the present. James, son of the deposed James II (James VII of Scotland) in the Glorious Revolution of 1688-1689, laid claim to the English throne as the Old Pretender in the Jacobite uprising of 1715.[7] Alexander Glen's sympathy with the unsuccessful campaign of the Earl of Mar in behalf of the Stuarts forced his resignation as provost. Yet he did not suffer the forfeiture of property imposed on some Jacobites in the eighteenth century who took a more active role in opposition to the Hanoverians. Alexander Glen's property would pass intact to his eldest son, James.

By the time of the Jacobite uprising in 1715, Alexander Glen was the father of eight children. His wife was Marion Graham, the daughter of James Graham who had served in Edinburgh as bailie, a Scottish municipal magistrate similar to an English alderman. The increase of the family came with regular intervals of one to two years, beginning with James in 1701. The Parish Register in Scotland was not complete in the early eighteenth century and does not list the birth of James. By the time the subsequent children arrived, the family recorded the birth of each in the Register. As the eldest son, James was designated heir to his father on August 28, 1722 and came into possession of the lands of Longcroft, Magdalens, and the life rent of Bonnytoun.[8] The responsibility of being the eldest son weighed heavily on the character of the future governor. On numerous occasions he demonstrated concern for the welfare of younger siblings, particularly his sisters.

Andrew Glen, the second son, was born and baptized in 1702. Andrew's only daughter, Elizabeth, married George Ramsay, the eighth Earl of Dalhousie in 1767. She became the executrix of the estate of Governor James Glen when he died without heir in 1777.[9] Consequently, many of the valuable records and the best portrait known to exist have passed down through generations to the sixteenth Earl of Dalhousie who resides in the Dalhousie private castle in Brechin, Scotland.

The third son, Dr. Thomas Glen, was born in 1704 and was educated at the University of Edinburgh and the University of Leiden in the Netherlands. Brother Thomas followed James to South Carolina and took an active role in politics in the Commons House of the Assembly in addition to his practice of medicine.

There were two other sons, Alexander born in 1705 and John in 1710, and four daughters: Marion (b. 1707), Agnes (b. 1708), Elizabeth (b. 1712), and Margaret (b. 1713).[10] Agnes married David Bruce of Kinnaird in 1735. As his second wife, she assumed responsibility not only for her own children but also for James Bruce, son of David's first wife.[11] James was known as the Abyssinian Traveller because of his travels in Africa to discover the source of the Nile River. Both James Glen and his brother, Thomas, took great interest in James before their careers took them to Carolina. Margaret Glen accompanied the governor to South Carolina where she met John Drayton of Drayton Hall and became his third wife in 1752.[12]

James Glen grew up as a young man during the intensive period of transition of the Union of England and Scotland in 1707 under the name of "Great Britain." While many changes occurred, some things remained the same. The Treaty of Union abolished the Scottish Parliament and provided for sixteen Scottish peers and forty-five Scottish members of the House of Commons to serve in the British Parliament in London. The Scottish Privy Council continued under the merger with the proviso that it could be altered by Parliament. Alteration came swiftly, for it was eliminated the following year. The Union recognized the Hanoverian succession to the Crown as Protestants, and it preserved the Established Presbyterian Church of Scotland which has continued in its official position to the present. One of the other major areas of continuity was the preservation of Scottish courts and the laws and customs relating to property and civil rights. The Court of Session, the supreme civil court in Scotland, continued under article nineteen of the Union, though eventually appeal from it could be made to the House of Lords in London. This Court of Session included fourteen Lords of Session who sat in the "Outer House" as "Lords Ordinary" and as a group of fifteen with the Lord President as a court of appeal. Six of these judges sat as the Court of Justiciary under the Lord Justice Clerk as the supreme criminal court of Scotland with no appellate provision.[13] Glen as a lawyer would have significant contacts with these courts both as a friend of judges and as a litigant in cases before the Court of Session.

The administration of Scotland by the central government in London during the first half of the eighteenth century involved a variety of officials. In addition to the Secretaries of State for the Southern Department with jurisdiction over colonial affairs and the Northern Department over foreign affairs, there was a third Secretary of State part of the time with primary concern for Scotland. Correspondents with these secretaries from Scotland included the Lord Advocate for Scotland and the Lord Justice Clerk. Duncan Forbes, fellow Scotsman and friend of Glen, served as Lord Advocate from 1725 to 1737 and then succeeded to Lord President of the Session in 1737. Andrew Fletcher, later raised to the peerage as Lord Milton, also a friend of Glen, was Lord Justice Clerk from 1734 to 1748 and then Keeper of the Signet from 1746 until his death in 1766. The First Lord of the Treasury in London had much to do with the administration of Scotland through such boards as the commissioners of customs and salt duties and the commissioners for excise duties. Sir Robert Walpole as First Lord of the Treasury emerged as prime minister during the 1720s and continued in office until 1742 at a time critical for the aspirations of James Glen.[14]

One may well ask how the provost of a small Scottish burgh[15] not only attained the appointment of royal governor of South Carolina, but was also the recipient of other appointments: keeper of the royal palace of the Stuarts in Linlithgow where Mary, Queen of Scots, was born and where James VI of Scotland (later James I of England) resided part of the time; keeper of the castle of Blackness on the Scottish shore;[16] watchman of the salt duty at the port of Bo'ness, one of the commercial competitors to Linlithgow itself; and inspector for Scotland of seizures of prohibited and uncustomed goods.[17]

Several factors contributed to these achievements, notably James Glen's experience in local government, his interaction with other political leaders, and his marriage. First of all, as noted previously, James inherited the family tradition of service as provost of his native city of the royal burgh of Linlithgow. In preparation for a career of service, Glen, like the prominent Duncan Forbes and hundreds of other Scots, went to the University of Leiden for his legal education.[18] The Scots were more interested in studying Roman law applicable to Scotland than the common law of England.

Walpole as prime minister sought the support of Scottish delegates in Parliament and turned to John Campbell, the second Duke of Argyll and his brother, Archibald Campbell, the Earl of Islay (Ilay) and later third Duke of Argyll, for assistance. Islay became the most influential manager of Scottish support and patronage during the 1720s and 1730s with the able assistance of his *sous ministre*, Andrew Fletcher, later Lord Milton. The two were so successful that by the 1730s the Argathelians as followers of the Argylls gained dominance over their opponents, the Squardones, and they held "the majority of judicial and administrative posts in Edinburgh."[19] Islay was sometimes referred to as the "king of Scotland."[20]

The success of these efforts was based in part on the attention devoted to local elections of Scottish delegates to Parliament. In royal burghs such as Linlithgow, the election of parliamentary delegates was the function of town councils. Therefore, as one scholar concluded, "it proved impossible to separate municipal from parliamentary politics."[21] Still operating under the provisions of the act of Parliament of 1681 under King Charles II which stipulated property qualifications for the freeholder franchise,[22] Scotland authorized the freeholders of each shire to designate in annual meetings the roll of electors. It was mandatory to be on the roll of freeholders either to vote or represent the shire.

James Glen had a twofold involvement in selecting members of Parliament—as a member of the town council and as a freeholder in Linlithgowshire. Elected to the Linlithgow town council in September 1724, he was unanimously selected as provost the following month, serving in this office from 1724 to 1726 and again from 1730 to 1736.[23] He participated several times in the selection of Scottish members of Parliament in conference with other burghs. For example, in April 1725, he was selected to serve as town commander to meet with other representatives from the burghs of Linlithgow, Sellkirk, Lamerk, and Peebles to pick a representative to Parliament.[24] Again in May 1734, he was the town commander in the meeting of the burgh of Lanark for choosing a member of Parliament. The Linlithgow town council commended his action in the selection process.[25]

Glen's position as provost provided other opportunities to meet with political leaders in Scotland as well as to journey to London in behalf of the interests of his local burgh. Each year as provost he was designated as town commander to be its representative to the annual convention of burrows held in Edinburgh, usually during the summer. Following these meetings, he reported to his town council on the discussions and actions of the group of interest to his own local area. In 1733 he was appointed by the town council to proceed to London to request money for debts for public works for Linlithgow from the House of Commons. Authorized expenses not to exceed £300, he completed a successful mission in getting a new gift of two pence on a pint of ale from the Commons to continue for twenty-one years after the expiration of the previous authorization.[26]

Glen's participation in the selection of members of Parliament from Linlithgowshire became more complex when disputes over the identification of eligible voting freeholders came before the Court of Session, the supreme civil court in Scotland that met in Edinburgh. Under the provisions of the same 1681 act of Parliament for the franchise, freeholders of a shire were specifically authorized to revise the roll of barons and freeholders with the right to vote. This involved alterations as required by the death of former members with resulting changes in inherited property or by the acquisition of property by others "held immediately" of the Crown and valued at 400 pounds Scots per year. By a summons of November 19, 1733, Glen was among seventeen others called before the Court of Session to explain their procedures and justify their decisions in denying the addition of eight applicants for admission. This extensive case of Thomas Sharp and others versus George Dundas and others was among several that dealt with the difficult problem of controversial election procedures in the eighteenth century.[27]

Experience on the town council also initiated Glen to the controversies of political action that foreshadowed his later conflicts with the South Carolina Assembly as governor. One dispute arose in the council over the vote for new members in September 1725. When the initial count was taken, there was an even split of twelve to twelve, with one David Young stating that "he had voted none in that case." Glen as provost then cast the deciding vote for the installation of his favorite, John Bucknay, and proceeded to swear him into the Elite (Elyte) with the appropriate oath of fidelity. The clerk of the council, favoring candidates of an opposing faction, refused to enter the name of Bucknay on the minutes and stated that he would mark "res gesta as it really happened." Glen then took the minute book away from the clerk to record the vote, whereupon the leader of the opposing faction, Bailie Higgins, had the clerk record the minutes on a separate piece of paper with the election of their candidate.[28] At a subsequent meeting on September 18 with Glen absent, the council voted to accept the minutes of the clerk and rescind the action recorded in Glen's minutes. On September 23 this conflict spread to a dispute over the seating of various deacons as representatives of guilds, with the faction of Bailie Higgins again prevailing.[29]

When the council next met in October on the first day after Michaelmas of the same year, the usual day for electing magistrates of the burgh, Glen and his supporters took sterner measures to challenge the opposition. Bailie Higgins protested that the town council house was "presently full of hidden persons not concerned to be there" with the "doors locked fast." Glen explained that he had ordered a guard to preserve the peace. When the doors were finally opened, there came forth several guild representatives with their "accomplices having guns Swords hallberts and other offensive weapons." As one Edward Spense made his way up the stairs, he was "in a very violent manner attacked . . . and received a great cutt in the head with a broad sword." Order was finally restored, and the final voting went against the Glen group with another provost elected to succeed him.[30] At meetings the following year, Glen remained on the council with protests of the validity of elections the past year and with John Bucknay still demanding his seat on the council.[31] The future governor was experiencing the ups and downs of political conflict and was learning to accept defeat as well as success in competitive situations.

Provost Glen also confronted other snares in political administration that threatened a legal process against him before the Court of Session. The legal complaint came from William Bell, Esquire, and others who alleged that they had been wrongfully imprisoned upon orders from Provost Glen in the tolbooth, or prison, on High Street. The accusation included both James Glen after relinquishing the office of provost and his brother, Andrew. The town council of Linlithgow considered the complaint valid and proposed to pay the claim of 392 pounds Scots, with plans to sue Glen for reimbursement of the full amount. Before this legal process reached the courts, Glen provided a compromise with the approbation of the burgh's legal adviser, Mr. Craigie. Glen was to supply the 392 pounds Scots out of the rent that the town paid him for the Loch Milne.[32]

Glen rebounded from this legal difficulty and was again elected provost in 1730, continuing to serve to 1736.[33] He again participated in the selection of members of the British Parliament, as noted previously, and also experienced some of the varied functions of the town council. During the interim of his position as provost, for example, the town council in July 1727 had sent an address to King George II expressing condolence upon the death of his father and congratulating him upon accession to the throne.[34] More routine matters involved such problems as complaints that two new pews in the kirk (church) had been constructed higher than the previous ones, thus depriving some attendants from both seeing and hearing the minister. After a visit to the kirk, the council ordered a return of the pews to their former height.[35] Even more mundane was the problem of mad dogs and the necessity in 1736 of mandating that all dogs over four months old be wormed within fourteen days, upon penalty of 3 pounds Scots for each day neglected. The more serious problem of rabies evoked orders that any owner of a dog bitten by a mad one was to destroy his canine within twenty-four hours or suffer penalty. Furthermore, any owner of a dog or other beast that died of madness was obligated to bury the victim three feet underground within six hours, again under penalty of noncompliance.[36]

Glen's relationship with leaders influential in distributing patronage, in addition to his experience as provost, contributed to his success in obtaining royal appointments. He had the support of Duncan Forbes, Lord President of the Session at the time of Glen's appointment as royal governor. Forbes of Culloden rejected sympathy with the Jacobites who persisted in opposition to the rule of the Hanoverians, George I and George II. Their most disastrous defeat came under Bonnie Prince Charlie at Culloden in 1746. Forbes worked with the Duke of Argyll and his brother, the Earl of Islay. Islay had the greatest influence in appointments of Scots under Sir Robert Walpole at the time of Glen's selection. He was assisted by Lord Milton who was Lord Justice Clerk in 1738.[37] Milton not only assisted in handling the finances of Islay, but he also rendered service to Glen in the administration of heritable bonds and the arrangement for money needed from Scotland while Glen was detained in London.[38] Lord Dalhousie of Scotland supported Glen for royal appointments and also assisted him in financial arrangements while in England.[39]

Glen's visits to London first involved official missions for his town council and subsequently his negotiations for the benefits of his position as royal governor. He had substantial assistance from Spencer Compton. Son of James, third Earl of Northampton, Compton was educated at Trinity College, Oxford. Under King George I he became speaker of the House of Commons in 1715 and a member of the Privy Council the following year. He was a favorite of King George II and in 1730 attained the rank of Viscount of Pevensey and Earl of Wilmington. The same year he succeeded to the post of Lord President of the Privy Council and continued in influential positions during the time of Glen's appointment as royal governor. Wilmington was even made First Lord of the Treasury upon the defeat of Walpole in 1742, and he nominally became prime minister but never fully exercised authority in the position before his death the following year.[40] He was never married, and Horace Walpole described him as "the most formal solemn man in the world, but a great lover of private debauchery."[41] It is clear that Lord Wilmington was the most influential person in obtaining Glen's appointment as royal governor in 1738. Glen's letter the following year noted his long and expensive stay in London and added that it would have been more precarious had he "depended upon the promise of one of less worth and weight than Lord Wilmington."[42] In 1740 another letter to Lord Wilmington referred to "When your Lordship procured for me the Government of Carolina."[43]

Glen's marital status was most likely an important factor in this relationship. Some sources state that Glen was never married. Yet collections of private correspondence make several references to Governor and Mrs. Glen.[44] *Burke's Peerage* identifies Elizabeth Wilson, granddaughter of Sir William Wilson (baronet), as the wife of Glen.[45] The support that Glen received from Lord Wilmington lends credence to the gossipy diary of the Earl of Egmont, which states that Glen married the illegitimate (natural) daughter of Lord Wilmington and that Sir Robert Walpole, even at age sixty-four, had taken on a new mistress, one of the sisters of Governor Glen.[46] No extant record has been found to identify which sister, but most likely it was the youngest, Margaret, who later came to Carolina while Glen was governor. Such sexual relationships in eighteenth-century England were not too unusual. The Earl of Egmont goes on to say that Sir Robert Walpole, later the Earl of Orford, exerted his political influence to have his illegitimate daughter declared officially as the Earl's daughter, an action that Egmont noted "cannot please the female sex."[47] Extensive research has not determined whether or not Glen was married more than once. Egmont as one of the Trustees for the colony of Georgia also recommended to the Duke of Newcastle the appointment of Glen with the rationale that his connection with administration officials would be beneficial to the new colony.

The implementation of royal appointments in the colonies was administered through the Secretary of State for the Southern Department with the assistance of the Lords Commissioners of Trade and Plantations, popularly known as the Board of Trade. The Duke of Newcastle, brother of Henry Pelham, headed the

Southern Department at the time of Glen's appointment in 1738. The Board of Trade had assisted as a recommending body in the administration of British colonies since its creation in 1696. In response to orders from King George II, the Board submitted a draft of the commission for Glen to be "Our Governor in chief and Captain General."[48] Soon after, as Glen later wrote, "I kiss'd the King's hand for the government of S. Carolina."[49]

Glen also received appointments in the customs service, which was charged with the dual responsibility of collecting revenue and supervising trade regulations. His office as watchman of the salt duty contributed to the annual collection in Scotland of £9,000 to £10,000. Following a two-year hiatus in the salt collection when the British House of Commons abolished the salt duty, the government revived it on Lady Day in 1732 and it continued unchanged to 1742. Walpole merged the Scottish and English boards of customs commissioners to improve efficiency. The great majority of the collection of the 12 pence per bushel duty on Scots salt came from the largest ports of Kirkcaldy, Prestonpans, Alloa, and Bo'ness. Regulations forbade customs officers from service in their own burgh or village, but Glen was eligible for Bo'ness which had become a challenger to his native Linlithgow. The position of customs and salt commissioner was a prestigious one in Scotland with a salary per annum up to £30.[50] Glen, however, seldom appeared on the service record for Bo'ness with his extended stays in London.

Glen's delay in taking up the reins of royal governor extended to 1743 primarily over disputes about salary. Prior to this time, the royal governors of South Carolina had received an annual salary of £1,000 from the Crown as commander-in-chief of military forces in the colony payable from funds established for the independent company of foot. After the founding of Georgia in 1732, however, the Crown had unified the military command of units in Georgia and South Carolina in 1737 under the command of General James Edward Oglethorpe as leader of Georgia and committed the £1,000 to him. While Glen still held his inherited property in Scotland with the limited approximate annual income of £600,[51] he negotiated for additional payments and resented the deprivation of the award previously received by South Carolina governors. He was so outspoken in manifesting "much spleen" in criticism of Oglethorpe that the Earl of Islay cautioned him to get along with Oglethorpe if he expected any favors from the government.[52]

Glen elaborated in detail on the inconsistent and inadequate financial provision for his appointment. Writing to Lord Wilmington in 1740, he noted the very high income in Barbados where both Robert Byng and Lord Howe as governors had a salary of £2,000 plus £1,500 for equipment. Even in South Carolina, Governor Robert Johnson had a salary of £1,000[53] with approximately the same amount for equipage.[54] In a petition to Sir Robert Walpole and the Lords of the Treasury, Glen further bemoaned the deterioration of income formerly provided governors of South Carolina that approximated £3,100 per annum. This amount, Glen asserted, had included £1,000 as salary plus £600 as profits of the independent company, £200 annually from each of the positions of naval officer and vendue master, and £100 from the licensing of all public houses. Additional increments of £500 by the provincial Assembly for country salary, another £500 from fees and perquisites, and the £120 per annum for house rent exceeded the £3,100. Unfortunately, Glen continued, General Oglethorpe then had the salary for commander of military forces and the profits of the independent company, and the Crown by royal sign manual had appointed other persons as naval officer and vendue master. The South Carolina Assembly had moved the licensing of public houses to other appointees, and the profits from other fees and perquisites had declined to only £250. Furthermore, the local Assembly had reduced the country salary to £300 and threatened to withdraw it unless the Crown provided the usual salary of past years.[55]

Persisting in his concern over salary, Glen noted the necessity of maintaining a life-style commensurate with planters of the colony and reiterated the perennial problem of being dependent on local assemblies for basic salary.   Crown officials were aware of this concern and had considered a variety of solutions in other royal colonies to encourage the independence of their royal appointee. For South Carolina in the 1730s and 1740s, there were three possible sources: use of royal quitrents where adequate, diversion of funds from other colonies particularly from the West Indies, or payment directly from the British Exchequer.[56]   Glen's appeal persuaded the Board of Trade to recommend the full £1,000 in 1740,[57] but it was not until 1741 that the Lords of the Treasury agreed to £800, with funds to be drawn from the 4½ percent duty of Barbados and Leeward islands.[58] Glen's royal instructions specifically stated that he was not to "receive any Gift or Present from the Assembly or others on any Account or in any Manner whatsoever without Our express Licence . . . upon Pain of Our highest Displeasure and of being recalled."[59] Permission was given to have the Assembly provide a house or house rent out of public services, an issue that proved to be a bone of contention for Glen on several occasions. Officials also authorized efforts to have the Assembly establish a fixed and competent salary for the governor with the assent of the Crown, but this step was never achieved in the colony.

Glen's appointment as governor included not only his royal commission but also an extensive set of instructions to guide him in representing the British Crown and protecting its royal prerogative. It was traditional for new governors upon arrival in America to present their royal commission. A sixteen-page document, Glen's commission of 1739 repeated many of the royal dictates of the past. He was to have a Council of twelve members with three required as a quorum, and he was authorized in case of a smaller number to make temporary appointments to be confirmed by the Crown. With advice of the Council, he could call General Assemblies to make laws that were subject to review by the King and Privy Council within three months. Glen received veto power over legislation and authority to "prorogue and dissolve" General Assemblies. In addition to the usual supervision over courts, public money, and land grants,

Glen was empowered to raise and command military forces, but his commission specifically stated that his actions were "not to interfere with or derogate from the Powers and Authorities" previously given to Oglethorpe for Georgia and South Carolina. The governor was also to have power to collate persons to churches and to be vigilant in taking and administering oaths that would uphold Protestantism and guard against the claims of Jacobites and "Popish Recusants."[60]

Even more detailed guides followed with the 110 instructions of September 7, 1739, which were similar to directions for royal governors in other colonies. In fact, during the 1720s the South Carolina governor was asked to share his instructions with the new governor of North Carolina. Glen's instructions were almost identical to those prepared for his predecessor, Colonel Samuel Horsey, who took his oath of office on August 1, 1738, but died of apoplexy and palsy on August 19. Glen did have the opportunity to confer with the Board of Trade several times to react to his instructions. Crown officials then agreed, upon suggestion from Glen, to delete the portion of article thirteen prohibiting the governor from allowing the Assembly and its members "any Power or Priviledge" not allowed to the House of Commons in England.[61] For the governor's benefit, they also modified article twenty-six to permit the Assembly to provide him with a house or money in lieu thereof for house rent until an appropriate dwelling could be supplied.[62] The critical question in number ninety-nine on paper money was altered to reconcile it with the Order in Council of March 22, 1739, requiring the borrower to pay part of the principal toward the sinking of new bills.[63] Later, in 1753, Glen had the opportunity to review and evaluate in much greater detail this extensive set of directions for the benefit of colonial administration.[64]

Glen's long delay in proceeding to the colony left the prime responsibility for administration of South Carolina in the hands of the lieutenant governor, Colonel William Bull, Sr. Yet he conferred from time to time on matters of general policy with the Board of Trade. The question of major land grants for colonization was a frequent issue. For example, Glen opposed land petitions by John Hammerton and Henry McCulloch,[65] but he gave a more positive reaction as he attended with William Livingston in 1741 relative to his request for 200,000 acres for the settlement of 1,000 Protestants. Only one white settler was to be required for 200 acres. Insufficient support for the Livingston venture, however, transferred the authority later to John Hamilton in 1749 for "Hamilton's Great Survey" along the south side of the Saluda River.[66]

Glen also met with the Georgia Trustees in England to discuss problems of mutual interest to both colonies. In September 1741, for example, he discussed with the Earl of Egmont and other Trustees the thorny question of regulation of Indian trade and the possible number of Indian traders to be licensed by each colony. No final solution was worked out for this highly sensitive issue, but Glen's attitude reflected a sincere effort to resolve the question satisfactorily to both colonies, even though he was still resentful of Oglethorpe's having part of the salary previously paid to South Carolina governors.[67]

Glen's delay in taking up his duties in Carolina evoked reactions both in England and in the colony. Sir Archibald Gant, for example, identified himself as a friend of Lord Carteret, one of the eight original Carolina proprietors and the only one that had not yielded his shares to the King. Gant in his "Memorial" asserted in 1742 the apparent lack of interest in Glen going to Carolina and suggested that Lord Carteret's support of him for governor might influence his appointment with the Duke of Newcastle. He also stated that Newcastle "hath no favour for Mr. Glen."[68] Robert Pringle, fellow Scot and merchant immigrant to South Carolina, erroneously reported about the same time that Glen had been made governor of Jamaica.[69]

Pringle's correspondence with his brother, Andrew, in London and other friends reflected the impatient anticipation of the new governor's arrival. Robert wrote in 1740 that Glen "is very much wanted amongst us," and again in 1741 he stated that we have "Great Expectations. He is much wanted & wish'd for here as we have in a Manner no Government here at present, neither have had for some time past."[70] Some English merchants, however, had doubts about Glen's appointment and were emboldened enough when reading about this in the newspaper to write the Duke of Newcastle in 1738 expressing their concern. Noting that the position of royal governor "Requires a Person of abilities and great experience," the merchants expressed their fear that "this Gentleman may be wanting, who, we are informed is young and a Stranger to Publick Affairs, either Civil or Military." Their major concern was in the "Interests of Trade."[71] Amid the variety of views about his appointment as royal governor, Glen finally set sail for Carolina aboard the *Tartar* Man-of-War in October 1743.

What cultural baggage did Governor Glen bring with his Scottish heritage, his English experience, and his legal education in the Netherlands? Scholars differ about the extent to which there is a "recognizable Scottish character." Such attributes have been suggested as pragmatism, honesty, concern with logic, and love of independence for the home land.[72] Glen, like Duncan Forbes, eschewed the Jacobite struggle to maintain Scottish independence and did not suffer the mistake of his father. With his English experience and his marriage to the daughter of Lord Wilmington, he fitted more into the mold of anglicization characteristic of many upper class Scots of his time.[73] He was pragmatic in politics and willing to engage in devious political manipulations. Yet conscientious in devotion to duty, he followed a work ethic comparable to Puritans and was obviously concerned with money. Religious influences were also a factor in Scotland with the dominance of Presbyterianism embracing Calvinism as interpreted by John Knox. Glen was a member of St. Michael's Church in his native Linlithgow but discoursed little, if any, on such theological issues as predestination. He was more concerned as a royal appointee in his role as the King's representative in a colony with an established Anglican Church and his legal authority in administering this institution.

2

Governor Glen Takes Command

I found the whole frame of Government unhinged.

James Glen, 1744

After a tedious passage of eleven weeks on the *Tartar* Man-of-War, Governor Glen arrived in Charles Town on Saturday, December 17, 1743, at the inconvenient hour of three o'clock in the morning. Traditional gun salutes acknowledged his arrival and a variety of both formal and informal welcoming ceremonies followed during the remainder of the day. As the *Tartar* came to anchor, the clerk of the Council and master in Chancery came aboard to extend the compliments of Lieutenant Governor William Bull, Sr., and the Council and to direct him to the landing wharf. Fort Johnson had saluted the governor in passing with fifteen guns. Broughton's battery in White Point Garden at the end of Church Street added another fifteen-gun welcome; Granville's bastion north of the creek along Water Street followed with eleven guns; and Craven's bastion on the Cooper River side near the end of present Market Street concluded the initial serenade with seven guns. Both Edmond Atkin and Charles Pinckney of the Council greeted Glen and conducted him through two lines of the Charles Town regiment of foot soldiers to the Council chamber. Glen's commission was read appointing him captain general, governor, and commander-in-chief of the province. The official delegation then returned toward Granville's bastion preceded by the provost marshall with the sword of state[1] through the two lines of troops. The clerk of the Council announced the official publication of Glen's commission that was followed by a roar of three huzzahs and another discharge of guns from the bastion and the regimental troops. Upon his return to the Council chamber, Glen took the oath of office both as governor and as chancellor of the court before later returning to Broad Street to enjoy the special entertainment prepared for this official occasion.[2] The governor no doubt enjoyed the elaborate ceremonies upon his arrival, for early in his career he displayed his enthusiasm for the formalities of both political and military events. The Assembly had just adjourned the day before until January 10, so Glen awaited his opportunity to deliver his first message to its members.

The Assembly of South Carolina had the traditional two houses: the lower body of the legislature known as the Commons House, and the Upper House as the Council with the two additional duties of executive advisor to the governor and with him to serve as the highest judiciary body in the Chancery Court. These agents of government were the leading officials in the provincial government over some 65,000 colonists with the threatening imbalance of only 25,000 whites to 40,000 blacks, most of whom were slaves concentrated in the plantations of the low country.[3] Some slaves had participated in the Stono slave revolt in 1739 in efforts to flee to the Spanish in St. Augustine. White planters and merchants dominated the provincial economy, while blacks made significant contributions in such areas as rice culture from their African experience.[4] The wealthiest low country planters accumulated several plantations supervised by overseers with possibly hundreds of slaves, while less affluent ones more often directed their crops in person with the assistance of only a few slaves. Smaller farmers in townships to the interior had few or no slaves and more often cultivated such crops as corn and wheat as well as the herding of livestock. The major group of merchants operated out of Charles Town with some mercantile activity at the ports of Beaufort and George Town. Often engaged in the slave trade, they also imported a variety of goods from England, wine from the Madeira Islands, and rum from the Caribbean. They exported products such as rice, lumber products, deerskins of the Indian trade, and indigo after the experiments of Eliza Lucas Pinckney in the 1740s.[5] Some entrepreneurs such as Henry Laurens combined the role of planter and merchant as well as participating actively in the political life of the colony and the emerging new nation.[6]

Glen made his first official message to both houses of the Assembly on January 11. In optimistic fashion, he praised their "Loyalty and Zeal for his Majesty's Person and Government" and promised to make the colony's "Welfare and Prosperity my peculiar Care." Acknowledging that "Bad Governours and Magistrates are the greatest Grievance that any Province can be afflicted with," he pledged his conscientious effort in administration and challenged members of the Assembly to fulfill their duties in legislation and to be mindful of the most effective use of finances both within the colony and in the support of England in war with Spain. Vowing to "prefer the Public Good to my own private Advantage," he, perhaps with tongue in cheek, stated that "Whatever Salary you give I shall be contented with, not in the least doubting but you will enable me to live suitably to the Dignity of my Office as Governour of so flourishing a Province."[7] This contentment was not always later displayed in controversy over payments by the Assembly both for salary and for housing. The Assembly gave gracious responses to Glen's first speech, congratulating him on his safe arrival and "the kind and affectionate Manner" of his address and pledging cooperation in promoting the "Safety and Welfare of the Province."[8]

Beneath this rosy facade of harmony in the internal working of the government, Glen was quick to perceive the problem of distribution of power among governor, Council, and Commons House that pervaded his entire administration. "I found the whole frame of Government unhinged," he wrote to both the Duke of Newcastle and the Board of Trade. In challenges to the royal prerogative of the British constitution and the explicit authority of his instructions, the governor found his powers "parcelled out" to many individuals over whom he had little control. Many commissioners were appointed by, and responsible to, the Assembly, while others had received their positions from patrons of England.[9] The only offices he controlled, he later complained, were justices of the peace and commissions in the militia, offices with little profit that were difficult to fill.[10] The most acute conflict, however, centered on practices that challenged the authority of the governor and hence the royal prerogative. As he conscientiously spent his first few weeks in the colony reading journals to get abreast of public matters, he was dismayed to find that in 1739 the Council as Upper House had excluded the governor from debate on legislative matters on the grounds that it was of an "Unparliamentary nature."[11]

Past governors had consciously or unconsciously yielded to encroachments on the royal prerogative. Governor Francis Nicholson during the 1720s had enhanced the status of the Council by changing tenure to one of good behavior rather than the former pleasure of the proprietors. He had also deliberately evaded his instructions by letting the Council elect its own president and, indeed, even select its new members and compile a list of qualified persons for future consideration of membership. He followed a similar path in yielding to the Commons House by approving most of its bills and by permitting it to select the public treasurer and other officials receiving public salaries. These actions seriously diminished the royal prerogative of the governor. Governor Robert Johnson served first as a proprietary governor from 1717 to 1719 and later as royal governor from 1730 (appointed 1729) until his death in 1735. While demonstrating a conscientious approach to his royal instructions, he likewise was willing to ignore or disobey them occasionally without being challenged by the Board of Trade in its passive approach to strict adherence to royal mandates.[12] With Glen's long delay in arrival, lieutenant governors such as Colonel William Bull, Sr., were less mindful of royal dictates and more inclined to yield to the preferences of fellow colonials. Records of the Council revealed that, contrary to the King's instructions, business had been conducted by only three, two, or even one member present without the governor. Such records, Glen noted, had not been forwarded either to the Board of Trade or the Secretary of State for some three years.[13]

Glen's early concerns went beyond these matters of the political process as he inspected the fortifications of Charles Town. Cannons sent from England were still not mounted, and the ones in place had no aprons or tampions to cover the muzzles. Temporary measures were taken to cover them with tar and tallow. Further inspections revealed a careless night watch of the town, leaving the hundreds of barrels of powder insecure in case of threats from another slave insurrection or from the Spanish. Still other disturbing conditions of the night watch occurred when fires at night with high winds threatened the many wooden buildings. Glen ordered the night watch to notify him in case of fires, and he even joined the bucket brigade in carrying water to extinguish the flames.[14] Such actions demonstrated his energetic approach to the challenges of his office, yet they could enhance the concern of some Assembly members in posing threats to powers they had gradually accumulated in past years.

The defense of Charles Town continued to be a critical issue with the war with Spain still smoldering. Spain had continued in possession of Florida from its early settlement by Europeans. The founding of Georgia in the 1730s had increased Anglo-Spanish tension, particularly following General James Oglethorpe's aggressive challenge. He established Fort Frederica as a "military town" on St. Simons Island and set up a series of fortifications reaching toward the Spanish. These included Fort St. George on San Juan Island just across from the mouth of St. Johns River, which the English maintained was their rightful border rather than the Altamaha River much farther north as the Spanish asserted. Efforts to reconcile these border conflicts had been the subject of the Treaty of Frederica in 1736 between Oglethorpe and the Spanish governor of Florida, Francisco del Moral Sánchez. The Spanish governor was under the viceroy of New Spain with headquarters in Mexico, and the viceroy in turn was responsible to the King and the Royal and Supreme Council of the Indies in Spain. Despite this treaty and the subsequent efforts of the Convention of El Pardo near Madrid in 1739 to promote peace, other conflicts continued. Spanish resentment of the *asiento* lingered even though revoked the same year. It had authorized by the earlier Treaty of Utrecht in 1713 English importation of 4,800 slaves into Spanish colonies and trade by one 500-ton English ship each year.[15] The Spanish coast guard (*guarda costa*) attempted to curtail British trade, and one Captain Robert Jenkins reported to the British House of Commons that a Spanish captain boarded his ship, *Rebecca*, near Havana and "took hold of his left ear and slit it down with his cutlask."[16] His display of the ear which he claimed resulted from the Spanish assault provided the name for the Anglo-Spanish War of Jenkins's Ear that erupted in 1739.

English efforts in prosecuting this war involved both naval operations in the Caribbean and attacks and counterattacks along the Georgia-Florida frontier. The naval expeditions were successful for the English in capturing Porto Bello in November 1739; but they failed disastrously against Cartagena in April 1741, and against Santiago in Cuba the following July. Meanwhile, General Oglethorpe organized attacks against the Spanish in Florida. He came in person to South Carolina to appeal for assistance, supported by his official status of commander of Crown forces in South Carolina as well as Georgia, a position that still rankled Governor Glen in England. Nonetheless, South Carolina responded with authorization for 400 troops and the promise of an additional

100, organized under the command of Colonel Alexander Vander Dussen. Taking part of his 900 white troops and some 1,100 Indians by land and part by water, Oglethorpe was ready to assault St. Augustine to challenge the new Spanish governor, Manuel Montiano, successor to Sánchez. The planned attack on June 5, 1740, failed as naval units were unable to bombard and neutralize the fort because of shallow waters and the presence of six Spanish half galleys that had slipped in with supplies from Havana. Oglethorpe's alternative of a siege of the city also failed. This can be attributed to the lack of initiative of his troops, the alert responses of the Spanish, and the approaching hurricane season that forced the withdrawal of British naval forces.[17] The widespread criticism smearing English participants set off partisan views that have echoed over the years between South Carolina and Georgia historians. South Carolina historians have not been timid in criticizing Oglethorpe and defending Vander Dussen and his forces by contending "how groundless are the charges . . . carelessly made against the South Carolina contingent."[18]

Governor Glen found himself in a sensitive position as the investigating committees of the two houses of the South Carolina Assembly pointed the major accusing finger at Oglethorpe in a separate report printed by the editor of the *South-Carolina Gazette* in 1742.[19] The Assembly ordered its publication in England by its agent, Peregrine Fury; but Fury's role also as agent for Oglethorpe's regiment and the influence of Oglethorpe's sister, Anne, resulted in its being turned over to Governor Glen, who was prevailed upon by the Georgia Trustees not to release it.[20] Fury was blamed for failing to follow the Assembly's order and was later removed as agent.

Oglethorpe was more successful in resisting a major Spanish assault in 1742, despite the failure of South Carolina to provide timely assistance. His influence among Carolinians after the failed Florida mission was suspect, for one visitor to Charles Town reported to the Earl of Egmont that "they cannot hear the name of Col. Oglethorpe, but they fall into such a rage as sets the very dogs a barking."[21] As the Spanish planned their attack from St. Augustine, Governor Montiano of Florida became commander of ships and troops sent from Cuba. The exact number in the expedition has not been determined, with estimates varying from thirty-three to fifty-six ships and from 2,000 to 7,000 soldiers. The Spanish were able to move past the string of forts Oglethorpe had attempted to reinforce. They overwhelmed Fort St. Simon after a bitter fight and prepared to march on Fort Frederica, the major target of the campaign. The campaign reached a climax in the battle of Bloody Marsh in July 1742, when Oglethorpe's forces ambushed the enemy and killed or took prisoner some 200 Spaniards. The hazardous terrain and the partial deception by a contrived note of the true strength of the English contributed to the victory over Montiano's superior contingent in number. Oglethorpe's aggressiveness, the role of the effective Scottish Highlanders, and the assistance of Indian allies were also important factors in the outcome.[22] One Spanish sergeant exclaimed that "the woods around Frederica were so full of Indians that the devil himself could not get through."[23] British ships on the horizon also threatened to trap the Spanish fleet in Frederica River. South Carolina finally agreed to provide assistance after the actual Spanish invasion of Georgia, but Georgians had only ridiculing jibes for the South Carolinians who arrived on British ships too late to catch the retreating Spaniards.

After arrival in Carolina the following year, Governor Glen went much beyond his initial survey of fortifications to assess the strengths and weaknesses of the whole colony and to provide more cooperation with Georgia against Spanish threats. Charles Town, he wrote to Crown officials, was located on a neck of land between the Ashley and Cooper rivers, and the port was protected in part by a sand bar seven miles below the town prohibiting the passage of ships with over twenty guns. Any vessels passing with the required assistance of a pilot then came under the walls of Fort Johnson, built in 1708, some three miles below Charles Town. At the fort, Glen continued, there were thirty-three pieces of good cannons along with a supply of shot, powder, and muskets. Twenty-five men were on duty at the fort and an additional 100 could reinforce them in case of an attack. He also noted a total of 1,000 men well armed in the town, and he speculated that even blacks could be used to assist in using the 1,500 muskets in the armory, assuming that their fidelity could be trusted since most were native born. This view, however, was not shared by all South Carolinians who remembered the Stono revolt of 1739. One major area still exposed, Glen added, was the neck of land extending from the town to the country, and he reported this need to the Assembly for consideration.[24] The state of protection for the outlying ports of Beaufort and George Town were also matters of concern in view of the Spanish knowledge that they could be entered by ships of fifty to sixty guns. Lieutenant Governor William Bull, Sr., had been unable to persuade the Assembly earlier in the war to provide adequate security for these ports. Since Fort Frederica in Georgia formed part of the network of protection against the Spanish, Glen in consultation with the South Carolina Council responded to the several requests from Captain William Horton of Frederica by sending two 12-pound cannons and two 6 pounders along with shot, 1,500 weight of powder, and 1,000 weight of cannon balls.[25] The governor thus continued the spirit of cooperation with Georgia, promoted by his contacts with the Trustees while in England as well as recognition of the benefit to both colonies.

The war with Spain posed serious threats on the high seas as well as to the coastal ports of Carolina. Ships of opposing nations were fair game under letters of marque such as the one issued to Aeneas Mackay in March of 1744 for his ship, *Friendship*. Fortified with ten carriage guns, this British-owned ship set sail for London with authorization to capture vessels of the King's enemies. The British ship, *Loo*, operating during the previous months with similar authorization, had the puzzling experience of capturing Monsieur Jack Dansen who had papers identifying him in the service of the French while another set of documents in Spanish, recovered after being thrown overboard, appeared to have him in the service of Spain for purchasing quicksilver. The latter identification proved to be erroneous.[26] Soon thereafter the *Loo* itself was captured by the Spanish and aroused anew the concern of ports such as Beaufort of Port Royal about inadequate security. While there had been provisions for British men-of-war to call at such ports, residents sought more than a small galley or two for their continuous defense, preferably ships with over fifty guns. "We are subjects, not slaves," the inhabitants of Port Royal complained in their "Remonstrance" of September 1744.[27]

Ports such as Beaufort and Charles Town were points of exchange of prisoners in the Anglo-Spanish conflict. In September 1744, for example, a flag of truce from St. Augustine brought twelve English prisoners who were exchanged for some twenty-six Spanish.[28] Cartels were arranged for payment of the expenses for these transfers, as evidenced by the receipt of 890 pieces of eight by the sloop, *Postillion*, for delivery of fifty-seven Spanish prisoners in Havana. Governor Glen, in turn, authorized the public treasurer of South Carolina to pay Gabriel Manigault and Captain Edward Lightwood over 383 pounds currency for the price of hiring the *Postillion* for this mission.[29]

South Carolina ports were also the destination of immigrants from Europe, primarily German Protestants who had earlier received encouragement and financial assistance under the township schemes of Governor Robert Johnson in the 1730s. Neutral in affiliation, they became innocent victims in the war on the high seas. Governor Glen reported to the Commons House in October 1744 the capture by the Spanish of some 265 immigrants just a few leagues east of the Charles Town bar.[30] They were whisked away to Havana. Glen asserted that they were individuals of consequence in their own country, and he stated, perhaps with some exaggeration, that they had several thousand pounds sterling in gold, household furniture, and clothes. The Commons House responded by dispatching a small vessel to Havana to determine if the immigrants still wished to reach South Carolina. Glen with his legal training opined that while a ship on the high seas might be a legal prize, the passengers who were not British citizens certainly were not.[31] Complex though this international situation was in the Anglo-Spanish conflict, it had become more entangled as France joined Spain against the British in King George's War in March of 1744.

Meanwhile, Governor Glen turned his attention to domestic problems of the colony and attempted to make his way through issues that often found the Commons House, Council, and governor vying for control with the governor attempting to follow his instructions and protect the royal prerogative. Partial solution of the improvement of the collection of quitrents came easily from action prior to Glen's arrival. The departure of the contentious Henry McCulloh, the King's commissioner of quitrents, cleared the way for the 1744 quitrent act. It provided for the identity of quitrents due on lands under jurisdiction of the Crown in the transition to a royal colony by requiring memorials of deeds of transfer within eighteen months from all persons holding such lands with details of location and the amount of the rent. The act also prohibited further grants to large landholders with royal grants who had failed to satisfy their cultivation requirements.[32]   Although not providing extensive revenue from which some government officials other than the governor received their salaries, the total annual collection in South Carolina from 1745 to 1751 did increase beyond the previous high of over 1,500 pounds proclamation money to over 2,100 by 1748.[33]

The diverse interests of members of the Assembly led to conflicts over legislation. The Commons House in the early 1740s had a preponderance of planters over merchants. In 1742, for example, out of forty-four members of the Commons, twenty-seven were planters, thirteen were merchants, three were lawyers, and one was a placeman, a royal appointee who was frequently a protégé of a leading British official in London. Three years later the total of thirty-nine members of the Commons included twenty-eight planters, ten merchants, and one placeman.[34] Inventories of the estates of members of the Commons are available for ninety-five individuals during the decade from 1741 to 1750. These inventories cover personal property including slaves, but not an evaluation of landholdings. The range of value in pounds sterling for these ninety-five estates extended from one as low as 201-300 to a high for two over 30,000. The largest number of seventeen were between 5,001 and 10,000, while thirteen were valued between 1,001 and 1,500, and eleven between 1,501 and 2,000.[35]

The Council with twelve members also had a greater number of planters than merchants, though with a smaller variation. For the forty-nine members of the Council from 1720 to 1763, there were eighteen planters, sixteen merchants, four lawyers, nine placemen, and two not easily classified in these professions. The average worth of a sample of merchants of £7,503 exceeded the average of the estates of planters of £6,500, but this did not include wealth in land.[36] Where a member was both planter and merchant, he was included in a category with greater assets. Although there was usually a higher number of planters in the Assembly, they frequently yielded to the leadership of merchants and lawyers who most often resided in Charles Town.

When the tax bill of 1744 required an oath by individuals to certify their total personal property including bonds and mortgages, the merchant-dominated Council as Upper House rejected it. Requirement of the oath for money at interest and extension of the requirement to the town hit directly at merchants. They objected to the potential injury to trade and to the inherent challenge of the oath to personal honesty. They also maintained that merchants were different from planters because of the merchant's need to carry on trade by credit and to invest in bonds for receipt of interest.[37] Letters to the *Gazette* debated at length the validity of precedents in English history for such requirements.[38] Governor Glen had a high regard for both groups and attempted to steer a neutral course. Nonetheless, the merchants' protest was so strong that two of them, Isaac Holmes and John Hume, had the governor's coach stopped in the streets of Charles Town to hand their petition directly to him.[39]   Glen considered the petition irregular, but the Upper House delayed to hear the complaints. Eventually, the bill became law with the governor's approval.[40] Glen's favoring the planters over the merchants on this issue opened him to criticism such as the remarks of Robert Pringle, merchant and fellow Scot, in his well-known letterbook. In January 1744, Pringle stated that Glen "Seems to Gain the Love & Esteem of the People." But by October of the same year after the tax bill had passed, he asserted that Glen "is not much to be Depended on and seems to beguile & want Resolution."[41] The governor was not immune from criticism from even one with a Scottish background. Clearly, the economics of trade prevailed over a common national origin.

Subsequent tax bills contained the required oath and renewed the Upper House-Commons struggle over their respective powers. The 1745 tax bill passed the Commons House by the narrow margin of fifteen to fourteen with the fifteen members opposing an amendment to exclude the oath. The Upper House rejected the bill by an equally close vote of four to three.[42] Irritated by this rejection, two members of the Commons House proposed to Glen that he sign the bill without passage by the Upper House. They acted "in a private manner, not by order of the House," but they assured the governor that a majority of the Commons would support the action.[43] Lawyer Glen refused to be part of such an unconstitutional ploy, and it was not until January of 1746 that a similar tax bill passed with the oath still included, for merchants by then found it less detrimental to trade than originally anticipated. They had also been favorably impressed with the substantial amount of interest recorded.[44]

Money requirements raised other issues as the periodic need for special expenses faced all of the American colonies at some time. By the eighteenth century, several colonies had turned to the issuance of paper money and had usually stipulated a time period for its withdrawal by collection of additional taxes. The scarcity of specie of gold and silver in the colonies, exacerbated by imperial restrictions on their export from the mother country and the frequent expense of military campaigns, were the prime contributors to the need for additional mediums of exchange. By the 1730s the Crown permitted issuance of paper money but required by instructions of governors that laws for this purpose include a suspending clause for their approval.[45]

South Carolina as a royal colony had issued 120,000 pounds in paper money in 1723, with Governor Francis Nicholson violating instructions by his approval. He received strong censure from the Crown for this action, and the protest of both colonial and British merchants resulted in disallowance of the act. The colony gradually turned to two other alternatives for paying creditors: issuance of public orders and provision for tax certificates by the treasury. Both mediums were subject to redemption within a specified time limit, and both were acceptable for taxes and duties, though not legal tender.[46]

Governor Glen attempted to come to grips with this money problem. His ninety-ninth instruction set out specific conditions if such issues were to be continued. This instruction referred to a 1736 currency act of the Assembly that had authorized the emission of 210,000 pounds in paper bills of credit with 100,000 of it to replace earlier issues. The instruction noted the objection of the Crown to a clause in the above act permitting a 10 percent discount on inward trade if paid in gold or silver. This unequal value in relation to other colonies violated an earlier law of 1707 by drawing currency from one colony to another. The ninety-ninth instruction reiterated two major guidelines for money bills: the acts were to include a suspending clause for Crown approval, and they should provide for the borrowers to repay part of the principal in the "sinking" of bills on a designated schedule.[47]

Aware of the snares in currency issues, Glen exhorted the Commons House on May 17, 1744, that payment for quitrents, provincial taxes, and negotiations for trade *without* new emissions of paper money would provide high commendation of the Assembly from the Crown.[48] Here the governor in the early years of his tenure was attempting to influence the Commons by use of the carrot based on pride rather than by coercion with an imperial stick. Yet the demands for coastal protection during King George's War led the Commons House to attempt an issue of 40,000 pounds in paper money without a suspending clause for payment of sloops hired by the governor and Council. Glen vetoed the measure and rejected another attempt to issue 16,000 pounds. For this action the Board of Trade agreed and praised him for following his instructions. Keep up the good work, the Board commended, and "you will always meet with our approbation and the Support of the Government."[49] Glen continuously sought such approval, but his action brought vigorous objections from the Commons, which refused to make other provisions for the expense.

The Commons House turned to more constructive matters and sought to upgrade its membership by enhancing property qualifications for members beyond the stipulations in the election law of 1721. This effort had support from conclusions of a grand jury in 1742 which asserted that qualifications were "too small and may be of ill Consequence." Consequently, in 1744 the Commons proposed to require 300 acres of a freehold estate for voters, or the value of 60 pounds proclamation money in freeholds such as houses, lands, or town lots. For members of the Commons House, the higher requirement would be 500 acres of land and twenty slaves, or the value of 1,000 proclamation money in freeholds as above. The bill also barred from the Commons any officeholders who received "a yearly salary from the public."[50] There was an additional provision designed to promote toleration of religious dissenters who were more often directly affected by the emotional appeals of the Great Awakening. The measure provided that instead of being required to take an oath on the Bible, members of the Commons could demonstrate their loyalty by swearing "according to the Form of their Profession," or as later stated, to hold up the hand and swear "by the Living God."[51] These efforts became entangled in conflict with the Commons as the Council attempted to assert its independence as the Upper House and refused to act on this bill for over a year. When pressed by continuous messages from the Commons to act or explain its failure to do so, the Upper House responded in 1745 with resolutions in acid pen:

Resolved that this House hath an indisputable Right to read any Bill lying before them, and to send the same to the Lower House when only they please, or, if they shall so see fit, not to read such Bill at all.

Resolved that this House is not accountable to the other House, or to any Power whatever, for their Reasons for not reading or sending down, or for not dispatching any Bill lying before this House, or for any of their Proceedings whatever relating to such Bill.[52]

The Commons retreated from its aggressive stance, and after a conference between the two houses, both agreed to proceed with the business before them. The Council as Upper House finally approved the election bill but demonstrated a final act of independence by retaining the swearing of the oath on the Bible, or "on the holy evangelists" as the act stated. The Commons accepted this provision.[53] The governor stood aside in this skirmish between the two bodies of the Assembly.

In that same year of 1745, Glen was more involved in the question of the time period for election of legislative bodies and the frequency of meeting sessions. The models for Parliament in England emerged from seventeenth-century experiences with the conflict between Cavalier and Roundhead. The Triennial Act of 1641 required the election and meeting of Parliament at least once in three years, a stipulation confirmed in 1694 after the Glorious Revolution in the time of William and Mary. The Septennial Act of 1716 extended the life of the legislative body to seven years. Imperial officials persistently attempted control of colonial assemblies by royal instructions to colonial governors for calling and dissolving them.

As South Carolina made its transition from proprietary to royal colony, the Commons House in September 1721 continued an earlier triennial provision for the life of an Assembly for three years and increased the frequency of required sessions from annual to every six months. Soon after Glen's arrival, the Commons House began tampering with these provisions by first proposing biennial elections and then in 1745 actually passing a bill for annual elections. By 1747 this arrangement had proved unsatisfactory and was returned to the two-year limit for the life of each Commons House. Glen, attempting to get along with the Assembly, gave his approval to these measures, his instructions notwithstanding.[54] He consequently received sharp criticism from Crown officials as both the 1745 and 1747 measures were disallowed. Thereafter, South Carolina returned to the 1721 Triennial Act for the remainder of the colonial period.

Glen also reacted in October of 1745 to the question of what should constitute a quorum in the Commons House. The precedent from England found the House of Commons setting its quorum as far back as 1641 when it stipulated less than one-tenth of its members for business. In proprietary South Carolina, a 1716 quorum was much larger, with sixteen out of thirty-one members being required—more than 50 percent. Three years later the quorum rose to nineteen out of thirty-six, still more than 50 percent.[55] The figure of nineteen for a quorum continued to the time of Glen's tenure when the Commons House had increased to over forty members. Even though now below 50 percent, Glen thought the requirement was still too high. As tension increased with the aggressive efforts of the Commons House to encroach on the royal prerogative, Glen criticized the manipulation that this quorum allegedly permitted. "A Party of pleasure made by a few of the Members," Glen complained, "renders it often impossible for the rest to enter upon Business, and sometimes I have seen a Party made to go out of Town purposely to break the House as they call it (well knowing that nothing could be transacted in their absence) and in this manner to prevent the Success of what they could not otherwise oppose."[56] Glen's complaint and subsequent objections by the Board of Trade failed, however, to change the quorum requirement. William Henry Lyttelton, Glen's successor as governor, was also unsuccessful in similar efforts and the quorum of nineteen continued for the remaining years of the colonial period.

Glen was even more concerned about the Council, particularly in view of his exclusion from its sessions as the Upper House of the legislature and possibly, too, his lack of influence over its members in its executive role. He protested his exclusion from the Upper House and its contention that his presence was of an unparliamentary nature. He actually distorted the English constitution in asserting that the King's throne in the House of Lords confirmed that the King and the Lords were one house for legislation.[57] In 1745, the Council reluctantly consented to his presence in the Upper House but on condition that he not participate in debates and not even speak to explain his instructions, upon penalty of further exclusion.

The Council's views on restricting the governor received emphasis in Edmond Atkin's report in 1745 for the Committee on Style, entitled "The Committee appointed to enquire into the Constitution, State and Practice of the Legislature of this Province."[58] While the report, in rather laborious detail, was more critical of the encroachment by the Commons House on the prerogatives of the Upper House in legislation, it also reviewed the errors of previous governors, particularly Governor Francis Nicholson. It concluded that William Bull, Sr., as acting governor had rectified some of the past practices and had maintained the proper balance among the branches of government, but it asserted that Governor Glen had again upset that equilibrium. Stating that the governor as the King's representative was "himself a different and separate Branch of the Legislature," the report contended that Glen "hath no more Right to be present with the Council in their Legislative Capacity, than with the Assembly."[59] This report notwithstanding, Glen continued to sit with the Upper House, but it again revived the exclusion of the governor some five years later.

Glen also reviewed the membership and attendance of Councillors and reported his conclusions in 1746 to the Duke of Newcastle and the Board of

Trade. He agreed that twelve members of the Council were satisfactory. A greater number would lessen its authority, and a smaller group would entail absentees, not only for legislative business but also for its judicial responsibility as the Court of Chancery. Glen's commission stated that three would constitute a quorum for the Council, but his fifth instruction mandated that five members were required to act except in emergencies when this number could not be assembled.[60] For the Court of Chancery seven members were needed along with the governor. Glen noted that four Councillors were in England: John Colleton, John Fenwick, John Hammerton, and Richard Hill. Joseph Blake and Edmond Atkin planned to go there in the spring. Joseph Wragg was ill, and James Kinloch wanted to go to New York for his health.   Among those remaining, two were at opposite extremes of the province: William Bull, Sr., to the south near Port Royal and John Cleland to the north at Winyah.[61]

Eugene Sirmans in his *Political History* erroneously dismissed Glen's complaint about Council attendance as "prattle" and "sham." He stated that the lack of a quorum in the Upper House during this time resulted only once, but he carelessly supported this assertion with documentation from the record for the Commons House rather than the Council or Upper House. Furthermore, Glen's *explicit complaint* in his 1746 letter referred to inadequate numbers for the Chancery Court which, as noted above, required seven members.[62] A review of the records of the Upper House and Council meetings in 1746 and 1748 reveals that attendance at times was, indeed, small and with several meetings without the required number for the legislative quorum of the governor's instructions.   Lieutenant Governor Bull was often absent, and Glen was sometimes not present. The Upper House and Council continued to consider items of business, even without the required quorum.[63]

The governor was authorized to make recommendations for new members of the Council when vacancies occurred. Glen's submission of seven persons in 1746 revealed to some extent the strategy he followed during the 1740s for political influence. He did not align himself with either the strong merchant faction in the Assembly or the followers of the Bull family with a substantial number of planters. He did attempt to improve Council attendance and to gain support for his own actions. His recommendations were partially based on the expediency of location, with all seven nominees residing in Charles Town with ease of attendance at meetings. Six of them also held provincial appointive offices. There was also a Scottish connection, with James Graeme and James Michie as lawyers and John Lining as a Scottish doctor. Graeme became one of the staunchest supporters of the governor and later defended him in the Choctaw revolt controversy. Graeme had the support of Glen's brother, Dr. Thomas Glen, who by 1749 was a member of the Commons House from St. Helena Parish. Graeme became chief justice of the colony in 1749 and was appointed to the Council in 1750 but served only two years before his death in 1752. James Michie, planter as well as lawyer, judge of the vice-admiralty court, and member of the Commons House, was finally appointed to the Council in 1755 near the end of Glen's tenure and served until his death in 1760. Dr. Lining never became a Councillor.

Among the other four persons recommended, three eventually did serve on the Council. Glen had included Chief Justice Benjamin Whitaker, former speaker of the Commons House, on the list but had reservations about his membership because he obtained leave to go to England for his health. Whitaker never received appointment to the Council. Alexander Vander Dussen, soldier, planter, and member of the Commons House, did serve on the Council from 1746 to 1755. Hector Beringer de Beaufain, native of France, collector of customs, and member of the Commons House, also served from 1747 to 1756. Othniel Beale, merchant from New England, holder of several commissions, and member of the Commons House, like Michie, was not appointed until 1755 but continued with a distinguished record until 1773. With five out of seven this was not a bad record of achievement when compared with the six nominations later of Lieutenant Governor William Bull, Jr., that were completely ignored.[64] Yet Michie and Beale came too late to give Glen much support. The Crown also appointed seven other members of the Council during Glen's tenure who were not recommended by him, so he did not succeed in controlling the Council by this procedure. Glen also had to confront Edmond Atkin who had been on the Council since 1738 and often followed an erratic course, asserting the independence of the Council and often vigorously opposing the governor. Glen did succeed in getting the Board of Trade to check on absentees in England and to force the resignation of John Hammerton in 1748 because of absences.

The governor continued his efforts to restore what he viewed as the proper balance of government with appropriate recognition of the royal prerogative. In letters in 1748 to the Board of Trade and the Duke of Bedford, successor to the Duke of Newcastle as Secretary of State for the Southern Department, Glen again discoursed at great length on the extent to which he found the "whole frame of Government unhinged."[65]

The General Assembly, Glen stated, selected and controlled the tenure of the treasurer who received and disbursed all public money collected for the Crown. The Assembly also appointed other officials such as the commissary, the Indian commissioner, the comptroller of duties on imports and exports, and the powder receiver. Furthermore, much of the executive duties of government and administration, Glen continued, were "lodged" in an array of commissioners, including the "Commissioners of the Market, of the Workhouse, of the Pilots, of the Fortifications, and so on without number." Even "Ecclesiastical Preferments" were in the hands of the people, although the governor's instruction delegated him the "Power of collating to all Livings." Ministers changed their parishes and received money imposed by taxes without notice from the governor. This situation, Glen opined, probably explained why the governor was not prayed for in any parish, although supplications were regularly offered for the Assembly while in session.[66]

Most critical of all, Glen continued, was the governor's inability to exercise constitutional powers. The Crown by various laws of the Assembly had lost its "principal flowers and brightest Jewels." The governor then was "stripped naked of Power, and when he can neither reward the virtuous and deserving, nor displace or punish those that offend, it must be difficult for him to keep Government in order." Glen concluded with a flourish: "God Almighty in his moral government of the World is pleased to make use of both love and fear, of promises and also of threatnings."[67]

Many of these problems facing Glen had their origin during the proprietary period, with usage over time solidifying the gradual transition of more authority in the hands of the Commons House. The position of treasurer and other revenue officers was a case in point relating to funds provided by colonial legislatures in contrast to Crown income from such sources as quitrents, fines, and imperial duties of customs. As far back as 1691, the Commons House in South Carolina assumed the responsibility of nominating and appointing the treasurer whose duties were to receive taxes and other fees imposed by the legislature and to dispense them upon authorization by all branches of the legislature.[68] Dispute over combining the office of treasurer with that of speaker of the Commons led the legislature to pass a statute in 1707 stating the right from past years to nominate the public receiver.[69] Both Governor Nathaniel Johnson and the Council, apparently unmindful of the precedent it confirmed, agreed to this measure, which the Commons House later used to assert the right to appoint all officials responsible for provincial revenues. The proprietors disallowed this measure in 1718 as "inconsistent with and contrary to the Usage and Custom of Great Britain."[70]

Nonetheless, the transition from proprietary to royal control permitted the Commons House in 1720 to proclaim the continuation of the privileges of the act of 1707. The Council, attempting to recoup its authority, insisted with the passage of the treasurer act of 1721 that revenue officers should be appointed by agreement of both houses of the General Assembly.[71] The Commons resisted at first and contended that its authority to nominate was a right long established since the 1707 act, and, furthermore, that as representative of the "whole people," it should have the authority of appointment of officials responsible for the people's money. To counter the governor's claim of control by authority of his instructions, the Commons House introduced the concept that his present instructions were applicable only to laws of the future, not to laws and privileges from the past[72]—a bit of clever sophistry and an early glimmer of the position later asserted more directly that only royal officials were bound by instructions, not the people of the province. Despite these arguments, the Commons House had to yield to the position that nominations were to be made by both houses of the Assembly to operate under a commission from the governor. At the same time, it was able to achieve the de facto recognition of having its nominees accepted for the various revenue positions. Beyond the treasurer, this included the commissary general with responsibilities for providing military supplies, Indian presents, and payment for land surveys for poor Protestant immigrants. It also provided for the powder receiver who was authorized to collect one-half pound of gunpowder for each ship entering the ports to enhance the defense of the colony, and for a number of minor officials throughout the province.

Glen's protest of 1748 regarding his lack of control over the treasurer alerted the Board of Trade to this major example of encroachment on the royal prerogative. While agreeing that the treasurer act of 1721 should be disallowed, the Board never made such a specific recommendation to the King and Privy Council. Its subsequent instruction to Governor William Henry Lyttelton for repeal of the statute failed to implement changes.

Glen's protest of lack of power over "Ecclesiastical Preferments" also fell victim to past colonial laws and practices. His commission specifically stated that he was authorized "to collate any Person or Persons to any Churches, Chappels or other Ecclesiastical Benefices" under the Crown whenever vacant.[73] Instruction number seventy-two reiterated this authority by reserving from the general powers of the Bishop of London in the colony the right of the governor to "Collating to Benefices, Granting Licences for Marriages & probat of Wills."[74] As other colonies such as Virginia had experienced, however, Glen found that the Commons House, by its 1704 and 1706 acts of establishment of the Anglican Church,[75] had provided for the Anglican freeholders of parishes to elect their own ministers who served from year to year without the more secure induction under authority of the governor. And so it continued throughout the remainder of the colonial period.

A review of Governor Glen's efforts to fulfill the obligations of a royal governor from his arrival in 1743 to 1745 reveals mixed results. Before leaving Britain after his appointment in 1738, he had plenty of opportunities to examine his commission and his 110 instructions. But week by week he discovered that the political realities in Colonial South Carolina did not adhere fully to the pattern set forth in imperial orders. There were many precedents to the contrary. The Commons House had encroached on the royal prerogative in various ways, such as the selection of the public treasurer, the issuance of paper money without appropriate provisions for redemption by a sinking bill, the denial of the governor's power to make Anglican religious appointments, and the ignoring of English precedents for the time periods for elections of the Assembly. Glen also did not achieve full rapport with the Council either in its role as the Upper House of the Assembly or its executive function as advisor to the governor. Dispute persisted over the right to attend legislative sessions of the Upper House. For the Council in its executive role, attendance was often irregular and the governor was unable to get the appointment of all members recommended. Furthermore, established members such as Edmond Atkin from his appointment in 1738 were often uncooperative, for Atkin often asserted an independent role in interpreting royal mandates. Nonetheless, Glen worked diligently and with great energy to learn about the needs of the colony, including such areas as the fortifications for Charles Town and the defense needs at the other ports of Beaufort and George Town.

The governor did not align himself directly with either the influential merchant faction or the planter group in the Assembly usually associated with the Bull family. He attempted to steer a neutral course, although he did have to take a position in favor of the planters over the merchants in the tax bill issue of 1744. This was an early glimmer of Glen's admiration for the plantation tradition which he later emulated. On the other hand, he recognized the potential benefits of mercantile activities, which he was later to explore in the Indian trade.

Much of what Glen did came from his own initiative, motivated by his conscientious attempts to follow his commission and instructions to uphold the royal prerogative. Correspondence with imperial officials was limited during these early years. The Board of Trade was in a period of little supervision of colonial affairs. The Board, created in 1696 by the King's commission to undergird the royal prerogative in opposition to Parliament, received the title of Lords Commissioners of Trade and Plantations. It was appointed "for promoting the Trade of our Kingdom, and for Inspecting and Improving our Plantations in America and elsewhere."[76] Acting as a committee of the Privy Council, it collected information about the colonies, made recommendations to the Privy Council, and corresponded with royal governors. The Board's limited participation during this period was caused in part by the inefficiency and illness of its president, Lord Monson, from 1737 to 1748, as well as by the increased exertion of authority over colonial affairs by the Duke of Newcastle as Secretary of State for the Southern Department. For example, the Board sent only nine letters to colonial governors in 1746 and only eleven in 1747.[77] This sporadic activity was soon to change with new appointments to the Board about the time Glen encountered difficulties in the Choctaw revolt. The Choctaw affair is part of the many concerns of the next chapter on Indian affairs, which also engaged the governor's major attention during these early years.

3

International Conflict and the Role of Indian Allies

The Fate of this Country is so interwoven and inseparably connected with Indian Affairs that we must always be attentive to every thing that concerns them and be watchful to prevent French Influence there.

James Glen, 1746

The international alignment of warpowers on the southern frontier became more complex at about the time Governor Glen arrived to assume full duties as chief executive of South Carolina. France had concluded with Spain the Second Bourbon Family Compact in 1743, the continuation of a series of agreements more closely relating the interests of Bourbon rulers. Diplomatic events on the continent of Europe had united Sardinia and Austria in a defensive pact in 1743 as a counter to the threat of the Spanish Bourbons to territories in Italy. This spurred France to proceed with the Second Bourbon Family Compact and to join Spain in challenges to English aggression in Georgia, the English threat to Florida and Louisiana, and the competition for Indian allies and Indian trade. France consequently declared war on England in April of 1744 and joined forces with Spain in the war in the colonies known as King George's War, the American component of the War of Austrian Succession in which England had been allied with Austria since 1740.[1]

The role of Native Americans in the colonial struggle took central stage and launched Governor Glen on a course that dominated much of his energy and resulted in one of his most effective areas of administration. His initial ethnocentric reaction to the role of Indian leaders belied the more sympathetic position of his later experience. In a letter of February 6, 1744, he referred in a cynical tone to his time spent in creating kings for "those mighty Indian Monarchs" who had come down. He then continued, "I remember Roselli at the

Hague petitioned the States either to be made professor of Divinity or to be allowed to keep a Coffee house. These Gentlemen seem glad of their Commission to be King but I believe would be better pleased to be Kitchen boys at Newcastle House."[2]

These comments notwithstanding, Glen proceeded to learn about the many tribes adjacent to South Carolina and to assess their potential in the international conflict at hand. The Yamassees, who had seriously threatened Charles Town in the Yamassee War of 1715, were still hostile but had fled to the protecting arms of the Spanish near St. Augustine following their defeat. Glen sent agents to survey the population, the number of gun men, and the nature of Indian trade, as well as surveyors to compile maps of tribal locations. By 1748 he reported the results to the Duke of Newcastle as Secretary of State for the Southern Department and the Board of Trade.[3] Edmond Atkin, Charles Town merchant in the Indian trade and member of the South Carolina Council since 1738, submitted a report in 1755 to the Board of Trade that also included estimates of Indian population as well as a plan for imperial supervision of Indian affairs.[4] His figures were in essential agreement with Glen's. The population figures in subsequent paragraphs are the eighteenth-century estimates of Glen and Atkin. Peter Wood has recently completed a general review of population changes in the colonial South for whites, Indians, and blacks from 1685 to 1790.[5]

The Catawbas were living along the Catawba River near the present boundary of North and South Carolina with a population of 300 to 500 fighting men. Glen suggested 300 "Bravest Fellows,"[6] while Atkin listed 320[7] and other sources range as high as 500. Known as the Esaws in the late seventeenth century, they were identified as Catawbas by 1710, and by the time of Glen's arrival in 1743 they contained a diverse collection of over twenty dialects and languages. While they have traditionally been classified as Eastern Siouan, recent scholarship recognizes that some of them may have spoken Siouan, but they appear to have been culturally identified with the Cherokees, and others may have spoken their Iroquoian language. Usually pro-English in allegiance, the Catawbas had occasional conflicts with other pro-English tribes. They were threatened by Indian allies of the French and also suffered from the long-standing feud with the Iroquois nation in New York.[8]

The Cherokees of Iroquoian linguistic classification were identified in four divisions: the Lower Cherokees on the upper waters of the Savannah River and along the Keowee and Tugaloo rivers in upcountry South Carolina; the Middle Cherokees on the Tuckasegee and the upper waters of the Little Tennessee between the Cowee and Balsam mountains in western North Carolina; the Upper or Valley Cherokees along the Valley River and the north side of the Hiwassee River in northern Georgia and southwestern North Carolina; and the Overhills south of the Cumberland ranges along the lower waters of the Little Tennessee in eastern Tennessee. A South Carolina survey in 1715 had listed sixty towns with a total population of 11,210.[9] James Adair, Indian trader and author of the valuable *History of the American Indian* published in 1775, stated that their number had been drastically reduced from epidemics by one-half.[10]   Glen described them as only ninety miles from some of the South Carolina settlements with not over 3,000 fighting men in the 1740s,[11] the same figure listed by Atkin.[12] Usually pro-English in allegiance, they had competition among towns for political authority that presented a constant challenge, particularly as the Overhill town of Chota asserted its claim to dominance.

The Creek or Muskogee Confederacy of the Muskhogean language family consisted of the Lower Creeks along the Chattahoochee River in present-day Georgia and Alabama with their headquarters in Coweta, and the Upper Creeks along the Coosa and Tallapossa rivers in present-day Alabama, including the Tallapoosas, Abeikas, and Alabamas. Glen suggested a total of 2,500 gunmen for the combined group,[13] while Atkin assigned 1,200 to the Lower Creeks, 1,180 to the Upper Nation, and an additional 185 Savanoes (Shawnees) incorporated from the north for a total of 2,565.[14] The Creeks were noted in past years for their efforts to remain neutral in the international struggle by European nations, particularly under the leadership of Old Brims as "emperor." The Lower and Upper groups, however, did not always agree on their relationship to these nations.

The Chickasaws, also of the Muskhogean language family and at one time in union with the Choctaws, inhabited the northern part of present Mississippi along the upper waters of the Tombigbee and Yazoo rivers. They were consistently allies of the English and had a reputation as the bravest of warriors. Glen listed a reduction of their number to 200 to 300 men,[15] while Atkin's report gave a total of 480 with 350 in their central location, 80 at a camp bordering the Upper Creeks, and 50 who had moved to the Savannah River to be close to South Carolina.[16]

The Choctaws of the Muskhogean language family were the largest of these tribes and lived west of the Creeks in present Mississippi in an area extending from the upper waters of the Pearl River to the Tombigbee River. A report of 1739 gave a total of some 5,000 warriors with a total population of between 15,000 and 20,000.[17] Limited opportunities to gain information on this distant group led Glen to suggest at least 6,000 warriors,[18] while Atkin used a captured report from the French governor of Louisiana, Marquis de Vaudreuil, to list 3,600 men.[19] Usually pro-French in their allegiance, the Choctaws attracted great attention from Governor Glen and others in efforts to win them over to the English.

Within the colony of South Carolina there remained smaller tribes that were known as settlement or tributary Indians. While the tributary system was not as extensive as the Virginia experience that began with the Powhatans in 1646,[20] it did exist as early as the seventeenth century when the colony required the Coosa tribe "to pay a dear skin monthly as an acknowledgement or else to loose our amitie."[21]   The Yamassees had departed after their unsuccessful war in 1715, but several smaller tribes continued with a limited number of approximately 400 warriors. Though not of great significance in providing protection of the colony, they still demanded the attention of the governor and the Assembly. This was evident in the provision for the following gifts in March 1744 to the Peedee Indians on their visit to Charles Town: a gun and knife for the three head men, a knife for other males, a looking glass for the three women, plus bullets and vermillion (paint) to be divided among the group.[22]

After France entered the war against England, Governor Glen and the Council pondered possible attacks that would threaten Mobile and Louisiana as well as the Spanish in Florida. Aware of the potential for Indian allies, the governor and Council proposed as early as 1745 a possible scenario against the French that was taken to England by John Fenwick, a veteran legislator of South Carolina with long years of service in the Commons before membership on the Council from 1730 to 1746, including two years as its president.[23] The plan advocated the use of Indians (Cherokees, Chickasaws, Creeks, and possibly the Choctaws) to assist in assaulting French fortifications. These attacks would include Fort Toulouse in Upper Creek country near the junction of the Coosa and Tallapoosa rivers and other French strongholds en route to the conquest of Mobile and New Orleans. Assistance from the royal navy would be required, with possible use of up to four ships from Jamaica. Since there was uncertainty about cooperation from Georgia, South Carolina was to assume responsibility for directing the project. Fenwick presented this plan to the Board of Trade in 1745, but both the Board and the Duke of Newcastle simply filed it for possible future discussion.[24]

As the international conflict lingered on, Glen revived the 1745 plan in early 1748 and spelled out more specific details for Newcastle and the Board of Trade. He advocated the erection of four forts among the Indians: one in the Choctaw nation with 100 men, one among the Upper Cherokees with fifty men, a smaller fort among the Chickasaws in proximity to the Creeks with twenty-five men, and one among the Catawbas also with a contingent of twenty-five. Glen included the information he had on the limited strength of both the Spanish and French. In St. Augustine there were only 600 soldiers, and several companies had incomplete complements of fifty men in areas from Mobile and New Orleans to the Illinois country. Glen proposed attacks on these settlements under the direction of Admiral Sir Charles Knowles[25] with 300 men from General Dalzel's regiment in the Leeward Islands, another 300 from the regiment of Governor Edward Trelawny[26] of Jamaica, General Oglethorpe's regiment in Georgia, and the three independent companies in South Carolina.[27] Alexander Vander Dussen,[28] a member of the Council, was selected to present this proposal in person to the Board of Trade. While Glen's plan had considerable merit in view of the small French and Spanish forces and limited wartime supplies, it evoked minimum attention with the war coming to a close with the approval of the preliminary articles of peace of Aix-la-Chapelle. The Duke of Bedford succeeded the Duke of Newcastle as Secretary of State for the Southern Department in February of 1748 and temporarily had greater interest in this scheme. The final approval of peace terms, however, turned it aside as well as the uncertain negotiations with the Choctaw Indians. Glen had thus presented two plans for British conquest on the southern frontier, even though neither was implemented by imperial officials. Nonetheless, he would submit others in the future to respond to what he considered the duty of colonial governors.

The governor's earliest crisis in Indian relations involved the attack in 1744 upon the Catawbas by the Natchez (Notchees), a refugee group from the extreme French attack in the 1730s that scattered this sun-worshiping tribe from the area of present Mississippi with their authoritarian Sun Chief. The Natchez had murdered seven drunken Catawbas, scalped them, and cut out their tongues. Anticipating the traditional clan revenge of the law of blood (*lex talionis*), the governor intervened and persuaded the Catawbas to delay acts of retribution. Meanwhile, Glen brought the Natchez leaders to Charles Town and convinced them to turn over the heads of the guilty attackers. The colony then pickled these remains and hastily transported them to the Catawba leaders who accepted this as satisfactory revenge for the cruel and cowardly attacks. The Catawbas by this process moved toward greater dependence on the colony to resolve its external relations, while Glen expressed optimism for this arranged agreement as lessons to neighboring tribes. At the same time, he again reacted negatively to native society: Indians "whatever is said of them and of their native Simplicity and honesty, are a savage, cruel, perfidious, revengefull sett of Men."[29]

The Cherokees were to play a more dominant role in Governor Glen's career. Among the villages of the four divisions in the precontact period with Europeans, the Cherokees had virtual autonomy in political affairs. The administration of village councils included "white" officials with civil authority frequently based on heredity and "red" officials for war and military action whose positions were more often dependent on exemplary individual exploits. These leaders apparently functioned for several purposes or in several poses. These purposes included the hunt, clan obligations of revenge and social customs such as marriage, religious festivals, or agricultural pursuits under the "white" leaders, and war under the "red" banner of leadership.[30]

Contact with the English colonies brought pressure on the autonomous villages to develop more central authority for the full Cherokee nation in diplomatic negotiations. One step in this direction came from the incredible efforts of Sir Alexander Cuming, a Scottish baronet and member of the Royal Society. Having come to Charles Town with an interest in collecting scientific information, he journeyed to the Cherokee country in 1730 as his attention turned to Cherokee politics. He visited several Cherokee villages, armed with "Pistols, a Gun, and a Sword," and persuaded them with his oratory to make the pro-English Moytoy of the Overhill villages their "emperor."[31] Superficially at least, this moved the Cherokee nation from an aggregate of independent villages to a more explicit structure for tribal government, although this external influence did not persuade most Cherokees to modify their traditional autonomy. Cuming then prevailed on seven Cherokees (two chiefs and five warriors) to travel to England where the Board of Trade seized the opportunity to conclude a treaty to "brighten the chain of friendship." The agreements provided for Cherokee recognition of subjection to English jurisdiction. In return for promise of more trade, the tribe was to assist the English against their enemies and to yield to English law both Indians and whites guilty of murder.[32]

This English intervention over political leaders was oblivious to the internal relationships among the Cherokees. Chota of the Overhill villages was the oldest of regional councils, the town of shelter and the mother town. A position such as "emperor" would normally belong to the Uku of Chota. Moytoy, however, was from Great Tellico, which was colonized from the Valley towns and, therefore, did not have the long-standing prestige of the Chota leaders. Upon Moytoy's death in battle in 1741, South Carolina attempted to perpetuate its control by naming his thirteen-year-old son, Ammonscossittee, as "emperor" with the Raven of Hiwassee as guardian. Hiwassee, however, was a Valley town that further intensified the friction over superiority in Cherokee affairs between Chota and other towns.[33]

Governor Glen in October 1744 received a message from the new young "emperor" that he had heard of the governor's arrival and planned to come down to Charles Town, but with news of the English war with France, he postponed his trip until spring. At the same time, the "emperor" added, this would permit his young men to continue their hunt and help pay off their debts to traders; he reiterated his desire to visit "to set and talk and Smoak a Pipe of your good Tobacco."[34]

Glen was not content to confer with Indian leaders only in Charles Town. Characteristic of his energetic approach to administration, he was willing to travel extensively to all parts of the province. In February of 1746 he reported to the Duke of Newcastle that he visited Port Royal and reviewed the militia at Fort Frederick. The heat was excessive, he lamented, and he was seized with a violent fever. He had also traveled to Winyaw, the most northern part of the colony, where he reported that his visit evoked great satisfaction since he was the first governor to travel to the area.[35]

The increased Anglo-French tension led Glen to visit the Indian country. He noted in February of 1746 that Indian affairs were in good shape with visits of both Cherokee and Catawba leaders to Charles Town, and with the Indians having changed his title from the more traditional "Brother" to that of "Father."[36] By May, however, he perceived deterioration in Indian affairs thanks to French meddling. The Cherokees informed him that twenty French Indians and two Frenchmen were among them as agents and wanted to construct a French fort in their villages. The Creeks had attacked the Euchees, and the Chickasaws had raided the Catawbas with several killed and some 100 women and children taken captive. With this alarming news, the governor persuaded the Assembly to authorize pay for horsemen at £ 0:15:00 per trooper per day to accompany him to meet with several tribes.[37]

Glen conferred first with the Catawbas near the Congarees in the vicinity of present Columbia and discouraged them from a raid of vengeance against the Chickasaws. Moving on to Saluda near Ninety-Six, he met some sixty Cherokee leaders and their "emperor" who, he reported, was greatly impressed with this show of force that brought together the largest armed group of colonials thus far assembled in the area. The Cherokees warned the governor of the French threat, particularly to their westernmost towns of the Overhills, and agreed to act in consultation with him, but they were not yet enthusiastic about the suggestion for an English fort in their bounds for their own security.

Glen then moved on to Fort Moore at Savannah Town just across the river from present-day Augusta, Georgia, for meetings with the Chickasaws in the area and with leaders of the Creeks. He effectively warned the Chickasaws about attacks on the Catawbas and their pilfering of outer settlements, but he was unsuccessful in persuading the Creeks to attack the French Fort Toulouse as they continued to adhere to the traditional role of neutrality of Old Brims. In these conferences the governor found that the Indians had their own agenda of self-interest which they vigorously pursued.

With an eye to proper credit from imperial officials in England, Glen elaborated in detail about the hardships endured as a result of the incessant rain and the limited number of tents for the expedition. The men were forced at night to lie on the wet ground with cover only from the bark of trees, resulting in a variety of fluxes and fever for which his medicine chest provided only a partial remedy. The flooding waters, he continued, forced them to swim horses across the streams and to create boats from buffalo hides sewed together by bark to keep ammunition and provisions dry in crossing.[38] Impressed with this extra effort, the Board of Trade commended Glen for his extensive activity.

Regulation of the valuable Indian trade was a perennial problem leading to a variety of experiments and continuing the challenge for its control by governor, Council, and Commons House. While still under proprietary jurisdiction, the Assembly finally passed the 1707 act for regulation of the Indian trade after controversy with Governor Nathaniel Johnson over the extent of authority of the Commons House. The act stipulated that traders obtain licenses for trade with all natives except the nearby settlement Indians, and it authorized nine commissioners and an Indian agent who was required to spend at least ten months each year among the Indians.[39] At the same time, it put specific restrictions on traders from other colonies and set off the embittered controversy with Virginians. They protested to imperial officials the requirements for Virginia traders to pay a fee of £8 and to post a bond of £100 in Charles Town. The Crown issued an order in council prohibiting the South Carolina practices of both the 1707 act and subsequent legislation of 1711,[40] but South Carolina continued to squeeze out its competition from the Old Dominion.[41]

South Carolina again tampered with Indian trade regulations during the aftermath of the violent Yamassee War as it instituted a public monopoly of the trade in 1716. Proposed earlier by planters in the Commons to correct trade abuses, the monopoly was successfully resisted by merchants in the Upper House until approved during the confusion following the war. The monopoly provided that the commissioners named in the act by the Commons House handle the trade and establish three "factories" or trading posts at Fort Moore, Congarees, and Winyah.[42] Even though additional "factories" were set up to meet the Indians' complaints, opposition from both London and local merchants led to its repeal in 1718 and 1719 as the colony turned to a compromise with a combined public and private trade.[43] The public corporation continued at a reduced level, and private traders were licensed by the appointed commissioners. This compromise gave way to a complete return to private trade in 1721, and supervision reverted to the status of 1707. A total of three commissioners appointed by the Commons then attempted to control the trade and traders to avoid abuses in the system. In 1723 Royal Governor Francis Nicholson succeeded in returning control of Indian trade to the governor and Council, but the complexity of the frontier task led to a return of the responsibility to the Commons House which then turned to a single commissioner under its control.[44] This system, though obviously encroaching on the royal prerogative, was still in effect when Glen became governor.

Amid the conflict of the Anglo-French struggle in King George's War, the more distant Choctaw nation presented both an opportunity and a trap for Governor Glen. There were three Choctaw divisions based primarily on cultural/geographic influences. The Western division was along the watershed of the Pearl River, the Eastern one along the Tombigbee, and the Six Towns along the Pascagoula and Chickasawhay rivers. The different social moieties of inholahta and imoklasha were distributed among all of these divisions, with matrilineal exogamous moieties containing six or eight clans each. Politically, each division appeared to negotiate separately in its own best interest.[45] Interestingly enough, Sieur de Bienville, commander of the French at Mobile, attempted the same effort in behalf of the French as the English tried among the Cherokees to have one political head represent the entire Choctaw nation. The French recognized their leaders by bestowing medals on them as medal chiefs, including at one time the supreme chief, the war leader of the nation, and the three division chiefs.

Although traditionally pro-French, the Choctaws showed signs of discontent with inadequate French supplies in trade as early as the 1730s which eventually resulted in the Choctaw revolt of the 1740s. One of the central figures in this conflict emerged through French recognition of his exploits in wars against the Natchez and Chickasaws in the 1730s. He was popularly known as Red Shoe or Red Shoes, from a term in French, *soulier rouge*, that applied to leaders of different groups. Known also by his Indian name of Shulush Homa (Shulashummashtabe), he had by the 1730s developed an interest in English trade through marital connections with the Chickasaws. After the French attempted to discipline him by curtailing trade, he journeyed in 1738 with John Campbell, Indian trader, to Charles Town where Lieutenant Governor William Bull, Sr., completed a treaty of peace and commerce.[46] Through these efforts, he continued to draw from both the French and English to build a faction mainly among the Western division. Some support also came in part of the Six Towns, most evident in his close relationship with Mongoulacha Mingo as the medal chief of the Chickasawhay villages.[47]

There is confusion about the initial steps in the reopening of Choctaw trade during King George's War involving the role of James Adair, noted Indian trader among the Chickasaws for many years. His *History of the American Indian* was designed in part to support his extensive claims for reimbursement of his alleged expenditures in the Choctaw trade. Edmond Atkin also wrote about the Choctaw revolt and challenged Adair's claims as well as being highly critical of Governor Glen. Adair stated that he had initiated efforts in 1746 to open the Choctaw trade "by virtue of the pressing engagement of a prime magistrate of South Carolina," obviously Governor Glen.[48] The governor also gave his own account of this revolt in his message to the Assembly; his account was never published, but it is now available in the Glen Papers in original manuscript in the South Caroliniana Library.[49] Intended in part to deny the claims of another trader, Charles McNaire, for reimbursement, it provides still another account of the Choctaw crisis but has the limitation of Glen's efforts to rationalize, or at times to conceal, his role in what turned out to be an embarrassing failure.

According to Glen, James Adair visited him at his country home in 1745 and discussed ways of harassing the French on the Mississippi, a visit that Atkin asserted never occurred. Glen stated that Adair minimized the potential of assistance from the Chickasaws because of their reduced population but Adair hastened to propose "upon proper Encouragement" to work with fellow Chickasaw trader, John Campbell, to bring about a revolution among the Choctaws in favor of the English. In response, Glen noted that he hesitated in promising financial assistance from the Assembly which was not then in session, but he hoped Adair would undertake the task.[50]

In the Choctaw nation, Red Shoes in 1745 attempted to strengthen the English connection. He negotiated a peace with the Chickasaws through the "Blind King" (Imayatabé le Borgne), with assistance again from trader John Campbell.[51] The hostility of Red Shoes to the French in the same year increased as a result of the aggression of a French soldier from Fort Tombigbee who forced his attention on a favorite wife.[52]

In the following year the French attempted to discipline Red Shoes for his English negotiations. They withdrew his French medal, and he was conspicuously absent from Mobile in March and April when French presents were distributed.[53] Meanwhile, the followers of Red Shoes, stepping up the efforts for English goods, murdered three Frenchmen in August, supposedly in retaliation for the earlier killing of three English traders by the French. Red

Shoes sent the scalps to the Chickasaws for renewed peace with the tribe, and the scalps were to be forwarded to Governor Glen. The scalps, however, were later turned over to the Pakana, a part of the Creeks near Fort Toulouse, rather than completing the original plans of this grisly business.[54] The invitations for trade motivated John Campbell and other unlicensed traders to take supplies to the Choctaws, who rejoiced in this revival of trade. This gave such a boost to the pro-English group that twenty-five towns were claimed in support of Red Shoes, approximately half of the nation.[55]

Red Shoes then sent his brother, Little King (Imataha Pousouche or Minko Puskus), and the head men of fifteen towns to Charles Town to renew peace with South Carolina and to promote further trade of critical supplies of powder and ammunition which were urgently needed to counter French activities among the Choctaws. By April 10, 1747, Little King and his entourage had reached Charles Town and completed a treaty by April 18 with Governor Glen and the Council.[56] The Commons House only agreed to a long list of presents for the Choctaw delegation and procrastinated in taking further steps to maximize the opportunity for solidifying agreements with the visitors.[57] Nonetheless, Little King, in return for promises of trade and friendly relations with the English, did agree to resist the French and to provide security for traders along the path near the French fort built on the Tombigbee River in 1736. He also agreed to assist in capturing this stronghold, to cooperate in building a fort within the Choctaw nation, and possibly to assist the Creeks in assaults on Fort Toulouse among the Alabamas. In response to the determined request for a trader to accompany the delegation on their return trip, Governor Glen introduced Charles McNaire to the Council and, upon its approval, identified him to Little King as the key person in delivering presents and trade goods.[58]

Who was Charles McNaire? He certainly was not an experienced Indian trader; moreover, he was unacquainted with Indian languages. He had been an unsuccessful seafarer and was now willing to seek his fortune on the frontier along with his merchant friend, Mathew Roche. Unknown to the Council at that time, Glen had decided to seek profit from the Indian trade by attempting to give McNaire and his associates a monopoly of the Choctaw traffic in a company in which he himself would invest along with a small group of friends. His investments were made under the name of Mathew Roche, and stock was also issued to his brother, Dr. Thomas Glen, Jordan Roche (uncle of Mathew), and James Maxwell with trading partners, including Thomas Maxwell, Arthur Harvey, and John Vann.[59]

Little King reluctantly left Charles Town ahead of McNaire with plans to wait at Fort Moore near present Augusta for the trading caravan. McNaire delayed seven or eight weeks until June 10 before his train of 200 horses was ready. Proceeding to the Upper Creek nation, he left many of his goods at a store near the Alabama fort. After delays that were never fully explained, he finally reached the Choctaws on September 25 with only part of his goods after requiring twice the length of time usually required for this travel. He gave presents or trade goods estimated at a value of 400 pounds Carolina currency, or approximately £57, and reported an exaggerated claim that forty-two Choctaw towns had declared for the English while only four remained loyal to the French near Fort Tombigbee.[60]

When McNaire and Little King were en route, Red Shoes was killed by hired assassins of the French on June 22, 1747, while accompanying the Creek trader, Elsley, on his way to the Choctaws. The village of Red Shoes confirmed Little King as his successor, and although the French also threatened to kill him, he survived until his natural death in 1749.[61]

Meanwhile, James Adair had been active in his position as a Chickasaw trader. Only four days after the treaty in Charles Town with Little King, Governor Glen had written a private letter to Adair on April 22, 1747, inviting him also to encourage the Choctaw revolution.[62] Adair also claimed, which Glen later denied, that he was designated a public agent and the governor had stated that, if he succeeded among the Choctaws, the governor hoped the colony would compensate him for his services. If not, Glen would recommend favorable action by imperial officials in England for him and John Campbell. While Glen may not have identified Adair as a public agent, it is clear that he did promise to recommend a reward for Adair's action. McNaire's scarcity of goods led him to obtain assistance from Adair for supplies of powder and ammunition for the Choctaws.[63]

Still more supplies were needed to sustain the pro-English factions. McNaire along with Little King returned to Charles Town by December 29, 1747. They had several meetings with Governor Glen along with Mathew Roche but, according to Atkin, without an official meeting of the Council. The secrecy of the meeting involved the attempted monopoly of the trade and Governor Glen's provision of a proclamation for McNaire's use to exclude other traders from the Choctaw for fear of overburdening the trade. Supplies were furnished as presents to the delegation in the amount of 100 arms, 1,500 weight of powder, and 3,000 weight of bullets. McNaire took these to Maxwell's plantation in January 1748 and delivered them in the presence of Little King to John Vann,[64] Indian trader and partner in the company that Adair dubbed the "Sphynx company" because of its secrecy.[65] McNaire returned to the Choctaw nation by the end of March, but Little King waited in the Upper Creek nation for Vann, concerned about returning without the desired supplies. Unusual delays in delivery again resulted, with the material not arriving among the Creeks until early July, a trip that ordinarily required only twenty-five days rather than nearly six months. Vann and Harvey were then ready to proceed from the Upper Creeks to the Choctaws but again waited twenty-one days for a Choctaw guard to escort them past the threatening Tombigbee fort. When the escort arrived, the traders changed their mind and decided to return for fresh horses and go by way of the Chickasaws, a safer route that would have been a better initial choice. The delay postponed Little King's return until August.[66]

By this date, McNaire's direct participation in the Choctaw trade was near its end. While proceeding through the Creek and Chickasaw nations en route to the Choctaws, he had displayed Governor Glen's proclamation to exclude other traders. Adair, miffed at this exclusion, referred to it as a "scare-crow of bees-wax" written on a sheep-skin with a "threatening lion and unicorn."[67] McNaire made his final departure from the Choctaws in August of 1748, returned to Charles Town, and by September of 1749 had departed for England to pursue payments for his services.

Efforts continued to encourage the pro-English Choctaws as civil war erupted in conflict with pro-French towns. A Choctaw delegation with the heads of two towns had reached Fort Moore by December of 1748. The following month they were conferring with the Council in Charles Town with overt requests for their own individual presents, a very unusual procedure in Indian diplomacy. With McNaire out of the way, Governor Glen identified John Pettycrow's (Pettycrou's) offer to deliver presents to the Choctaws at the cost of £5 for each horseload of ammunition. Alarmed by the report that the pro-English Choctaws were reduced to such straits that they were "obliged to fire glass Beads, instead of Bullets," colonial officials agreed to send supplies by Pettycrow to the Creeks and Chickasaws as well as the Choctaws—twenty horseloads for the Choctaws and some forty or more for the Creeks and Chickasaws. These supplies went by boat to Augusta for Pettycrow on October 15, 1749, and he then proceeded to the Chickasaws by November 25 where he waited thirty-seven days for a Choctaw guard. After fifty-two days for the journey from Augusta, he began visiting Choctaw towns in January 1750, with Pouchimataha, one of the chiefs still holding out against the French. Pettycrow counted twenty-four towns that were still friendly to the English with some 1,322 men, a likely exaggeration, before he returned to Charles Town in February with this inflated report.[68] Two years later, he again planned to return to Choctaw country, but the murder of one of his trading party en route prevented him from continuing. English support among the Choctaws had obviously declined with the renewed vigor of the French and the excessive delays and bungled efforts of South Carolina representatives.

Inadequate trade goods and delayed deliveries were important economic factors in the failure to sustain pro-English influence, but they were only part of the story. Vaudreuil's persistent efforts in behalf of the French and the long tradition of French support among the Choctaws militated against the English efforts. The Indians also had their own agenda, and their pursuit of these goals have often been overlooked by writers of Native American history. Among the Choctaws, the peace chiefs and the honored men of the nation had priority in receipt of presents and other benefits; war chiefs accepted this tradition but were not immune to aspirations for similar amenities.[69] Red Shoes as a war leader and medal chief had only fragmented support among part of the Choctaw towns. When civil war erupted following his assassination, the leaders of many towns deplored the slaughter of Choctaws by other Choctaws and exerted influence in returning the nation to its status quo with traditional support for the French.

Even with a steady flow of English trade goods, it was problematical that the Choctaws could be won away from the French as the French continued for a few more years in their international struggle for dominance in North America.

As complex as the events of the failed efforts among the Choctaws may seem, the sequel of conflicting claims by traders for payments and the controversies over their validity was even more entangled. It embroiled all levels of government from both houses of the Assembly, the Council, Governor Glen, and imperial officials in London, particularly the Board of Trade. McNaire and Adair were the major claimants. Reactions to their efforts involved Governor Glen in several shifting positions and in a power struggle with other colonial officials.

Despite the inefficiency of his efforts and the unfavorable results on the Choctaw alliance, McNaire petitioned the Assembly in May 1749 for reimbursement for expenses and alleged losses in the trade of 11,748:5:0 pounds.[70] This petition proved a dilemma for Glen because investigation of it could lead to identification of investments by him and his friends in the monopolistic project, and emphasis on its failures would undercut his claim to the Board of Trade of success in winning over the Choctaws. Glen, therefore, began to disassociate himself from involvement with McNaire. But McNaire had considerable support in the Commons House. Two of his partners, John Roche and James Maxwell, and seven of his creditors were in the Commons, including Andrew Rutledge as speaker and Dr. John Rutledge. Three other creditors were members of the Council, including Charles Pinckney. McNaire had further support from William Pinckney as commissioner of the Indian trade and James Crokatt as provincial agent in London—another creditor.[71] The sympathetic committee on Indian affairs in the Commons recommended payment of 2,000 pounds currency, but the full house voted only 1,000 to assist McNaire in pressing his claims in England.[72] Glen did not openly oppose these efforts of McNaire at that time, but he criticized his failure in private denunciations before later overtly denying his service as a public agent.[73]

The plot thickened as McNaire's supporters turned to the press in direct criticism of the governor. Mathew Roche as McNaire's partner penned a vitriolic denunciation. Its printing was announced in Peter Timothy's *South-Carolina Gazette* of February 26, 1750, under the title of "A Modest Reply to His Excellency the Governor's Written Answer To the Affidavit of Charles M'Naire & Mathew Roche, Concerning The late Revolt of the Chactaw Nation of Indians from the French to the British Interest."[74]

Such an assault on the chief executive of the colony was not to be taken lightly. Glen requested the Commons House to open an investigation of the failure of McNaire and associates to deliver presents to the Choctaws within a reasonable time.[75] As a possible counter to McNaire's claims, Glen invited James Adair back to Charles Town to testify with official protection from legal action by his creditors. This move backfired, however, as it became evident that Adair was also critical of the governor. Roche repeated these criticisms in the "Modest Reply," with other printed complaints by Adair also announced in the *Gazette*.[76]   Adair's anger was no doubt enhanced by his having been excluded from the Choctaw trade for a time by Glen's proclamation used by McNaire. This second assault led the governor to refer Adair's criticisms to the Council, which requested the attorney general to consider the possibility of libel.[77]

The Choctaw affair was a major issue as the Assembly reconvened in May of 1750. Upon resubmission of Mathew Roche's petition accompanied by a copy of his "Modest Reply," the Upper House cited Roche for contempt and had him arrested. These criticisms, it stated, was "a High Contempt of the Dignity of this House."[78] Action in the Commons House centered in the committee on Indian affairs where Glen's position improved with the addition first of his friends, Isaac Mazyck and Isaac Holmes, on May 10 followed by the further addition to the committee the next day of his brother, Dr. Thomas Glen.[79] The governor then presented his side of the story to the Council but refused to table his speech for the record. The next day he gave the same information to the committee on Indian affairs of the Commons House after the Upper House committee refused to continue, according to Edmond Atkin, because of the governor's "unparliamentary interruptions." Glen again refused to make his speech a matter of record.[80] Consequently, it did not become part of the official documents, and it has hitherto been unavailable to scholars. A copy of this speech, however, in Glen's own hand with revisions of his drafts, is now available in the Glen manuscripts recently obtained from Scotland by the South Caroliniana Library.[81] Glen vigorously condemned McNaire's failure and vehemently denied having made him a public agent and having agreed to support reimbursement for his trading expenses. Glen's denial relative to McNaire was more credible than similar assertions for Adair.

Following these committee meetings, Glen apparently went to Atkin's house and explained that he did not table his speech for "fear Atkin would cut it to pieces." Atkin as chair of investigating committees of both the Upper House and the Council was critical of the whole Choctaw affair. Atkin agreed with Glen in denying McNaire's claims, but he was equally critical of Glen's claims for a Choctaw alliance. He did agree with most of Glen's narrative of events, except for the statement that Glen had met with Adair in 1745 to initiate action among the Choctaws. Adair, according to Atkin, had gone to the Indian country in 1744 and did not return to Charles Town until 1747 with Little King.[82]

Adair, nonetheless, had submitted his petition for reimbursement for his services to the Assembly and had added his criticism of the governor in a letter to the Council. Although the Council as Upper House endorsed his petition, the Council reacted negatively to Adair's harsh criticism of the governor and submitted his letter to the attorney general, who rendered a prosecution charge of seditious libel.[83] Both Adair and Mathew Roche were thus challenged for their denouncements of the governor. The Upper House accepted Roche's apology for his statements on May 10. Yet he fared badly, for six of his creditors, including the speaker of the Commons House, filed suits against him for debts from loans for the Indian trade. Glen later joined the legal actions against Roche for his loans, and Roche was forced to declare bankruptcy in July 1750, with Glen and his uncle as preferred creditors since both were heavy investors in the Sphynx Company. Roche was later arrested by the provost marshal and imprisoned as a debtor. His estate was sold by the provost marshal, with his uncle, Jordan Roche, as executor.[84]

Meanwhile, Governor Glen had taken another questionable step by attempting to strengthen his position in the Assembly against the claims of McNaire and others. Samuel Venning, a packhorseman, came to Charles Town with a letter from Pettycrow that gave an overly optimistic view of the pro-English faction among the Choctaws with appropriate credit to the governor's role. Glen then obtained an affidavit from Venning that was critical of the earlier efforts of McNaire and associates. Glen included this affidavit with his direct attack on the claims of McNaire and Roche in his letter to the Assembly on May 17, 1750.[85] The Council viewed Venning's affidavit with suspicion and attempted unsuccessfully to get Glen to turn over his Choctaw papers to the Council. When the report went to the Commons House, a very heated debate resulted in the Glen versus McNaire contest, with Chief Justice James Graeme, a fellow Scot, as the major proponent for Glen against Dr. John Rutledge. The Commons equivocated on the question of Choctaw presents and hinted that Glen might have to share responsibility for failure, but it categorically deemed Roche's "Modest Reply" a seditious attack on the governor—a defeat for the Indian traders.[86]

Atkin, longtime foe of the governor, and some other members of the Council, as the Upper House, were not so willing to dispense with this controversy and attempted to continue the investigation of the Choctaw affair when the Commons was ready to adjourn. Trader John Campbell had also submitted through Isaac Barksdale a petition for payment for his efforts, the most worthy of all petitions, but the Commons adjourned with Glen's approval without giving it consideration. Glen maintained that the Upper House could not continue in session with the Commons having adjourned, and finally the Upper House did cease its meeting without formal adjournment. Its investigation was never completed.[87]

The persistent Glen tried one more move to attack McNaire and his associates. He turned to the grand jury of the October sessions court of 1750 in efforts to prosecute Mathew Roche and Peter Timothy of the *Gazette* for publication of the "Modest Reply." Another heated debate resulted between supporters and critics of the governor, with Chief Justice Graeme in behalf of Glen versus Charles Pinckney and Dr. John Rutledge, a repeat of the battle that had occurred in the Commons. These charges, however, were finally dropped, but not without bitter acrimony over the proper reporting of the jury's verdict.[88]

The governor emerged from this conflict with good support from the

Commons House, if not from the Council led by Atkin. In November Glen commended the Commons: "You divested your selves of all passion and prejudice, you made a strict search after Truth; and, having found it, you silenced Slander; and for once put a stop to all false and fictitious Claims upon the Public."[89] The Commons responded with gracious expression for "so just and mild an Administration" and with pledges to "use all means in our power to maintain and support, as well for the general Good of the Colony, as the happiness of your Excellency's Administration, which we heartily and unfeignedly wish may be long and prosperous."[90]   Glen, constantly seeking approval, was so pleased with this commendation that he passed it along to the Board of Trade.

The Board of Trade, now in a time of transition, was not so sanguine about news from Carolina. The conflicting reports about the Choctaw revolt and the obvious shortcomings in South Carolina's efforts were most unfortunate for Glen in this transition period. The death of Lord Monson in 1748 brought a new era for the Board of Trade, with George Dunk, Earl of Halifax, as the new president. Committed to reform and a much more active role over colonial affairs, Halifax and other reform members of the Board reviewed reports from colonial governors and challenged inconsistencies and failures to uphold the royal prerogative. Halifax, incidentally, was also striving for greater power by attempting to become a member of the King's Cabinet—an ambition never realized.[91] Glen became particularly vulnerable with the loss by death of such past supporters as Lord Wilmington in England and the Earl of Dalhousie of Scotland.

The Board of Trade singled out the problems of the Choctaw revolt and sharply criticized Glen as the acid pen of Halifax was clearly evident in its changed attitude.   We lament due care in conveyance of presents to the Choctaw, the Board lashed out, and then it continued its denunciation by expressing surprise that Glen by October of 1748 did not have an explanation for the failure in July.   You should "act with more Prudence & Circumspection," it added in exasperated tones.[92]   Glen responded to these criticisms by still maintaining in 1749, using Pettycrow's flawed information, that there was still support for the English among the Choctaws. At the same time, he expressed dismay at the Board's criticism when he expected commendation for his efforts.[93] The slow pace of trans-Atlantic communications found the Board in November 1750 still reminding Glen of the Choctaw fiasco[94] and extending their critiques to a variety of other procedures analyzed in subsequent chapters.

As this chapter has shown, Indian affairs were major concerns for Governor Glen and South Carolina. The colony was in the most strategic and most critical position for negotiations with Native Americans on the southern frontier. The governor also displayed a penchant for Indian affairs and a commendable skill in negotiations, as is evident in the peaceful resolution of the Catawba-Natchez conflict. In contrast to some governors who had little interest and little aptitude in Indian relations and who at best were willing to confer only on their home turf, Glen was willing to travel to distant frontiers and undergo the hazards of rough terrain and inclement weather to meet face to face with many different tribal leaders.   Such negotiations provided favorable contacts with Cherokees, Creeks, and Chickasaws, even though he was not always able to persuade them to undertake major campaigns against the French in view of their own agenda of self-interest.   In the case of the Creeks, there was also a long tradition of neutrality relative to the aspirations of competing European powers.   The failure to win over the Choctaws resulted in part from the incorrect assessment of continuing French influence and the inefficient efforts to get trade supplies to the tribe.   Governor Glen was also guilty of the unethical and possibly illegal efforts to monopolize Choctaw trade by the secret organization of a trade company. Subsequent negotiations would later continue and vigorous efforts would be made to bring greater assistance from tribes willing to assist the British in the ongoing struggle for North America.

4

Between Scylla and Charybdis

Nothing can be more repugnant to Reason, more contrary to the Constitution, more opposite to the Laws, Customs, and Practice of Great Britain.

James Glen, 1751

While the controversies over the Choctaw revolt raged over several years, Governor Glen continued to walk a tightrope in the three-way contest among governor, Council, and Commons and at the same time to encounter increasing harassment from the reform-minded Board of Trade. The local contest at times involved the governor versus the Council, the Commons also against the Council, and, most critical of all for Glen, the challenge of the Commons not only to uphold past encroachments on the royal prerogative but also to expand them further.

The increased activity of the French and Spanish in sending privateers along the South Carolina coast during the winter of 1747-1748 led Governor Glen to counter these hostilities. Such action became necessary because the Royal Navy had withdrawn the *Aldborough* in August of 1746 from the coast, and the *Adventure* operating out of Beaufort had suffered damage in an October storm. Glen then authorized fitting out the *Non-Pareil* and the *Pearl* to patrol the coast and turned to the Commons to provide expenses.[1] The Commons agreed to bear the cost but unfortunately planned to use public orders for the funds, authorizing first 30,000 pounds currency that was later increased to 40,000.[2] Public orders were simply another version of paper money, so Glen, mindful of his royal instructions, refused to endorse this procedure without approval from Crown authorities.[3]

The Commons then attempted to impose tighter restrictions on expenditures in Indian affairs. Controversial exchanges resulted over the extent of the cost of Indian presents and the nature of payments for Indian visits. Probing further the specific authorization for expenditures and preferring to have the commissary general provide for Indian delegations to Charles Town over whom it had supervision, the Commons aggressively insisted in May 1748 on an inspection of accounts before its approval for payment.[4]   Glen responded that most expenditures had been authorized with the advice of "the General Assembly or of the Council," but noted that some decisions had to be made when neither was available.[5]

The governor in June responded to the arrogant message of the Commons in May.   He stated that he would be agreeable to respond if "you shall endeavor to take Notice of any Matter in such decent Manner as is consistent with the Respect that is due to the chief Magistrate of this Province and the Honor of your House."   He added further that "Sarcasms are indeed unbecoming the Gravity and Dignity of any one of the Branches of the Legislature and therefore it will be right for your House still to avoid using any.   I shall use none."[6]

The same month of June found other tensions between governor and Commons House as the Commons urged approval of the additions to the act of 1746 that would authorize two justices and three freeholders to rule on debt suits over 20 pounds currency (4 pounds proclamation money) and under 75 pounds currency (15 pounds proclamation money).[7]   The rationale for this proposal was that the fees and charges in the court of commons pleas often exceeded the total of the debt and hence were disadvantageous to both the plaintiff and the defendant.   Aware of opposition to this bill by the Board of Trade because of the absence of a suspending clause, Glen refused to approve the measure a second time.   He explained that he had been criticized for approval of the 1746 measure as "contrary to his Instructions," although he had not yet received official notice from either the Board of Trade or the provincial agent of its disallowance.[8]

Despite this charged air of disagreement in 1748, Glen unwisely again raised the question of his salary and his house rent.   As the eldest son and heir to his father of land properties in Scotland he was not destitute, but he continued to try to improve his fortune through direct payment of salary, house rent, and specific governor's fees.   He had earlier claimed half of the money provided by the Assembly to Lieutenant Governor William Bull, Sr., while he served as acting governor with Glen still in Britain.   This was a traditional practice in past years. But the Commons in 1745 concluded that Bull was not expected to share these payments since they were "intended as a grateful Acknowledgement from the People of this Province for his Honour's good Services during the Time of his Administration."   William Bull, Jr., as speaker of the Commons, signed a resolution relative to his father in March 1748, reiterating the same position.[9]

Still, Glen pressed on in his efforts to bring his payments in line with those of earlier governors.   He objected to the new tax bill of 1748 with its tax on public salaries.   While stating that the fee on his salary and house rent was "scarce worth mentioning," he still complained that he had heard that no governor in America now paid such a tax and no previous governor in South Carolina had ever made such a payment.   Furthermore, Glen noted that his income from the public was less than former Governor Robert Johnson by 4,655 pounds currency, and he had also experienced diminution of income by no longer receiving fees for licensing public houses.   Earlier governors had apparently abused the authority by excessive licensing, and it was turned over to justices of the peace. In lieu of this reduction, there was the provision for the governor to receive 200 pounds currency as an equivalent of the fees, but Glen maintained that this amount in 1748 would be the equivalent of 600 pounds currency. He requested a resolution of this deficiency.[10]

The Commons appointed a committee of ten members on June 28 to consider Glen's request. It responded the following day with a report agreed to by the Commons refusing to make adjustments in any of these areas of complaint. Furthermore, the report called attention to the 700 pounds currency for the governor's house rent and reiterated the view of a former Assembly to favor this only if the governor retained his house in town rather than retreating to the country where he was less available for conferences.[11] Glen, like other royal governors, was forced to struggle with the failure of British imperial officials to provide adequate independent financial support for their appointees.

The governor occupied Belvedere out of the city in what was sometimes called the "Governor's House." As early as 1712 the Assembly had authorized the purchase of a tract of land within six miles of Charles Town to include not less than 100 and not more than 300 acres with a brick dwelling for governors. Two preceded Glen at what became known as Belvedere: Charles Craven under the proprietors and Robert Johnson as both proprietary and royal governor. The house and plantation of 144 acres were described in 1721 as being located on Oyster Point on a marsh of Cooper River. In the eighteenth century, the property was also owned by Gabriel Manigault and Thomas Shubrick, and by World War I it belonged to the Charleston Country Club.[12] The conflict in Glen's time over residence in or out of the city contributed to the tension between the governor and the Assembly.

The governor struck back vigorously at the Commons' refusal to make salary adjustments as he called both houses of the Assembly together on the same day as the report, June 29. He announced his veto on both the bill for expenses for the sloops and the additional bill to the justice act of 1746. He did assent to the tax bill but then abruptly prorogued the Assembly until August and left both his critics and defenders stunned by his swift action.[13] His critics quickly turned to the *South-Carolina Gazette* of Peter Timothy to air their complaints. The Commons committee stated its dismay to find that "His Excellency should, at *this calamitous Time of War*, appear *so unaffected* with the Miseries thereof to the People of this Province, as to *desire* the *Allowances and Exemptions*" requested.[14]

Appeals to public opinion by criticism through the newspaper was one of two major ways the Commons exerted pressure on the governor; another effective technique was to threaten direct appeals to imperial officials, which became more precarious for Glen with the reform-minded Board of Trade. The colony of South Carolina did not designate an official and exclusive public printer, but Peter Timothy followed the family tradition by becoming editor of the *Gazette* in 1746 and continued as a willing servant of the Commons.[15] In sycophantic fashion, he printed criticism of the governor submitted by opponents in the Assembly. He received substantial authorizations for public printing by the Commons, and later he was even elected to serve St. Peter Parish as a member of this body from 1751 to 1754.[16]

With the Assembly prorogued, the Commons directed a series of vicious attacks on the governor in the summer of 1748 in three successive issues of the *Gazette* under the guise of quotations from ancient days. From Cato's letters and quotations from Algernon Sidney, there was a long discourse on virtue and an exposition on the sharp contrast between the character of a good and an evil magistrate, the public being left to judge the identity of the evil leader. Maintaining that the government of the colony was more a commonwealth than a monarchy, the quotations again were critical of arbitrary leaders and included Cicero's statements on "The Right and Capacity of the People to Judge of Government." "Every Ploughman knows a good Government from a bad one," the *Gazette* asserted in championing the role of the Commons in representing every private man.[17]

The intensity of this conflict subsided temporarily, for the Commons did not again meet for nine months following its prorogation in June of 1748. The delay came in part by lack of a quorum and in part by the call for new elections after Glen dissolved the Assembly in November. The Crown had notified him that the election act of 1745 had been disallowed primarily because it had no suspending clause for Crown approval. Resuming activity in March 1749, the new Commons House was somewhat conciliatory, agreeing to pay for the two sloops as part of the tax bills of 1749 and 1750 rather than issuing public orders.[18]

The Commons, however, continued to challenge both the governor and Council in other matters. Patrols along the coast were still an issue in efforts to prevent the escape of runaway slaves to Florida. As early as April 1749, the Commons advocated the equipping of two scout boats for patrol and resolved to provide the expenses of 25 pounds currency per month for their commanders and 10 pounds currency per month and provisions for ten men for each boat. The Commons requested the governor to implement this proposal and impatiently inquired on May 15 about its progress in view of a report that several runaway blacks had stolen a large canoe and were escaping southward.[19] The following day the governor responded that he had submitted the proposal to the Council. Having obtained an estimate from the commissary of 4,000 pounds currency for the expense, the Council concluded that the emergency was not urgent enough for this expenditure. Furthermore, the Duke of Bedford as Secretary of State for the Southern Department planned to have the Crown provide three boats to protect the coast of South Carolina and Georgia, which it was believed would achieve the desired goal. The governor added that he would provide the two boats if the Commons still thought it necessary.[20]   Indeed, the Commons did still advocate this and stated that the opinion of the Council notwithstanding, "we think this House the only proper Judges of any Expence that shall be necessary."[21]   Glen accepted the decision but chastised the Commons for asserting that it alone had the right to determine expenses.   "A Position not to be allowed of in that Sense," stated Glen, "and which, if admitted, would tend to destroy the very Being of the other Branches of the Legislature, and, consequently, the whole Frame of Government."[22] The Commons recanted in part by acknowledging that their action did "assert a Right which we do not pretend to Claim, and is an Expression which escaped through Inadvertence."   At the same time, it added a resolution of its "undoubted Privilege of having the sole Right of giving the Money of our Constituents."[23]   And so the contest went on in the power struggle, with the Commons House tenaciously attempting to increase further its control.

Another irritating question arose the following month when the governor and Commons disagreed over what agent should represent the colony in London. The position of the agent was of long standing and had involved other disagreements in both the periods of proprietary and royal governments. It was the agent's duty to articulate the needs of the respective colonies to various imperial bodies.   The more contacts this appointee had with influential leaders in England, the better chance for favorable consideration of the colony's requests.   Some agents such as Benjamin Franklin later served more than one colony.   Among the many responsibilities of agents were efforts to obtain approval of colonial legislation and resist unfavorable parliamentary actions. They were also to promote the trade and economic developments of the colony, initiate and present petitions, and expedite legal appeals from colonial courts to the Privy Council.   They were to serve as a collector of information of benefit to the colony as well as a provider of data in support of colonial interests to both colonial and imperial officials.[24]

Control over the agents in South Carolina led to conflict between Council and Commons House as well as between the governor and both houses of the Assembly.   When Glen became governor, Peregrine Fury had held the office since 1731.   While the Commons House tended to exercise control over Fury through its committee of correspondence, Glen got along well with him and was not enthusiastic about the Assembly's decision to replace him in 1749.   The Commons had objected to some of Fury's actions in the past, such as the failure to print its report on the disastrous St. Augustine campaign in 1740 to which Glen had agreed,[25] but it was not until May of 1749 that the Commons voted against the motion to continue him as agent.[26]   The Upper House on May 27 was evenly divided on this proposal with a four to four split.   The Commons preferred James Crokatt, a London merchant with prior residence in South Carolina.   When the ordinance for his appointment from the Council and Assembly finally reached Glen, he lamented the removal of Fury as "an old, faithful, and able Servant, whose Conduct has been approved for many Years."

While he acknowledged the good reputation of Mr. Crokatt, he added that Fury "by his Interest and long Experience in the Affairs of this Province, must be superior to Mr. Crokatt in the Knowledge thereof."[27]   Yet Glen reluctantly acceded to this change. Even greater controversy over the agent would arise later when Crokatt wanted to resign.[28]

Meanwhile, before this conflict reemerged, relative calm prevailed between Commons and Council to 1754. Governor Glen realigned his political allies and sought more support in both the Commons and the Council. His efforts to exert more influence in the Commons, particularly in Indian affairs, had involved the leadership of Chief Justice James Graeme with assistance from Dr. James Irving and the governor's brother, Dr. Thomas Glen. Brother Thomas represented St. Helena Parish from 1749 to 1751 and again from 1752 to 1754.[29]   Graeme served as chair of the standing committee on Indian affairs and had minimized the criticism of the governor during the investigation of the Choctaw affair. Graeme, however, upon Glen's recommendation, was appointed to the Council in 1750 to provide greater support for the governor.[30]   The departure of Edmond Atkin, Glen's longtime foe on the Council, for England in October 1750 was also advantageous, even though Atkin continued as a Council member for the next six years in England.

Most important in these shifting alliances was Glen's changed relationship with the Bull family. Glen had earlier complained of little contact with William Bull, Sr., as lieutenant governor during his first few months in office. Later lamenting Bull's jealousy when changes were proposed, Glen noted the opposition by government leaders "who happened to have the management before his arrival, by all their friends and relations, and by all those who advised or concurred with these measures, who think themselves impeach'd and their proceedings arraigned by any contrary conduct."[31]   Glen had also unsuccessfully demanded, as noted previously, half of the money paid Bull, Sr., by the Assembly while acting governor with Glen still in Britain.

With his pragmatic approach to politics, Glen put these disagreements behind him in the early 1750s, and the Bull family was willing to work more closely with him for the mutual benefits of gubernatorial power. The Bulls were among the six leading planter families who were most influential in South Carolina politics during this period, including the Blakes, Draytons, Fenwickes, Izards, and Middletons. M. Eugene Sirmans, author of a dissertation on the Bull family, noted particularly the connections with William Bull, Sr., whose three daughters and two nieces had married two Draytons, two Middletons, and an Izard.[32]   Glen's position was further solidified by the marriage of his sister, Margaret, to John Drayton in 1752. The governor recommended Drayton for the Council in the same year and actually added him to its membership in 1754 by his authority of appointment when vacancies existed. The opposition of William Wragg and others to the seating of Drayton resulted in his not achieving his official position on the Council until Crown appointment in 1761 with service continuing to 1775.[33]   Glen also selected Lieutenant Governor William

Bull, Jr., to represent the colony in important negotiations in New York with the Iroquois which in 1751-1752 resulted in a renewal of peace with the Catawbas.[34] The governor's commitment to the relationship with the Bulls had a fitting climax in his eulogy to William Bull, Sr., upon his death in 1755. Glen commended Bull for his respect for the law: "He was careful in passing these Laws; he was vigilant in executing them; he procured Obedience to them, not so much by the Weight of his Power, as by the Authority of his own Practice, for no Man was more obedient to the Laws than he himself." The governor then added a personal note: "I was frequently benefited by following his Advice, more frequently by imitating his Example, and when I could not equal, I endeavoured to copy after him."[35] These were pleasing words to native South Carolinians.

Glen's efforts to gain greater support from the leading families in the colony came at a time when the Board of Trade continued to harass him about colonial encroachment on the royal prerogative, much of which had occurred before he took office. The Board under Lord Halifax had challenged Glen's claims to uphold the prerogative as early as 1748, particularly in his approval of the act relative to the qualifications of electors and the act authorizing two justices and three freeholders to determine actions of debt under 75 pounds currency. "It is with difficulty we can reconcile" your claims "with some parts of your past Conduct" in approving these acts.[36] Again referring to Glen's claims in 1750, the Board was even sharper in its criticism: "we cannot help saying with some concern, that we have seldom opportunity of Writing to you upon the affairs of your Province without being obliged at the same time to Complain of some Departure from your Instructions and often of a Notorious Breach of Prerogation."[37] Continually seeking approval of his actions both in the colony and in England, Glen was stung by these strident criticisms and began to take a sterner approach to upholding the royal prerogative. More and more the governor found himself steering a treacherous course between the mythical Scylla and Charybdis.

Glen's efforts to bring the colonial government back to the principles of the British constitution were manifest both in debates with the Assembly and in the exercise of his veto power. His challenge to the colony's long-established practice of selecting juries by ballot, though not resulting in a veto, did highlight the conflicting views of colonials and imperial officials. As early as 1682 under the proprietors, South Carolina began drawing juries by first compiling a list of eligible persons and then having a child take names from a box.[38] In 1748 Glen maintained that this did not follow the long-established practice in England and that the colony had no right to deviate from this practice under the claim that "she has improved the Constitution."[39] Glen was especially critical of the possibility that persons with "neither Estates in Lands or Goods" may thus serve on trials for treason or "to try the Lives and Fortunes of others." If this occurred, he exclaimed, "nothing can be more repugnant to Reason, more contrary to the Constitution, more opposite to the Laws, Customs and Practice of

Great Britain. "[40]

The Commons, in defense of this practice, cited British acts it deemed consistent with the colony's system and appealed to custom and precedent for the rationale that colonial procedures, once in operation and not initially challenged by Crown officials, could no longer be changed by royal interference but only by the Assembly. The conflicting views were to continue. Glen did finally give his assent to a new jury bill on May 4, 1751, without major changes. With his approval he maintained in a message to the Assembly "That you have the Honour to agree with me that Persons should have Estates or Properties of their own to be capable of being Jurors to try the Lives and Properties of others. "[41]

In April of 1751 Glen objected to the bill to divide St. Philip's Parish and provide an additional church to accommodate the increasing number of "People disposed to attend God's Service. "[42] While sympathetic to the need for another church, the governor had several serious reservations about the proposal. He reminded the Assembly that the King was the "supreme Head of the Church" and had the "supreme Right of Patronage of all Benefices. "[43] He was also critical of the Assembly's acts of 1704 and 1706 that curtailed the governor's right of church patronage and left the selection of clergy to local parishes. [44] His specific objections focused on other provisions. He was concerned that there was no provision in the bill for itemized expenses. He also questioned the creation of commissioners for this purpose selected by the Assembly as a self-perpetuating group without Crown approval. Furthermore, the commissioners were authorized to "draw Orders upon the Public Treasurer" without supervision by the governor. He noted that the new parish would have the privilege of sending three members to the Assembly, all to be accomplished without a suspending clause to obtain Crown approval before implementation and in a bill for which the title fails to cover all of its major provisions as required by my royal instructions. "I must obey my Master," he added. [45] Consequently, Glen refused to assent to the bill despite the rumor that complaints would be made to the King in case of a veto. The Assembly did not follow through on this rumored threat. It did, however, again turn to the *Gazette* to publish the governor's veto as an implicit criticism, [46] and it urged the colonial agent to seek approval of the bill in England. [47]

Ten days later on May 4, the governor imposed two additional vetoes that again aroused the ire of the Commons. One was the rather popular bill for "incorporating the Charles-town Library Society," vetoed for lack of technical provisions, but with Glen's promise to forward it to imperial officials in efforts to obtain Crown assent. [48] The second veto was more complex, with the revival bill of several Assembly acts which evoked a long message from the governor. The act for better regulating taverns and punch houses provided for shifting its income from payment to the Charles Town watch to the King's independent companies, but Glen found its status ambivalent and failing to reduce the number of houses as intended. He also opposed revival of the Indian trading law which needed alteration.   One of its major problems was the continuation of the authority of Indian commissioners to draw orders on the public treasury.   His greatest objection was the failure of the general duty law, scheduled for revival, to set aside part of its revenue as a sinking fund to withdraw paper currency in circulation, a perennial problem in colonial affairs.[49]

Exasperated by these vetoes, the Commons requested leave to adjourn until October, emphasizing their strong disapproval of the veto of the revival bill and lamenting that there seemed to be little "prospect of having any success to their best Endeavour for the public Service."[50]   A report from the frontier noted the death of four colonists by Cherokee Indians; therefore, with the security of the province in the balance, Glen declined to agree to adjournment.[51]   The Commons referred the Indian problem to a committee that continued its resentment of the vetoes by proposing to petition the King with criticism of Glen's handling of Indian affairs.   Because the Council committee was divided on this issue, no immediate steps were taken.[52]   The Commons did exert additional pressure on the governor by voting to strike out the 700 pounds for his house rent in the bill for the annual operation of the government.[53]

Official records fall silent on exactly how compromises resulted in this intense conflict between governor and Commons.   It is evident, however, that in the spring of 1751 Glen had to yield his position on most of these critical questions possibly in return for no complaint to imperial officials.   The governor issued a proclamation on Friday, May 31, proroguing the Assembly until the following Tuesday, June 4,[54] in sessions that reintroduced the controversial measures.   They included the revival bill and the provision for dividing the parish of St. Philip to include the parish of St. Michael which cleared the way for building the magnificent St. Michael's Church.   On June 14, Glen gave his assent to these revived bills, which had been slightly altered but still contained the original objections.   In a somewhat curious message, Glen noted his "very chearful Assent" to laws that he maintained did not violate the royal prerogative and are not "hurtful to the Privileges of the People."   He went on to say that the "good People of Carolina are not a set of stiff positive People; but reasonable and dutiful Subjects."   He then wistfully added that this would provide him with arguments, if necessary, to have royal instructions recalled if not for the good of the people.[55]   He was not quite so sanguine as he forwarded these acts to London in 1752 without reference to his earlier vetoes but with the following suggestion to the Board of Trade: "I hope your Lordships will not immediately lay these Laws before His Majesty for his approbation or disallowance as a little time generally shows that many of our Laws need alterations."   He did add the rationale that this "cannot be so easily done after His Majesty has confirmed them."[56]

Glen became more tentative in dealing with these crises as he attempted to respond to the criticism of the Board of Trade and at the same time maintain a working relationship with the Assembly.   In several ways he was more sympathetic to the needs and desires of the Carolinians, but he had to confront not only the increasingly hostile views of the Board but also the possibility of his removal as governor. His persistent desire for full approval by all with whom he worked faded into the background as he became more motivated to find compromise positions that would at least be partially acceptable by opposing groups. In reality, with his wavering course he did not completely satisfy either at this time.

Still another bone of contention pervaded the relationship between the governor and the Commons during this period—the authority over fortifications. Even though the Crown considered this responsibility to be the governor's, the South Carolina Assembly even during the proprietary period had provided for commissioners appointed by its own laws for a variety of these defenses. As a royal colony, the fortification act of 1736 was the most comprehensive statute that was still operative when Glen came to the colony. Although a copy of the statute no longer exists, its provisions can be ascertained from the journal of the fortification commissioners and related documents. The Commons selected the commissioners for an unlimited term, and the governor was to appoint new members as vacancies occurred. The commissioners were to operate under the supervision of the governor and Council, but, in fact, they were more directly under the Commons with authority to obtain money from the public treasurer and made reports of accountability to the Commons House itself.   Their concerns extended beyond Charles Town to other coastal forts and to magazines in the interior for which the Commons often issued detailed instructions.[57]

Soon after his arrival, Glen continued the traditional practice of involving the Assembly in policy decisions on fortifications. He stated that he was "willing to have the Opinion and Advice of both Houses," and he invited committees from both houses "to assist me in the said Service" and "in fixing upon a proper Plan and Place" for a new powder magazine.[58] As the Board of Trade pressed Glen to protect the royal prerogative and follow his instructions, he became more mindful of his commission that granted him power, with consent of the Council, to provide forts and other fortifications and his additional authorization to arm them appropriately and to dismantle as warranted.[59]

The governor, continuing his concern about the excessive power of commissions, procrastinated in filling vacancies on the fortification commission, which then had only five members (four vacancies having occurred with the expiration of a 1745 act). In January 1752, the Commons obtained a report from the fortification commissioners that Fort Johnson was "very much out of Repair," and "like bad Condition" prevailed in the batteries and other bastions around Charles Town. The commissioners also noted that the governor had been notified over two years before of the "ruinous Condition" of the fortification line along the north of the town, but they had received no response to this need.[60]   Again in March and April the Commons requested new appointments to the fortification commission, suggested use of fortification funds when available, and expressed further concern about the poor state of Fort Frederick at Port Royal.[61]

Glen provided an extensive response to these communications in May after a delay that occurred when the clerk of the Council misplaced a communication. First, Glen questioned the effectiveness of the 1736 fortification law for Charles Town which authorized openings in the parapet on Bay Street for all bridges extending 20 feet beyond the low-water mark and permitted sheds for perishable goods without the parapet. He thought Charles Town merchants should be prohibited from erecting buildings beyond the curtain line and from leaving 15-foot breaches in the town's defensive wall for the purpose of transporting goods to and from their wharves. Better, said Glen, that there be a plan to convert sheds into block houses and that proprietors of bridges have gabions to assist in defense in case of hostile invasions. He stated further that the fortification commission had provided inadequate information about the needs of Fort Johnson whose refurbishing needed the recommendations of a skilled engineer. For expert advice on this and other fortifications, Glen suggested the use of John William Gerard De Brahm, an immigrant military engineer from the Netherlands and formerly an engineer in the German Imperial Army. As for Fort Frederick, Glen was very pessimistic about its condition and value, stating that it was merely "a low Wall of Oyster Shells which a Man may leap over!" and should hardly be called a fort for "a Garden Fence is full as good a Security." One final caveat concerned the legality of the fortification commissioners as "contrary to the Prerogative of the Crown."[62]

Not surprisingly, this message evoked a vigorous reply. The Commons reiterated that Fort Johnson was necessary for defense of the Charles Town harbor but rejected Glen's suggestion of using De Brahm's expertise. In an overt display of xenophobia, the Commons stated that it was "inconsistent with good Policy to suffer Foreigners . . . to make Plans of our Works and sound our Channels; and much more so would it be in us to employ them in a Work that might tend to the loss of our Country." The report of the Commons went on to deny that the fortification commissioners encroached on the royal prerogative, claiming in hypocritical fashion that their appointment was "intended to ease His Majesty's Governor here of the trouble of . . . inspecting and superintending the building and repairing of Fortifications." In one final barb, the Commons challenged the governor for questioning a law passed before his appointment and contending that the law was still in force until repealed and should be implemented.[63] Glen still refused to fill the commission vacancies.

A destructive hurricane of September 15, 1752 wreaked havoc in Charles Town which, according to the governor, "proved fatal to the Lives of several . . . Subjects, damaged a great Number of Houses, entirely demolished our Fortifications, ruined the high Roads, broke down Bridges, and . . . spoiled the Crops."[64] Forced to stay in town rather than retreat to his country home in order to coordinate relief efforts, Glen noted that this was done "to the hazard of my Health and till both my Wife and I contracted very severe Distempers."[65] He immediately called the Assembly into special session and was forced to send it a written message as it assembled on September 27 because of his illness with fever.[66]

The hurricane notwithstanding, conflict continued over solutions to fortification needs. The Commons urged use of the money in the fortification fund, the appointment of additional commissioners, and the formulation of a petition to the Crown for relief. Glen wrote letters to the agent in London and the Board of Trade about the destruction of the hurricane but delayed sending a petition to the Crown for relief until more expert information was available. He obtained a plan from De Brahm without informing the Commons; subsequently, the Commons refused to pay the £60 expense for De Brahm's service.[67] Glen still declined to appoint additional commissioners, even though the Commons on November 25 stated its request was "for the last Time." The Commons, then resorting to its earlier tactics, threatened to "have recourse to His Majesty for His most gracious Opinion."[68] Glen chided the Commons that this suggested appeal was hardly "parliamentary Language."[69] The Commons then retorted in December with the most belligerent and acerbic message thus far in this dispute. It contained a concluding resolution to prepare a petition to the King "to set forth the Governours Conduct with respect to his refusing to order the Fortifications to be repaired." The hostile language of this message found in the *Commons House Journal* is more severe in tone and content than another version recorded in the British manuscript of this journal, an obvious effort of the Commons to appear to the Crown less arrogant in relations with the royal governor.[70]

Amid this heightened tension, a compromise resulted in which Glen and leaders of the Commons may have met. Stating that he did not have "any power of dispensing with the Laws,"[71] Glen agreed to make additional appointments to the fortification commission. In return, the Commons deleted from its report its intention to complain to the King about the governor's conduct relative to fortifications.[72] The Commons, however, still refused to seek De Brahm's assistance, until the outbreak of the French and Indian War in 1754 increased the danger to South Carolina. The Commons then abandoned their xenophobia and requested Glen to obtain his services. De Brahm came to Charles Town in April 1755 and prepared an extensive plan for fortification of the city from all directions. He supervised the reconstruction of the curtain line from the present area of Water Street to Gibbes Street, a project that extended over a year and a half at the expenditure of over £30,000. Apparently, the construction was unsatisfactory: the foundations on the beach sands were inadequate to withstand raging waves and heavy rains. Abandoning De Brahm's elaborate schemes, the colony made no further improvements until the arrival of Glen's successor, William Henry Lyttelton. Free of the years of tension between executive and the Commons and with war now officially declared between England and France, Lyttelton was able to obtain more funds from the Assembly for further work on fortifications in 1757 as recommended by British engineers located in Charles Town. These limited efforts proceeded under the old arrangement of general direction by the governor but with the commissioners of fortification sharing in the project and arranging for workers and materials.[73]   The completion of more effective reconstruction awaited the outbreak of the American Revolution.

South Carolina deservedly has been recognized for "The Harmony We were Famous For" in eighteenth-century politics.[74]   Based largely on the ideal of "country ideology," the society "shared a coherent body of ideals, assumptions, and beliefs concerning politics" that distrusted human nature but strove to preserve individual liberty and impose self-discipline with the assistance of "Christian virtue, education, and concern for . . . honor."[75]   Wealth was recognized as an essential ingredient for personal liberty in the "community of economic interests and social values."[76]   Government with the British constitution as the guide was the protector of property and individual liberty, with consent of the governed by virtuous representatives.   Such representatives in the local Assembly served as checks on potential abuse of power by the executive in the person of the governor in the colony.   This chapter has revealed the many challenges to the executive by the Commons House, and Chapter 7 demonstrates an even greater assault on the power of the Upper House as part of the Assembly without embodying extreme overt factions.   One scholar has concluded that "At the end of the colonial period South Carolina, alone among the original thirteen colonies, appeared to be neither blessed with a useful upper house nor cursed with factions."[77]   It is also very obvious that while "Harmony" may have prevailed in the general society, persistent conflict characterized the struggle for power among governor, the Council as Upper House, and the Commons House.

This conflict at midcentury, particularly between the governor and the Commons House, had turned more bitter and cynical.   The Commons had become more aggressive in face of Glen's actions to protect the royal prerogative.   The governor was forced to compromise on several issues to avoid direct criticism by the Commons to the imperial government at a time when his own position was insecure inasmuch as his former patrons were no longer alive to defend him before the Board of Trade and other officials.   His conflict was primarily with the Commons as he defended the role of the Council as Upper House to participate in legislation.   There were some disputes, however, with the Upper House over poor attendance and its attempt under Edmond Atkin's influence to embarrass the governor over the Choctaw failure and again to exclude him from its legislative sessions.   After Atkin departed for England in 1750, however, Glen ceased attending meetings of the Upper House, as would all subsequent governors in Colonial South Carolina.   In pragmatic fashion, the governor realigned his political position with greater affiliation with the planters led by the Bull family, an alliance that was further enhanced with the marriage of his sister to John Drayton of Drayton Hall.   This new approach tended to minimize criticism from the Council, but the persistent drive by the Commons House to gain increasing power continued unabated, with criticisms of gubernatorial vetoes.   Glen would have preferred not to impose some of these negatives, such as the division of St. Philip's Parish and the Charles Town Library Society, except for the fierce admonitions from the Board of Trade. The major challenges of the Commons House would later shift toward contesting the existence of the Council as an Upper House for legislation.

Governor James Glen of South Carolina painted by Peter Snyers in 1743. Used by kind permission of the Earl of Dalhousie.

Linlithgow Palace, St. Michael's Church, West Lothian. Governor James Glen was appointed Keeper of the Royal Palace of the Stuarts in Linlithgow and was a member of St. Michael's Church where he was buried in 1777. Photo: Dept. of Environment, West Lothian, Scotland.

Copper plate from the grave of Governor James Glen in Linlithgow, Scotland. It now hangs on the wall of the Capitol in Columbia, South Carolina.

5

Responding to Imperial Queries

To take Notice of the Advantages we bring to our Mother Country...it would be doing Injustice to South Carolina not to shew our National Value. South Carolina was perhaps more valuable to our Mother Country than any other Province on the Continent.

James Glen, 1749 and 1751

During these years of controversy over the exercise of power between the governor and Commons, there were areas of activity in which a more cooperative spirit prevailed. One of these involved the preparation of "Answers" to queries from the Board of Trade. Periodically, the Board sent queries to all the royal governors to fulfill part of its obligations to obtain information about the colonies on such subjects as the nature of government and administration of justice, the mix of population, natural resources, and the potential for trade. Many governors responded to these inquiries in brief and terse language that involved little time and attention in preparation.[1]

When Governor Glen received a list of queries in 1749,[2] he devoted extensive effort in a conscientious approach to a full report on each question. In a long letter of July 19, 1749, he forwarded his report to the Board of Trade.[3] Some twelve years later, a clerk in the office of the secretary of the colony took a copy of this report to England and published it with substantial editorial revision without Glen's knowledge or consent. Though published anonymously, it was generally recognized as the work of the governor. This 1761 publication had a typical eighteenth-century full-page title beginning with *A DESCRIPTION OF SOUTH CAROLINA; containing Many curious and interesting Particulars relating to the Civil, Natural and Commercial HISTORY of that COLONY.*[4] Several editions of this report have been published,[5] and it still stands as one of the most valuable comprehensive commentaries on South Carolina by a colonial contemporary.

Glen submitted his original draft to both the Council and the Commons House in preparation for the final version. In his letter of transmission to the Board, he stated that the Council approved his statements without change, and the Commons "after they had kept them almost a month, they returned them, without any alteration but in one Word."[6] The process was actually more complex. Upon receipt of Glen's report on May 5, the Commons made ten tentative suggestions the following day for revision,[7] but it then decided to appoint a committee of nine members headed by James Graeme, with Andrew Rutledge and Dr. John Rutledge added later, to submit recommendations.[8] By May 16, the committee provided reactions under sixteen paragraphs that were adopted by the Commons and forwarded to the governor with a statement of appreciation for being given an opportunity to review the document.[9]

Glen gave careful consideration to the suggestions of the Commons and by June 1 returned a message stating precisely what he accepted and rejected, also including his "Thanks for the Pains you have taken in perusing these Answers."[10]   Among the half dozen changes accepted, Glen agreed, for example, to describe the Cherokees simply as "Allies" rather than "strict Allies" in view of their recent contacts with the French. He also added to his description of his land purchase from the Indians that it was "at the Expence of this Province," but he declined to say that all of his activities in Indian negotiations were done with the advice of the Council and Commons, with expenses defrayed by the Assembly. He insisted that some powers were "inherent in the Crown" such as war, peace, and treaties, which could be used without the assent of the Assembly. He also revised his economic examples of production, prices, and extent of labor required for rice, corn, and indigo, including such changes as to state that slaves could attend six acres of corn with production from ten to thirty-five bushels per acre rather than Glen's higher figures.[11]

While agreeing to make these changes, the governor refused to include others that questioned his view of the royal prerogative or provided controversial information on defense installations and the threat from the Spanish in Florida. In response to the suggestion that he request power over pirates for trial, Glen asserted that he already had that authorization along with the admiralty courts, but he did agree to seek the opinion of the attorney general. He also contended that his more favorable assessment of Fort Johnson was correct and that his description of the strength of the Spaniards in St. Augustine was the same as that of other reliable sources.[12]

Glen's letter of transmission that accompanied the revised version of his report afforded an opportunity for more informal observations than the later printed version. For example, he reiterated that the Assembly was encroaching on the power of the governor, and he again complained that he was not able to reward the most deserving persons in the colony. He also interjected commentaries on the controversy over North Carolina's boundary dispute with

South Carolina and hinted that the governor of North Carolina might need a new set of instructions relative to this issue.[13]

The printed version of 1761 contained the essential information of Glen's report, with the exception of descriptions of defense installations in South Carolina and evaluations of the strength of the Spanish in Florida, which may well have been considered inappropriate for purposes of security as the French and Indian War continued. The editor of the printed version provided a table of contents, divided the report into ten sections, rearranged some material, and attempted, with mixed results, to improve Glen's literary style. For example, Glen's reference to the importance of Indians prompted him to write that "he has taken great pains to learn about them," a statement converted to the more formal expression that he thought it "highly necessary to gain all the Knowledge I could out of them."[14] Although this revision may reflect improvement, the editor left out Glen's intriguing and expressive comment that "Plenty is often the Parent of Luxury" and included only his statement "to correct and restrain Vices of Extravagance and Luxury, by my own Example."[15] Even more extensive were the editor's additions that expanded the printed version by approximately one-third; the editor added sections nine and ten as well as other descriptions of the production of rice, naval stores, and corn, along with trade reports and comments on paper currency and coins. Part of these additions came from a pamphlet of 1731 on *The Importance of the British Empire* and from the 1741 edition of John Oldmixon's *History of the British Empire*. The further inclusion of "a long catchpenny index" stretched the printed version to 110 pages.[16]

Unfortunately, some of the editorial changes made in England revealed inadequate knowledge of the Carolina scene. For example, linen cloth was described as being made by Irish immigrants in the township of Williamsburg in Virginia rather than the South Carolina settlement near Winyah Bay.[17] The editorial changes also showed a striking unfamiliarity with Carolina history, for rice was said to have been introduced in the year 1700 when an earlier date of around 1685 was more correct. The Assembly designated rice as a commodity for payment of quitrents as early as 1696.[18]

Section one of the printed report described the boundaries of South Carolina in latitudes and longitudes as well as the colony's relationship to other competing European countries of Spain and France. It also briefly identified the general location of the major Indian tribes of the Catawbas, Cherokees, Creeks, and Chickasaws.[19] The boundary conflict between North and South Carolina was included without reference to the new instructions for the North Carolina governor noted above. Acknowledging the claim from the right of discovery by Sebastian Cabot, Glen erroneously relied on Oldmixon's *History* which stated that Carolina was named for King Charles the Ninth of France, when, in fact, it received the name from King Charles I of England with a renewal by King Charles II. Also, identification of the claim of discovery should have been attributed to John Cabot, and not Sebastian Cabot. While Sebastian may have accompanied his father on the 1497 voyage, he later claimed credit for the discovery after the early death of his father on the second voyage in 1498.[20]

Section two emphasized the variety of terrain with its diversity of soil and with the high bluffs along rivers to the swamps and marshes nearer the coast. Interspersed were "large Indian old Fields" cleared earlier by the Indians and also "fine Savannahs, or wide extended Plains" without trees but with beautiful grass.   Glen then described in some detail the production of rice in "a wet, deep, miry Soil," including the planting in rows, cutting even when "a little green," threshing formerly by a flail but then improved with a wind-fan, and finally grinding in a mill made of wood followed by another winnowing before beating in a pestle and mortar. The report added examples of amounts of rice as well as corn and indigo that a slave could produce and the potential quality of production according to the nature of the soil. The governor added the general computation of the production of a "good working Hand" at four and one-half barrels of rice each year weighing 500 pounds, a total of 2,250. This figure is in general agreement with a recent study that suggests 2,000 to 2,500 pounds for a "prime field hand."[21] Heeding the Commons' advice, Glen added the advantage that could result by having the same worker engage in the production of indigo during the summer and the production of rice during the remainder of the year when demands were most laborious.[22] Even spare time for sawing lumber was included, or as Glen stated in his original report, "Leizure time for sawing."[23]

In section three Glen used the reports of Dr. John Lining, the Scottish immigrant physician noted for his metaphysical observations and early experiments in electricity. Glen included a summary of barometric pressure from 1737 to 1740, the amount of rain from 1738 to 1748, and a table of wind directions for one year. These observations were made three times each day: morning, two o'clock in the afternoon, and at bedtime. Glen added his own views on the variation of temperature from ninety-eight degrees Fahrenheit in the summer to ten degrees in winter but exaggerated the claim that no other people on earth suffered greater extremes. To illustrate the extent of the cold, he recorded the experience in February 1747 of a member of his family who retired for the night in a room without fire with two quart bottles of hot water. By morning the bottles had split and the water was solid ice. He noted further the destructive frost that night that killed over 300 of his orange trees and a large olive tree.[24]

Section four enumerated estimates of South Carolina population. Since no national official census was completed before 1790, population counts were based on a variety of sources during the colonial period. The number of 25,000 whites was extrapolated from militia rolls, and the number of 39,000 blacks was determined more precisely from the tax paid on them. Glen identified the immigration of over 200 families of Germans and others from British colonies, with only a few persons in debt having departed for Georgia with their slaves. Optimistically, he anticipated future increases occasioned by several favorable criteria, including, with a degree of self-pride, the claim of "a mild Administration of the Government."[25]

Section five described in greater detail the nature of government in the royal colony and made brief references to the different officers and how they were appointed or elected. Noting the power of the governor and Assembly to pass essential laws, Glen added the interesting commentary that such legislation should not be "repugnant to the Laws of Great Britain . . . beyond what Necessity may require." Determining that "Necessity" would involve Glen in a number of controversies. He again complained about the limited power of the governor, but he added the curious commentary that, although a virtuous person might be trusted with greater authority, perhaps there was as much power already as "can safely be delegated to a weak or a wicked Person." Glen certainly did not mean to imply that the limitations on his authority were justified. But he did not reiterate his complaint of the number of officers appointed by the Assembly such as the treasurer and commissioners for Indian affairs, and he simply stated that the clergy were elected by the people. He did observe that the positions of justices of the peace and officers of the militia appointed by the governor were of such little profit that it was difficult to fill them. In his description of the forty-four members of the Assembly elected by sixteen parishes, he lamented the inequality of representation that would continue to be a problem with western expansion.[26] This was, for example, one of the major unresolved complaints of the Regulators in South Carolina in the 1760s.

Section six explained the sources of public revenues from duties imposed on imported goods and from taxes on real and personal property. He hastened to add that "not one Commodity of the Produce or Manufacture of Great Britain" had a charge of duty. Among the expenditures from this revenue were the salaries of civil officers not provided for in quitrents, including such officials as the clergy, schoolmasters, colonial agents in England, and military personnel, and other items of expense for defense. He noted with gratitude the Crown's contribution for making gifts to Indian chiefs previously required from the Assembly.[27] Providing appropriate gifts in Indian negotiations had become a critical issue for the governor and the Commons before this time. Even with authorization of funds by the imperial government, conflicts over amounts and procedure for donations continued.

Section seven, relating to trade and maritime activities, provided the most vital part of the report for the Board of Trade. Glen was aware of the leading economic ideas of the time, known in England as mercantilism. Among its leading tenets were the national state's desire to accumulate treasures of gold and silver, to establish a favorable balance of trade for the mother country with colonies serving as a source of raw materials and an outlet for manufactured products, to stimulate the growth of the maritime marine, and to contribute to the strength of the royal navy.[28] The governor claimed to show "the national Value of *South Carolina*, in respect of Shipping and Naval Power" and its contribution "to the Prosperity of our Mother Country by the Consumption of such Commodities and Manufactures as she produces or supplies us with."[29]

Glen provided a number of charts to support this claim. One chart included the number of vessels loading in Charles Town from 1735 to 1748, with totals ranging from 190 to 257 and with the computation for three of these years of the value of freight amounting to as much as £108,497 for one year and over 1,500 seamen. The report then added a list of commodities and manufactures that were typical of imports from Great Britain.[30] While acknowledging the value of all imports by British merchants, he still expressed "Surprize and Concern" about their bringing in such quantities of Flemish laces, Dutch linens, French fabrics, and East Indian products of gold and silver lace. Such imports, he moralized, contributed to "low Circumstance" and militated against our "Increase both in People and Wealth."[31] The governor claimed no trade with foreign countries unless one counted the export of rice to Portugal, obviously ignoring the illegal trade to non-English Caribbean Islands and other ports which continued to expand during the eighteenth century.

Another more detailed chart listed the kind and amount of exports from South Carolina from November to November, 1747-1748, with rates in both sterling and South Carolina currency at the exchange value of one to seven. Among the leading exports were the following familiar products: 55,000 bushels of rice at the value of £618,750, 3,114 barrels of pork at £31,140, 5,521 barrels of pitch at £12,422:5, 720 hogsheads of deer skins at £525,000, 10,356 pounds of tanned leather at £18,123, and the not so familiar indigo with 134,118 pounds at £117,353:5.[32] Although experiments with indigo for its valuable use as dye began in the seventeenth century, it was not until the 1740s that it became the colony's second major staple crop, partly through the efforts of the young Eliza Lucas. Daughter of Lieutenant Colonel George Lucas stationed in Antigua, Eliza at age seventeen began managing his plantation in St. Andrew's Parish in South Carolina in 1739. During the early 1740s she planted her first indigo seed as well as experimenting with other plants such as ginger, cotton, and lucerne.[33] By 1746 some 5,000 pounds of indigo were being exported with the increase noted above to over 134,000 pounds in 1748. The total value of all these exports amounted to £161,365:18, or 1,129,561:6 pounds South Carolina currency. The final part of this important section included an account of products not indigenous to the colony that were re-exported from Charles Town from November to November, 1747-1748. These items were simply listed without an estimate of value and contained a variety of products of cloth; metal pieces; edibles such as flour, cheese, and fish; liquors including beer, wine, and rum; lumber products such as mahogany; and finally a limited number of mineral products identified as quicksilver, gunpowder, and grindstones.[34]

The last section by Glen, number eight, provided a brief survey of neighboring Indians and evaluations of their important role in the international competition with the French and Spanish. The governor included a general estimate of the fighting men of each of the tribes in 1748-1749, which was in general agreement with the later, more extensive, report in 1755 of Edmond Atkin, member of the South Carolina Council and later appointed superintendent of Indian affairs in the South.[35] The extent to which Atkin may have depended on Glen's report has not been determined. Glen described the local settlement Indians as having only a few families. Other important groups for the support of the British were the following: Catawbas some 200 miles away with 300 fighting men, Cherokees at a distance of 300 miles from Charles Town with 3,000, Creeks at 500 miles with 2,500, Chickasaws at 800 miles with 200 to 300 "brave Fellows," and the Choctaws at a greater distance, with Glen listing them only as "the most numerous of any Nation of Indians in America." The governor's assumption that the Choctaws had been secured to British interests reflected the confusion resulting from the unsuccessful Choctaw revolt. Glen also included brief references to Indians subject to Spanish influence in Florida and to the location and population of the French and their fortifications in the Mississippi Valley. He reiterated that the peace of South Carolina depended primarily on "preserving our Interest with the Indians" by continuing our trade and responding to the request for a fort among the Cherokees.[36] The governor devoted much of his effort during the remainder of his term to these goals.

Glen forwarded this extensive report to the Board of Trade with a feeling of satisfaction that—with the approval of both houses of the Assembly—he had completed a comprehensive and accurate commentary on the state of the colony. But, alas, he was rebuffed by the Board of Trade, in its increasingly critical attitude, for having consulted the Assembly at all since it considered the report a confidential communication from a royal appointee to royal officials.[37] The report did remain unknown to the public until 1761 when, as previously noted, a clerk from the colony brought a copy to England and printed it without authorization from Glen.

Even after the extensive effort on the report detailing the state of the colony, Glen attempted to respond to the variety of sporadic inquiries that continued to come from the Board of Trade. In providing answers to the queries, the governor continued to be motivated by his persistent conscientious approach to the duties of his office. By this date, moreover, he was aware of the Board members' changed attitude and more solicitous approach to administration. Consequently, he made extensive efforts even on minor inquiries with the hope of gaining approval of his actions. The Board's letter of July 1750 requesting information on the boundaries of the province did not reach the governor until November.[38] By February the following year, Glen had completed his research on the subject and forwarded another long communication relative to international competition for territory in North America.[39]

Glen identified briefly the role of early European explorers of North America and gave particular attention to the Southeast. In addition to John Cabot for England and Ponce de Leon and Hernando de Soto for Spain, he recounted the Spaniards' brutal assaults in Florida under Pedro Mendez de Aviles as the

Catholics destroyed the predominantly Protestant settlements of Jean Ribaut and René de Laudonnière in the 1560s.[40]

The most intriguing part of the report was the analysis of the legality of territorial claims by European nations which reflected his knowledge of Roman law and of Latin. Glen questioned the widespread belief in right by first discovery by citing the rather obscure example from ancient history in which the city of Acanthos belonged not to the Adrians who threw out the first line there but to the Calistinians who actually took possession.[41] *Quasi pedum positio* was superseded by *quasi sedium positio*,[42] according to Florentine editions of the *Digest*. Attempts, using these principles, to determine the validity of either French or Spanish claims to the Southeast were, according to Glen, irrelevant because they assumed the territory was uninhabited (*vacua*). *Vacuum domicilium* was, indeed, advocated by a number of authorities in the age of exploration and discovery. While Justinian's statement of *"quod antea nullius est, id naturali ratione occupanti conceditur"*[43] gave support to the area's supposed return to a state of nature with the withdrawal by both the Spanish and French, such was definitely not the case with the continued presence of the Indians (Indigina). These natives as original possessors had still to be considered, Glen emphasized, as the only proprietors with sole dominion. Therefore, the most legitimate title to land for the English came from the contracts with and purchases from the natives. With some degree of exaggeration, he maintained that the English had acted as friends of the Indians and had made fair purchases of their territory.[44]

Glen next spent considerable time and effort on his response to a letter of March 1751 from the Board of Trade requesting an estimate of the value of the colony of South Carolina. The Board had suggested that he search past journals for calculations forwarded previously. Having completed the survey of the journals of both the Council and the Commons, Glen lamented that this had not produced "the least trace of an Estimate." Furthermore, the drudgery of reading journals without indexes was "A sort of Study in which there is neither Entertainment nor Instruction."[45]

The governor did report an earlier suggestion by members of the Council and Commons that there were 30,000 to 40,000 slaves in the colony computed at a value of 1 million sterling. He added the further note that "all other things together" might double this for a total value of 2 million sterling. Expressing reservations about such casual figures and emphasizing the difficulty in computing general values, he did list a population of 40,000 blacks and over 25,000 whites. Blacks from Africa had been sold at £20, but many slaves were natives of Carolina and had been trained as coopers, carpenters, masons, wheelwrights, and other trades. Estimates of intrinsic value were "difficult if not impracticable," for one gentleman had refused 500 guineas (1 pound 1 shilling per guinea) for three of his slaves. The governor, again mindful of the principles of mercantilism, did conclude that since the population subsisted on production from the land without manufacturing, South Carolina was "perhaps more valuable to our Mother Country than any other Province on the Continent."[46] Glen missed few opportunities to assert the importance of the colony, even though he was often critical of the Assembly's challenges to the royal prerogative.

The effort to determine the nature of landholdings with amounts cleared for cultivation and the annual totals of quitrents was very difficult. Attempting to compute total acres granted on the basis of population and royal provisions for headrights of 50 acres per person, Glen ended up with a figure of 3,250,000, but he realized this was not accurate because many individuals had obtained more than the basic 50. For 1738 there were 2,465,364, but ten years later the amount was only 2,057,457. He used the 1738 figure as a guide and suggested that the total should be near 3,000,000. Noting the difficulty of this task posed by obstruction from the Public Office, he promised to pursue this matter further at a later date.[47]

Glen added some social commentaries on the quality of life in the colony following on his suggested figures for imports in 1750 of expensive items such as brandy, beer, cider, Madeira wine, rum, and sugar. He concluded that total expenditures in the colony for food, clothing, and other necessary items, apparently computed for whites only, were no more than £400,000. This amount might be apportioned as follows: 5,000 people with "plenty of the good things of Life" spent 2 shillings per day for an annual total of £182,500; 5,000 more with some conveniences spent 1 shilling per day for £91,250 annually; 10,000 at half this amount with the "Necessarys of Life" for £91,250; and 5,000 or 6,000 with a "bare subsistance" spent a groat (old coin worth four pennies) a day for £35,000. These general figures, Glen added, were probably below the actual costs of all the necessities of life except meat products. They came "dear to us," with many additions to the price in England including shipping, insurance, and the merchants' profits. Consequently, wages of good labor might appear high, with ship carpenters earning 45 shillings per day, house carpenters 40, bricklayers 40, and a smith 14 to 16 pounds per month.[48]

Glen's critique of these social and economic categories of whites suggests some of the major groups in each, although incomplete financial and property records prevent precise designations. Certainly, major planters with hundreds of acres and a substantial number of slaves along with leading merchants and the most successful professional group of lawyers and doctors came within the top classification of 20 percent with "plenty of the good things of Life." The next level of 20 percent with some conveniences most likely contained planters who owned moderate estates and around twenty or more slaves or field hands, less affluent lawyers and doctors, smaller merchants, and the most industrious artisans and shopkeepers—the last two limited in number in this category. The 40 percent with the "Necessarys of Life" comprised small planters or farmers who tilled their own fields or possibly had five or fewer slaves, and the largest number of artisans and overseers with the builders, cabinetmakers, and silversmiths among the artisans usually most successful. The bottom rank with the less certain estimate of 20 percent with a "bare subsistance" possibly included some small planters with no slaves, the least industrious artisans, a few women and children, some seamstresses and tailors, free laborers employed by small planters, and beggars.[49]

Turning to shipping and trade, Glen noted that a limited number of vessels was owned in the province, for the total registration of tonnage did not exceed 1,600 and part of that was owned by residents of Britain. Yet the colonists had built good ships for sale and had used the valuable resources of the area. These materials included oak wood, preferable to what was found in England, yellow pine for planking, and an abundance of masts and naval stores. Despite the limited number of ships owned in the colony, Cooper River sometimes appeared to be a "Floating Market" with canoes, boats, and pirogues bringing country produce to town and returning supplies to interior plantations.[50]

Since Glen had submitted detailed lists of exports in past years, in this report he chose to deal only with rice in terms of its value to both Carolina and Britain. For the current year of 1751, the governor anticipated the shipment of 80,000 barrels of rice then weighing on an average 550 pounds, which represented an increase of 50 to 100 pounds with larger barrels then being made. The price earlier that year was £3 per 100 pounds, which had now declined 10 shillings to 50 shillings. The total value averaging these two at 55 shillings produced 1,100,000 pounds Carolina currency, or £157,142:17:1 as the value for Carolina. Considering the price sold in London with added charges for duty, freight, insurance, and other petty charges, Glen suggested that the 80,000 barrels sold at over 5 pounds would provide a value of £442,000 for Great Britain. Continuing his explanation, he estimated that 62,000 barrels of the 80,000 would go directly to Britain, 12,000 to Europe south of Cape Finisterre on the northwest coast of Spain, and the remaining 6,000 to either the British West Indies or the neighboring northern colonies with different duties to the King for each.[51]

Where did all of these economic exchanges place South Carolina relative to the principles of mercantilism with the other colonies as a source of raw materials and an outlet for manufactured products from the mother country? There is the suggestion that the British West Indies complied most successfully with these goals, the New England colonies least satisfactorily, and the southern colonies in a midway position. South Carolina contributed significantly to the middle status through its exports of rice, indigo, skins, and other raw materials and its limited competition in producing manufactured goods. The British West Indies also interacted with mainland colonies in a number of ways. As one recent study states: "they served as a major market for colonial exports, particularly foodstuffs and wood products; they supplied a variety of goods that the continental colonists imported, processed, consumed, and reexported; and they provided an important source of foreign exchange that helped balance colonial accounts and pay for British manufactures."[52]

By 1752 the Board of Trade turned its queries more directly to administration of the colonies by requesting royal governors to evaluate their instructions. This evaluation was certainly needed, for time and again instructions for one governor after another were simply repetitions of past ones with only minor exceptions and with little variation from one colony to another. The requests extended to both general and trade instructions. It was somewhat surprising that only three governors responded with detailed reports: Glen of South Carolina, Henry Grenville of Barbados, and William Popple of Bermuda.[53] In addition to a conscientious approach to the duties of office and a persistent desire for approval by imperial officials, Governor Glen was no doubt pressured even more by the crescendo of criticism from Halifax and the Board of Trade about upholding the royal prerogative.

In 1753 Glen reacted to the 110 general instructions issued at the time of his royal appointment. He stated: "I have often read, revised, and considered" them. He then deferentially added that "I am sure I shall find abundant reason to admire (as I have often done) the wisdom that framed them, and shall therefore be apt to doubt my Judgement, and even experience its self, should I point out a few things which might be wished altered in them."[54] Nonetheless, he proceeded to deal with some of the critical issues of his administration with varying degrees of success in altering royal instructions.

The first recommendation related to the governor's authority in suspending members of the colonial Council. By his ninth instruction, he was required to have the consent of a majority of his Council; or in case of sensitive issues "not fit" to communicate to its members, the governor could proceed with suspension but with full reasons to be sent to one of the Secretaries of State and the Board of Trade, including an explanation for bypassing the Council. Glen advocated a simpler procedure for action by the governor alone for "good and sufficient cause," with a full account to be submitted to imperial officials.[55] The Board of Trade failed to heed this observation in the next formulation of instructions in 1755. In fact, it made the procedure more restrictive by requiring the approval of the Council "signified in council after due examination of the charges against such councillor and his answer thereunto."[56]

Glen reacted to another major issue in the administration of the colony relative to the power, or lack of it, of the Upper House in framing money bills. He noted that the dispute in which the Commons had denied its right in money matters had led the Privy Council to eliminate a clause in his thirteenth instruction that had been in his predecessor's list which was intended to strengthen the role of the Upper House. Having experienced the intensity of this conflict between it and the Commons, Glen was skeptical of an easy resolution of this matter, for he was of the "opinion that Assemblys who are always tenacious of what they think their priviledges, and perhaps sometimes grasp at powers that do not belong to them will not easily suffer a Council to interfere or meddle with these matters."[57] Certainly, Glen was fully aware not only of the challenge of the Commons to the Upper House, but also of the encroachment by the Commons on the governor's authority. His observation, however, did not result in changes in subsequent instructions.[58]

Another major conflict affected the governor more directly in his twenty-sixth instruction. This article forbade the receipt of "Gifts & Presents" by the governor and other public officials, and, if offered, such gratuities were not to take effect unless approved by imperial officials. A house or house rent for the governor, however, was permitted. Even more important was the effort to get the Assembly to establish a "Public Revenue" that would provide "a competent Sallary to the Governor" and other officers of the colonial government. In 1753 Glen agreed that this was desirable and "nothing cou'd tend more to the benefit of the People," but he was pessimistic for colonial officers had assured him that "all attempts are vain." Perhaps, he surmised, colonial officials might be more receptive to such a "Public Revenue" after sending their children to England for education and learning more about the British constitution.[59] This instruction continued in subsequent orders, and even the reference to the governor's rent was eliminated.[60] British failure to provide adequate compensation for governors independent of colonial assemblies continued as a weak link in the chain of imperial administration.

Glen reacted to one other critical issue regarding the status of persons eligible for jury duty that had been a matter of discussion earlier. His fifty-third instruction urged the passage of a law setting the value of estates, either in goods or lands, required for jury duty. The governor declared that this requirement was not being complied with from lack of knowledge of the constitution and possibly a "little wilfulness." Even though trial by jury was the "Badge of British Liberty" of men of substance and the King's desire was for the "happiness" of the people in this matter, Glen concluded that "the People refuse to be happy."[61] This article remained in the next set of instructions in 1755 but was dropped in the subsequent one of 1761.[62]

Glen's observations may have been a factor in getting minor changes effected in less substantial issues. Article thirty-five on forfeitures of estates, which Glen maintained contained contradictions, was revised by the instructions of 1755. Several other provisions, consistent with Glen's recommendations, were dropped largely because of the changing situations of the time. These included such articles as number eighty-four relative to the powers of General Oglethorpe who was no longer in America, claims to "any Office or Place" under the former proprietors in number one hundred and seven, and fulfillment of promises to Jean Pierre Purry in the settlement of Purrysburg in number one hundred and nine.[63]

In 1753 the governor responded in even greater detail in his observations on the twenty-three trade instructions issued in 1739.[64] He approached this task with greater apprehension, however. After studying the many regulations of commerce and navigation passed since the time of King Charles II during the Restoration, he concluded that they were "dark and difficult, they have been made at different times, and Penned by different Persons, who seem not to have had the same views of things." Yet he proceeded to make suggestions for possible alteration of instructions and correction of current practices. He claimed to be as disinterested as any governor could be on the basis of not being involved "in Trade directly or indirectly."[65] This was a questionable assertion in view of his earlier efforts in the Choctaw trade and his continued interest in trade as a source of income.

His first article of instruction had enumerated many of the commercial measures that articulated principles of mercantilism beginning with the reign of Charles II. It required the governor to take a solemn oath to enforce the many provisions regulating plantation trade and to prevent fraud and abuse of the customs. He was to implement the bounty for increasing imports of naval stores, restrictions of the Hat Act of 1732, and encouragement of the British sugar trade with the Molasses Act of 1733. Glen noted that he was convinced of considerable illegal trade in South Carolina. Prevention of this trade was difficult, however, for in contrast to the many officers used for regulation in England, there were few or none to observe, for example, the fifty-nine sailing vessels then in the port of Charles Town. Furthermore, the province had two more ports of entry at George Town and Beaufort and some 150 miles of open coast with rivers and creeks. Charles Town had only a collector, a naval officer, and two searchers. Glen maintained that another searcher and at least four waiters were needed there as well as a searcher and waiter at each of the other two ports. Improved enforcement would stop illegal trade and greatly improve the royal revenue. This critique notwithstanding, the governor recommended the continuation of the same article.[66]

Glen gave particular attention to his third instruction because of different interpretations among colonial officials and merchants. The issue related to restrictions that went back as far as the Navigation Act under the Commonwealth in 1651 and repeated in the act of 1660 that no commerce was to be shipped to or from the English colonies except in English ships or in ships of which the master and three-fourths of the crew were English. The 1660 act extended restrictions to exclude all foreign ships from the colonial trade. Glen noted that merchants believed that the Spanish should be permitted to import in their own ships to English colonies such products as gold, silver, logwood, and cochineal as a desired drug and be able also to traffic for European manufactures and East Indian goods that had been properly brought from Great Britain. Glen argued for a modification of restrictions that would permit some Spanish ships to trade with English colonies. The justification was that Spanish aggressive patrols of "watchful Dragons" and *guarda coastas* curtailed English shipment to Spanish as well as French and Dutch colonies. Consequently, Spanish trade was often substantial with the French and Dutch and gave these English competitors a distinct advantage in the acquisition of these desired products at a much cheaper price.[67] No immediate changes were made in instructions as a result of Glen's suggestion, but the creation of free ports in

Jamaica and Dominica in the West Indies by act of Parliament in 1766 partially implemented his ideas.[68]

The governor also had suggestions about his fourth instruction on the regulation of the rice trade which, as previously noted, had become the leading export from South Carolina. While he stated that the province had not abused the privilege of the Navigation Acts permitting by license the shipping of rice directly to Europe south of Cape Finisterre in Spain, he still advocated the same opportunity for South Carolina that the Sugar Islands had received to export to the northward. The ministry at one time had promised to permit this, Glen added. The most favorable change that actually resulted was by the act of Parliament in 1765 that reduced by half the imperial duty on rice imported to England if reexported promptly.[69]

At much greater length the governor reacted to the difficulties of enforcing the Navigation Acts and gave particular attention to the Staple Act of 1663 as a part of what he called the "Bulwarks of the British Trade."[70] The Staple Act endeavored to tighten control of colonial importing by requiring that all foreign imports to the colonies be landed first in England, thereby diminishing Dutch competition in the carrying trade, and hopefully creating stronger ties between the English colonies and the mother country. A few products were exempt such as salt for New England, wines from the Madeiras and Azores, and servants and horses from Scotland and Ireland.[71]

Glen cited two examples relating to the Staple restrictions and the difficult position of customs officers. One involved a Dutch ship that had deliberately traded its goods, even at night to private families, in Jamaica as a better market than Dutch Curaçao. An English naval officer seized the vessel but turned to Glen for prosecution because his family expenses prohibited him from initiating the costly proceedings. The governor did prosecute at a cost first of £1,000 and later an additional £400 with the delays and confusion over authority in the admiralty courts both in the colonies and in England. Even Glen's request about the status of the case to the Duke of Bedford as Secretary of State failed to evoke appropriate instructions for proceeding. The results, Glen stated, have "so terrified the Officers of the Customs that many of them are deterred from doing their duty."[72]

Naval officers were also criticized by the governor in the second example of violation of the Staple Act by one James Abercromby as master of the Dutch ship, *St. Andrew*. He claimed to have only bread and flour on board as he came from Philadelphia to Charles Town, but local naval officers, aware of his past guilty practices, discovered Dutch cambrics and calicoes for which he did not have the proper coquet, or certificate, as required by the Staple Act. One searcher proceeded with the seizure, but other naval officers were unwilling to join him or relinquish their share of the prize to become legal witnesses to the violation. The vessel departed at night without proper clearances, and the governor vowed to suspend the naval officers for their improper conduct.[73]

Glen's conscientious approach in responding to the many bureaucratic inquiries was time consuming but had only limited influence with the Board of Trade, which was then already pondering a change in governors for South Carolina. These responses, therefore, provide more enlightenment on the major problems of governmental administration of the province than a direct influence on British imperial policy. Glen's *Description of South Carolina*, as noted earlier, has been acclaimed as one of the most valuable contemporary commentaries on colonial America with its comprehensive coverage. Previous studies of the governor, however, have failed to identify and acknowledge his other valuable reports to imperial officials. He was the only governor of the American continental colonies, as previously noted, to submit substantial evaluations of both general and trade instructions. Among the seven other continental governors or lieutenant governors queried, Governor George Glinton acknowledged the request but only managed to submit a criticism of the New York Assembly. Glen's reports also reflected his deep concern and interest in Indian policy. The time and energy he devoted to negotiations with different tribes is the subject of the following chapter.

6

The Perils of International and Intercolonial Competition

South Carolina is extremely Jealous of any other Colonies intermingling with our Indians, by long experience we have become acquainted with their nature and Inclinations and have managed them so as to keep them steadily in the British interest.

James Glen, 1754

At mid-eighteenth century, the southern frontier experienced a temporary interlude of peace among the three major European powers competing for dominance—England, France, and Spain. The peace of Aix-la-Chapelle of 1748 ending the War of Austrian Succession and King George's War, returned boundaries to the *status quo ante bellum* but failed to deal with the conflict over control of Indian affairs. France superseded Spain as the major colonial competitor for the area. England's relations with Spain improved as the old irritant of trade in the Spanish colonies diminished following the English agreement at Madrid in 1750 to relinquish the *asiento* for a money payment of £100,000 by Spain. England had forced the *asiento* concessions in the Treaty of Utrecht of 1713 by which Spain gave a monopoly to England for importing slaves into Spanish colonies and agreed to permit one English ship of 620 tons to trade annually with its colonies. England also canceled the mutual debts between the British South Sea Company and the King of Spain.[1] The Spanish retreated to a defensive posture on the southern frontier, and St. Augustine, St. Marks, and Pensacola became primarily military outposts with less of the dynamic threat that had existed in the challenge to General James Oglethorpe and the new colony of Georgia.[2] Governor Glen reported in 1749 that St. Augustine had a total population of only 2,300 of all colors and that the number of effective military troops was probably no more than 100, although some estimates have suggested as many as 600.[3]   Nonetheless, Spain continued to make friendly overtures to the Lower Creeks, who negotiated for English trade but retained its resentment for the Anglophile Cherokees and for the Georgia settlers advancing on their vacated lands on the Savannah River.

France, meanwhile, was gaining momentum at midcentury in its bid to expand its American territory and influence over Indian tribes. Francis Parkman has likened the French empire in North America to a large animal with its head in the snows of Canada and its tail in the canebrakes of Louisiana.   The expansion in both areas was to affect South Carolina, although its southernmost thrust was of greatest concern. The lower Mississippi River area in Louisiana in 1748 had 12 companies of French troops and one Swiss regiment. While the table of organization listed 750 soldiers, the individual companies, authorized 50 men, had only about 15, and the actual strength of 9 companies included only 141 fusiliers.   Authorization in 1750 increased military strength to 37 companies, and the number of troops increased to about 2,000 in 1751 distributed over both Louisiana and Illinois country as follows: 875 at New Orleans, 475 at Mobile, 100 at the German village, 100 at Point Coupée, 50 at Natchez, 50 at Natchitoches, 50 on the Kansas River, and 300 in the Illinois country.[4]

Governor Glen finally realized that the efforts to win the Choctaws away from the French in the Choctaw revolt had failed. He, therefore, concentrated his activities on other tribes, both north and south, in new directions of unifying all groups sympathetic to the British in general agreements and thereby minimizing intertribal conflicts that sapped their strength. This approach was contrary to the opinion held by a few South Carolinians who still articulated the view from the days of the Yamassee War that it was difficult to assist the tribes "in cutting one another's throats without offending either. This is the game we intend to play if possible."[5]

The neighboring Catawbas with their long-standing feud with the Iroquois in New York were in a critical position. A decade earlier, Lieutenant Governor George Clarke of New York had obtained the assistance of General Oglethorpe of Georgia and Lieutenant Governor William Bull, Sr., in getting the Catawbas and Cherokees to accept a treaty with the Iroquois in 1742.[6] By midcentury there had been violations of the treaty, and the Catawbas and Iroquois were again on the warpath. The Catawbas were, indeed, fierce fighters as is evident in the encomiums of Governor Glen who described them as "the bravest Fellows on the Continent of America,"[7] and of Edmond Atkin who added that "In War, they are inferior [to] no Indians whatever."[8]   While inclined to pursue an independent course in providing their own security, they were hard-pressed by a series of developments that reduced the number of their fighting men. Savannah-Shawnees, having suffered at the hands of the Catawbas in earlier years, had then moved to the Ohio Valley and were eager to strike back when opportunities arose. French officials in Canada increased their campaign to win allies and encouraged strikes against the Catawbas who remained committed to the British. Even more critical was the ability of the Iroquois to attack the Catawbas operating from villages of the Cherokees who had renewed their peace with the Six Nations.[9]

Governor Glen and Governor George Clinton of New York worked together to begin negotiations to renew the covenant chain between the Iroquois and Catawbas. They first had to recognize the insistence of the tribes on their own procedures based on past customs whereby the Catawbas wanted a "token" to signify the invitation to negotiate, and the Iroquois were adamant that the peace talks be held at their traditional site in Albany rather than in Philadelphia, Fredericksburg, or Williamsburg as suggested by colonial officials.   The Catawbas finally acceded to the New York location and arranged for their king, or eractasswa, Hagler (Nopkehe), along with five other Catawbas to travel by ship for negotiations in the summer of 1751. Glen, detained by the crisis of the Cherokee-Creek conflict, selected Lieutenant Governor William Bull, Jr., to accompany the Catawbas on the mission with the same goals advocated by Bull's father a decade earlier.[10]

Glen sent along presents in behalf of the Catawbas to "bind the Treaty," and Bull read his letter to the Six Nations emphasizing his desire to keep all Indian allies of the English in peace. The Catawbas, he stated, were "desirous to bury in eternal Oblivion all that has happened in either side" and "to make Peace and bind themselves in one Chain of Friendship with their Brothers of the Six Nations and the other Northward Indians, the one End to be kept by the Governor of New York and the other by the Governor of South Carolina."[11] Bull sent a full and intriguing report on the procedures of the peace talks in July 1751,[12] and later provided the full text of the treaty.[13] One critical provision of the agreement was to have the Catawbas return to New York by water with the Iroquois prisoners then held in exchange for Catawba prisoners detained by the Six Nations. The Catawbas declined to return to New York in the fall because of illness in the tribe. Upon Glen's urging, they returned one prisoner by water in the spring of 1752; the only other remaining captive refused to travel by water, awaiting the visit of his kin to return by land.[14] While Glen was not the only promoter of this renewal of friendship and exchange of visits, both the Mohawks and the Catawbas thanked him profusely for his efforts as the Catawbas joyously expressed their appreciation that the Iroquois had come as friends rather than as before "with Bullets out of the Muzzells of their Guns."[15]

Glen was even more involved in Creek-Cherokee relations which had prevented his journeying to New York. Without full understanding of all the complexities of Indian culture, he had to confront not only the friction between Overhill Chota and other Cherokee towns, but also the divisions among the Creeks. Their loose confederacy of about sixty towns concentrated primarily in the two major divisions of Upper Creeks and Lower Creeks. The Upper Creeks of about forty towns, extending from the Alabama River on the west to the Ogeechee River on the east, lived along the Coosa and Tallapoosa rivers with three major divisions: the Alabamas near the junction of the two rivers flowing into the Alabama River; the Tallapooses with the principal settlements of Muccolossus, Tuckabatchee, and Tallassee; and the Abeikas with the principal towns of Coosa, Okchai, and Okfuskee. The Lower Creeks of twenty towns occupied at various times the Ocmulgee, Flint, and Chattahoochee rivers in Georgia with their principal settlements in Coweta and Cussita.[16]

Glen's predecessor, William Bull, Sr., had concluded an agreement with the Upper Creeks in Charles Town in October 1743 to build a fort to counter the threat of the French Fort Toulouse. The Commons House, however, failed to authorize expenditures for the project, arguing that it was not essential.[17] Meanwhile, the relations between Creeks and Cherokees fluctuated. The 1742 treaty between the Cherokees and Iroquois had led to the Iroquois being able to use Cherokee sites as a springboard for attacks on the Creeks, thereby intensifying the Cherokee-Creek conflict. As King George's War erupted in 1744, Glen attempted to mediate the dispute between them and to encourage the Upper Creeks to go against Fort Toulouse. While there was some support for this venture, the council of the Creeks reiterated their stand of neutrality and were soon again involved in conflicts with the Cherokees.[18]

As King George's War continued, Glen again attempted to solicit Creek support against the French at Fort Toulouse. In May 1746 he conferred at New Windsor near Augusta with several Creek leaders, including Chigelley, Lower Creek brother of Old Brims and one of his interim successors as guardian of Malatchi, son of Brims. Later in the summer, he invited both Lower and Upper Creek leaders to come to Charles Town. Several responded in late October, including the Gun Merchant (Enochtanachee) of the Okchais, the Wolf of Muccolossus (both Upper Creeks), and Malatchi of Coweta (Lower Creek), who was then beginning to exert authority as successor to his father. The usual presents were distributed, but the offer to build an English fort among the Upper Creeks met with mixed reactions. The most adamant objection came from Malatchi who had influence among the Upper Creeks as heir to Old Brims whose neutrality he continued to advocate.[19] Malatchi was more concerned with efforts to uphold Creek title to lands claimed by Georgia. In this effort he supported the claims of Mary Musgrove Bosomworth (Coosaponakeesa) and her third husband, Thomas, who sought to uphold their own claims to Creek grants as well as to obtain compensation for Mary's assistance to General Oglethorpe and the colony of Georgia. Mary was a half-blood, being the daughter of an Englishman and a Creek. In one heated argument with Georgia, she even asserted that she was queen of the Creeks, apparently on the basis of being the niece of Old Brims, first cousin of Malatchi, and elder sister in a matriarchal society on maternal lineage. However, the Creeks did not generally accept her position as queen.[20]

As the intermittent conflict between Creeks and Cherokees continued, the Creeks solicited Governor Glen's aid to mediate peace. But Carolina's relations with the Cherokees had deteriorated following the murder of a packhorseman in the Lower Towns and the capture of Carolina surveyors, George Haig and

William Brown, by Senecas of the Iroquois with access to the Lower Towns.[21] Through pressure from Glen, the Hiwassee-Tellico leaders forced the Lower Towns to execute the murderer of the packhorseman as they continued their efforts to dominate Cherokee policy. These leaders even planned to challenge competing Chota by warring on Fort Toulouse and bringing French counterattacks on the Overhills that would disrupt their peaceful coexistence with the French. The end of King George's War with the peace of Aix-la-Chapelle led Glen to urge cancellation of the attacks.[22]

Renewed efforts then followed for a Creek-Cherokee peace, although the French still complicated the process by bribing Acorn Whistler, an Upper Creek headman of the town of Ulchitchi, to attack Hiwassee of the Cherokees, which resulted in the taking of two scalps.[23] Eschewing the usual blood revenge, the Cherokees continued peaceful discussions of identifying separate hunting grounds for the two nations and of refusing passage to northern Indians who had been so disruptive in the past. Glen invited delegations from both groups to Charles Town. The Wolf of the Muccolossus and a few lesser leaders of both the Upper and Lower Creeks attended in September 1749, but Malatchi and the Gun Merchant declined. Cherokee leaders included the Raven of Hiwassee and the young emperor, Ammonscossittee. General agreements resulted by which the Cherokees promised not to permit northern Indians to pass through for attacks on Creeks, and both tribes consented to a Carolina embargo for trade violators and for injured parties to confer with the Carolina governor before resorting to the law of blood revenge. These hopeful arrangements notwithstanding, positive factors were diminished by illness of fever en route home, which led some to believe the French warning that the peace meeting was an English trap, and by attacks on Upper Creeks by northern Indians accompanied, according to some reports, by Cherokee warriors.[24]

Strict compliance with the agreements failed as northern Senecas continued to pass through Cherokee territory to attack Creeks. The Lower Towns (Cowetas) retaliated by raids on the Lower Cherokees as Malatchi and some 500 fighters inflicted great damage on Lower Cherokee towns. Glen hesitated to enforce the agreement of 1749 by placing an embargo on the Creeks because the Cherokees had failed to adhere to their commitments. Furthermore, Glen was aware that Georgia, as a matter of self-interest, would not cooperate with a trade embargo, and that there was always the specter of Virginia moving into the trade vacuum to displace the dominant role of South Carolina.[25]

The spring of 1751 brought even greater turbulence as the Cherokee Lower Towns sought their own vengeance: they not only retaliated against the Creeks but also damaged white settlements and threatened traders in many of the Cherokee towns. Glen took precautions by ordering traders out of the Cherokee country, but the Commons House went even further by imposing a trade embargo on the Cherokees,[26] unmindful of Glen's concern that this action would give the Creeks an unfair advantage over the rival Cherokees. As the contest for dominance over Cherokee affairs continued between Hiwassee-

Tellico and Chota, the resourceful Cherokees sought other alternatives to preserve their independent operations.   Chota was particularly active as Connecorte, or Old Hop, the Fire King, sent overtures to the French at Fort Toulouse and dispatched the Little Carpenter (Attakullakulla), cousin of Old Hop and the Cherokee Second Man, to Williamsburg to negotiate for Virginia trade.[27]

Colonel Lewis Burwell, president of the Virginia Council and acting governor, promised to encourage traders to the Cherokees and gave them presents worth £200 before their departure.   However, upon protest from Governor Glen that the Cherokee delegation consisted of obscure, unauthorized persons who were guilty of attacks against Carolina and whose statements about lack of supplies from South Carolina were false, Virginia officials agreed to insert an article in the *Virginia Gazette*. It warned the colony that the delegation had been in Virginia under false pretenses.[28]   Consequently, trade goods did not flow from Virginia.

Implementing the South Carolina embargo, Glen sent demands to the pro-English Raven of Hiwassee in June of 1751. Among the requirements to avoid the use of force were the turning over to Carolina the Slave Catcher of Conutory for injury to a colonist, the surrender of those guilty of recent murders at Oconee, and the proviso that Little Carpenter come to Charles Town to account for his anti-English activities. The governor referred to the Little Carpenter as a "Common Incendiary" and a "Disturber of the Peace."[29]   The Raven of Hiwassee, continuing a pro-Carolina position as part of asserting the dominance of Hiwassee-Tellico over Chota, accepted the demands and proposed to confer with the governor at Saluda to clear matters and demonstrate pro-English loyalty by delivering the scalps of two Frenchmen. Chota discouraged the meeting and continued to invite Lower Towns to move to the Overhills for greater security. The Raven of Hiwassee persisted in efforts to respond to Glen's demands, and Osteneco of Great Tellico agreed to travel to Charles Town where he conferred with the governor. These moves of compliance by Hiwassee-Tellico resulted in the withdrawal of the trade embargo and the return of leading traders such as Robert Goudy to Great Tellico.[30]   The sequel to this situation was another conference in Charles Town to prepare new trade agreements and remove past conflicts.

Chota, still flirting with the French connection and hoping for possible trade from Virginia, procrastinated and did not have representatives among the 160 Cherokees with twenty-two headmen. They included the faithful Raven of Hiwassee, Old Skiagunsta of Keowee, the Good Warrior of Estatoe, and Kitta-gusta of Joree. The young emperor became ill en route and had to turn back, while Osteneco was recuperating at home following his recent visit.[31]

The governor set the tone of the conference with his talk on November 13, 1751, identifying several attacks on Englishmen and noting evidence of bad talks among the Cherokees that threatened the security of traders among them. With special concern for the young people in the delegation, Glen with hyperbole and a dramatic flare described in ethnocentric terms the contrast of their present condition with that of days before English trade:

Instead of the admirable Fire Arms that you are now plentifully supplied with, your best Arms was bad Bows and wretched Arrows headed with Bills of Birds and Bones of Fishes or at best with sharp Stones. Instead of being decently and comfortably dressed in English Cloaths, you were forced to cover yourselves with the Skins of wild Beasts. Your Knives were split Canes and your Hatchets were of Stone, so that you spend more Days in felling a Tree than you now do Minutes.[32]

The Cherokees spent nearly three weeks in Charles Town before the conclusion of the conferences. By November 26 Glen, with members of the Council in attendance, read their agreements in a treaty of seventeen provisions. Reading the document was essential, for Skiagunsta of Keowee, noting his inability to write, declared that "My Tounge [sic] is my Pen and my Mouth my Paper. When I look upon Writing I am as if I were blind and in the Dark."[33]

The seventeen articles highlighted many of the major issues in Indian-white relations. English demands along with English promises and efforts were made to improve overall relations as well as specific trade problems. Major demands included the delivery of Andrew White (half-breed) as the murderer of a white man and the full indemnification of Bernard Hughes who had suffered losses as a trader in Stecoe. They also provided for the dispatch of the Little Carpenter as "Disturber of the Peace" to Charles Town to explain his behavior, and agreement by the Cherokees not to supply northern and French Indians with ammunition as well as preventing them from invading English settlements. In return, Carolina promised to compensate the Indians of Stecoe for loss by white robbers of 330 deer skins upon satisfaction to Hughes. The colony also agreed to return English traders to Cherokee towns with supplies of arms and ammunition, and to promote peace with the Lower Creeks similar to terms between the Upper Creeks and Cherokees. Specific trade regulations banished the sale of rum by traders and stipulated that Indians trade only in their own town and that traders traffic only in towns for which they had licenses. Furthermore, traders were prohibited from crediting any Indian for more than 24 pounds weight of leather (one hunt) upon penalty of not collecting the excess amount. The Indians were not to engage in robbery or detain any whites summoned by the governor. If serious violence resulted, provisions for the perennial question of handling offenders, either Indian or white, were spelled out in semi-legal terms. An Indian killing a white man was to be punished by the Indians as Carolina directed or be delivered up for punishment by the colony. The English persisted in such requirements, even though they violated the traditional values of Indian society. If a white killed a Cherokee, the colony promised to punish the offender "as if he had killed a white Man" and to invite the relatives of the deceased to witness the execution of justice. Another perennial question related to blacks in the Indian country whereby Cherokees were required to apprehend any "Negro or Mullatoo" deserting and traders were prohibited from taking there "any Negro' or other Slave." One final provision was designed to minimize conflict by prohibiting Cherokees from hunting any closer to white settlements than "the Place called the dividing Waters" near Ninety-Six, and by requiring medals to identify messengers sent by Cherokee headmen. Medals were accordingly distributed to some of the Indian leaders at the conference, with one designated for the absent young emperor.[34]

There was limited discussion of the perpetual question of building English forts among the Cherokees. The seventeen provisions related only to possible assistance from the Indians when a fort was built. In preliminary discussions, the Warrior of Keowee had requested not only a fort in the Lower Towns but also another one over the hills for protection of the Lower Towns who had migrated. In the informal discussions following agreement on the major articles, Glen promised a fort in the Lower Towns to be built in the spring and evoked promises for the Indians to cut poles and "to send ten Men every Day out of every Town" to assist.[35]

The Creek-Cherokee hostility still hung over the conference, for the Council urged Governor Glen to warn the Cherokees of the rumor of a Creek threat to waylay them en route home. This possibility alarmed the Cherokees to such an extent that they requested that 58 more guns be added for their protection to the extensive presents already distributed on November 23 in the Council Chamber. Glen had decided on his own to increase the number of guns by 25 but declined the higher figure of 58 because the Indians had already received 113. He concluded with a mild chastisement of the Indians for such requests, for he viewed the presents as a "free Gift of the King" which had already exceeded previous contributions.[36]

Implementing all provisions of the treaty was difficult, if not impossible. Contributing to unstable conditions were several obstacles, including rivalry within the Cherokee nation between Chota and Hiwassee-Tellico and the continuing conflicts between Creeks and Cherokees. Also operative were the continuation of intercolonial competition involving both Georgia and Virginia, the French threat, and the rank individualism of Indian traders oblivious to regulations. The evil influence of excessive sales of rum in trade was still evident. The Creeks, convinced that the Cherokees were still permitting or assisting Senecas and other northern Indians to attack them, reacted most violently as Malatchi led the Lower Creeks in a devastating raid against the Lower Cherokee Towns with the burning of Echoi and Estatoe.[37] During the remainder of 1751 and early 1752, Creek attacks continued, with several Lower Cherokee Towns being abandoned and with five attacks on Hiwassee, central to the Hiwassee-Tellico leadership. In response to appeals from the Raven of Hiwassee and other Cherokees, Glen was again reluctant to act because they had not fulfilled their agreements of 1751. For example, Cherokee leaders had failed to deliver the guilty Andrew White and urged his exemption from the treaty requirements on the basis of his brave fights against the Creeks and his expression of regret of the Oconee murder as an accident.[38]

The Creeks, however, overplayed their hand in attacking the Cherokees near Charles Town who were under the protection of Carolina. Cherokee hunters had sought refuge in Charles Town, had given up their arms, and had promised to maintain peace with the Creeks. Several Upper Creeks with Acorn Whistler, a headman formerly in the service of the French, were in town in April 1752 for unofficial talks with Governor Glen.[39] They even threatened to attack the Cherokee hunters in the center of Charles Town. As the Cherokees proceeded on their way out of town, some twenty-six Upper Creeks feigned friendship but suddenly turned on them and killed several and wounded others. Acorn Whistler, pretending innocence of the tragedy, departed Charles Town in haste. Soon, however, he was identified as the "Contriver, Promoter . . . Instigator, and sole Cause" of this mischief.[40] This audacious assault in the environs of Charles Town moved Glen to demand punishment for the offenders and to work for restoration of a Creek-Cherokee peace.

For assistance the governor turned to the controversial Mary Musgrove Bosomworth and her husband, Thomas, who were then in Charles Town making plans to visit England to urge their claims for land in Georgia and for payments promised by Oglethorpe and others. Mary, having strong clan connections among the Creeks, was able to urge aggressively the demands of Glen for retribution on Acorn Whistler and agreement for peace with the Cherokees. She finally persuaded Malatchi and other leaders of the Lower Creeks to agree to the assassination of Acorn Whistler.[41] It was done, however, by recruiting a relative of the Upper Creeks to carry out the execution under the guise of jealousy over a woman and threats on his own life. The young relative completed the task, and a messenger reported "*That the Business was done*, and *he hoped the Governor's Heart would be streight.*" The relative, however, was then killed to prevent revenge that might follow if it became known that the assassination resulted from English demands. In turn, Malatchi promised to work for peace with the Cherokees and agreed to come to Charles Town in the spring of 1753.[42]

By the end of May, Malatchi and over 100 Creeks appeared in Charles Town (99 identified from Lower Creeks and 18 from Upper Creeks) for a series of conferences with the governor and Council from May 30 to June 4. This activity consumed so much of Glen's time that he complained on the last day that he had "other Matters of Consequence to transact."[43] The major purpose of the meetings was to renew the Cherokee-Creek peace, and a secondary goal of the Creeks was to obtain lower prices for trade goods. A Cherokee delegation, however, was not present. Upon persistent questions from Malatchi and other Creek conferees about their absence, Glen gave the Cherokee explanation that the Lower Towns wished to attend but were unwilling to do so for the reason that the Overhill Towns opposed attending because of threats to their security at home from French and northern Indians.[44]

Malatchi as the major spokesperson for the Creeks reviewed in great detail the problems of the past and steps to correct these problems. He admitted that

"Blood had been spilt at your very Gates" under the influence of Acorn Whistler, and he noted Whistler's death in compensation.[45] He recounted another influence on the cultural traditions of the Indians by telling of revenge on a Chickasaw living in their nation who in a drunken rage had killed a white colonist. Anticipating the demand for satisfaction, Malatchi and other headmen identified the killer and arranged that the "Blood of an Indian was spilt for the Blood of a white Man," albeit that the uncle of the killer voluntarily sacrificed himself for the younger offender.[46] Day after day, Governor Glen learned more about the unfamiliar cultural traditions of the Native Americans.

Malatchi and other Creek leaders agreed to restore peace with the Cherokees without reiterating the details of a treaty. In response to Glen's desire to obtain peace with the Seneca and other northern Indians, Malatchi expressed approval but noted the difficult and prolonged negotiations that might be required.

One untoward incident marred what was otherwise an amiable conference. In response to the Creeks' urgent demands that the price of their trade goods be lowered, Glen stated that he did not have control over prices and that his consultations with both traders and merchants had revealed their inability to provide cheaper goods, or, in fact, goods as cheap as for the Cherokees which the Creeks had requested. The Cherokee locations were more convenient for traders, Glen explained, and Cherokee skins from more mountainous areas were thicker and brought a better price on European markets. Irritated by the inability to obtain lower prices, the Oakfuskee Captain turned in his commission from the governor; other young men, sulking, left the Council Chamber and refused the presents offered them. The Wolf King further complained that the "true Reason" for high prices was the quantity of goods the traders gave their "Wives and Women which they keep."[47]

The following day the conference concluded on a more favorable note as headmen apologized for the behavior of some of their young people, who admitted their error and sought pardon from the governor. The Oakfuskee Captain also requested the return of his commission and vowed to "continue a true Friend to the English until the Day of my Death."[48]

The positive results of the conference were, nonetheless, jeopardized when Malatchi and his Creek party encountered an ambush near Dorchester and one Creek was shot and scalped. Seneca tokens left near the body suggested an attack by northern Indians. A messenger hastily reported the incident to the governor. In his usual energetic hands-on approach to Indian affairs, Glen with supporting horsemen and part of the Independent Company hurried to the scene to assure the safe passage of the Creek delegation from the colony.[49] Upon his return home, Malatchi found some opposition to restoration of peace with the Cherokees, but eventually moderate voices prevailed and the peace continued well beyond Governor Glen's tenure.

Glen still had to contend with the rivalry among the Cherokees between the mother town of Chota and Hiwassee-Tellico where the young emperor, Ammonscossittee, still clung to authority over Cherokee towns. In April 1752, the governor sent a letter of explanation and apology for the "unhappy Accident" perpetrated by Acorn Whistler and the Creeks.[50] Old Hop responded twice in the same month with conciliatory but firm tones, blaming some of the recent tensions between Cherokees and Carolina on Shawnees among them and seeking better trade supplies from South Carolina.[51] Ammonscossittee, in search of the same goal of trade, went himself with his empress, son, and members of the Tellico council to Virginia in efforts to arrange the trade for which the Little Carpenter had been unsuccessful the previous year.   The new lieutenant governor, Robert Dinwiddie, and the Virginia Council received the delegation in Williamsburg and provided entertainment during their stay. On one evening the Cherokees were guests at the theater where the tragedy of *Othello* was playing. During the stage performance of fighting with swords, the audience was surprised when the empress became alarmed and requested that those near her prevent the actors from killing each other. On the following evening the Cherokee leaders were guests at a ball at the Palace celebrating the birthday of the King of England.[52] In negotiations, Governor Dinwiddie questioned the status of the Little Carpenter from his recent visit, and the emperor falsely asserted that he represented him.[53] Dinwiddie presented the delegation with numerous presents and suggested possible Indian traders from Virginia in keeping with the treaty of 1730, but he deferred to South Carolina as the major source of their trade.[54] The young emperor returned home without great success in trade, and his position of authority among the Cherokees continued to decline as Chota asserted its authority more aggressively.

The Overhill Cherokees positioned themselves for tough bargaining with Carolina by responding to Glen's request to assist the hard-pressed Chickasaws against the Choctaws and supporting French. Great Warrior Oconostata attacked the Choctaws with some 400 warriors, and the Little Carpenter collected French scalps along the Mississippi River as the Overhills turned away from the peaceful agreements maintained with the French since 1745.[55]

Soon after the departure of Malatchi and other Creeks from Charles Town in early June 1753, a Cherokee delegation from the Overhills and the Lower Towns arrived before the end of the month. Leading the Overhills was the Little Carpenter as the Cherokee Second Man, along with Oconostata as Great Warrior and Long Jack as headman of Tanase. The overshadowed Lower Towns had Skiagunsta of Keowee as their speaker. While Glen was interested primarily in discussing the Creek-Cherokee peace, the Little Carpenter and other Overhills focused on trade and noted that peace diplomacy would have to be handled by Old Hop, the Fire King and First Beloved Man of the Cherokees.[56] In rather arrogant fashion, the Little Carpenter referred to the promises for trade in the treaty of 1730 in England to which he had been a participant, and he requested that he be able to go to England to visit King George himself. He also demanded the release of friendly Shawnees imprisoned in Charles Town and declared that peace with the Creeks was contingent on their freedom. Other criticisms emphasized the failure of Carolina to provide trade and protection.

The Overhills expressed the desire for "a large Tree to be planted in our Nation," or in other words, a fort to protect them from their enemies.[57]   In keeping with traditional conferences with Indians, Glen presented presents, smoked the peace pipe with Old Hop's tobacco, and even issued new commissions to the Little Carpenter, Long Jack, and Osteneco as Judd's Friend and Second Warrior of the Overhills.   Skiagunsta of Keowee had his participation muted by the aggressive Overhills, but he eventually had his say in stating approval of peace with the Creeks and requesting a fort in the Lower Towns to assure their restoration.   He also noted that his heart was grieved as "the other Day the Warriors over the Hills, who are but Boys, talked madly."[58] Yet the Little Carpenter and the other Overhills became more agreeable as the conference closed.   Nonetheless, Glen conferred with traders from the Cherokees about the "impertinent Manner" of the Overhills and asked what would humble them and be "the best Means to keep the Cherokees under the Awe of this Government?"[59]   When told that forts should be built among them, Glen decided on a countermove to the assertive Overhills by deciding to build first among the more loyal Lower Towns.   A clever maneuver in the complexities of Indian diplomacy!

The Assembly finally authorized expenditures for a fort after many discussions about its value and much controversy over who should share the costs—the colony or the Crown?   The figure of 3,000 pounds current money was initially stipulated for the fort; the expense of acquiring the land site would come from funds from the Crown for Indian presents.[60]   The Commons eventually provided 5,000 pounds current money to cover all claims submitted by the governor.[61]

Glen, therefore, proceeded in October 1753 with an independent company of sixty soldiers and an additional fifty workers recruited at Ninety-Six who were also armed.   As he arrived in the Lower Towns, he received no welcome from Chota of the Overhills still claiming its superior authority, but his old friend, the Raven of Hiwassee in the Valley, traveled 100 miles from his home with his two sons to greet him.   The Raven of Toxaway of the Lower Towns provided an impressive reception a day later with a hundred warriors in a solemn eagle dance with eagle tails.   In ceremonial fashion, Glen responded by having his soldiers and workers align themselves in military formation and give a salute with three volleys.   Glen opined that more soldiers would have been appropriate, for "Indians mind appearances, and I am sorry to say that our Assembly minds expence sometimes too much."[62]

The Cherokees were willing to donate land for a fort,[63] but Glen stated his intent to purchase "a spot of Ground" along with enough land for soldiers to plant corn and potatoes, ranges for horses, pasturage for cattle, and adequate timber for firewood.   The cession was also to include a 200-foot road as a right of way for sixty miles from the fort to Long Canes settlement, the point of the last purchase in 1747. The Raven of Toxaway, after consultation with headmen, agreed on a spot for the fort east of the ford over Keowee River in what is now

Pickens County approximately fifteen miles northwest of the town of Pickens.[64] He then rode the boundaries with the governor.   In response to Glen's information about the tradition of sealing transfers with exchange of earth, the Raven dismounted and donated a handful of earth and added a hat full of water from the river with the comment that it was purer than the supply in Charles Town (an obvious reference to the recent sickness suffered by Cherokees when returning). Glen closed negotiations with the contribution of goods worth almost £100 in duffels, strouds, shirts, guns, powder, bullets, and paint. The Indians made one further request—to respect the graves of their headmen on the top of the hill identified by piles of stone, which Glen readily acknowledged would be railed for protection.

The governor supervised the construction of Fort Prince George, named for the heir to the British throne, after laying out its dimensions with instruments brought for that purpose. As later described for the Board of Trade, it was a 200-foot square with regular bastions and four ravelins of earth on the corners. It was made of earth scooped from the ditch that surrounded it and secured by fascines (bundles of sticks) and well rammed. The sharp-pointed stakes of lightwood in the ravelins were 10 feet long and were set 3½ feet in the ground. Elevation from the bottom of the ditch to the top of the embankment was 10 feet. The interior contained a banquette on which soldiers stood to fire, and it also encompassed storehouses, a guardhouse, and log barracks. Glen allowed each soldier one shilling sterling per day and provisions in addition to his usual compensation from the Crown and the colony.[65]

Before returning to Charles Town by December 11, Glen garrisoned the fort with a sergeant and sixteen men.[66] Its immediate effect was to restore stability to the Lower Towns and to permit the return of many of their people who had fled either to the Middle Towns, to the Overhills to escape Creek attacks, or to position themselves for trade with Virginia. Time and the weather took their toll. Rains eroded the embankments and washed dirt into the ditches, while the unseasoned green timbers deteriorated as the fort continued to be occupied for thirteen years. The fortification had more effect on internal relations among the Cherokees than its service as a bulwark of protection for the English frontier. The territorial area yielded by the Indians was relatively small and is not to be confused with the earlier purchase of 1747 and the later one in 1755 at Saluda. As the governor negotiated for the Saluda purchase, more generous Indians, referring to the Fort Prince George cession, stated "that the Land . . . was not worth Acceptance, it was like a small Shred from a great Piece of Cloth."[67]

While Governor Glen was providing the fort for the Lower Cherokees, he was already receiving urgent messages from Governor Dinwiddie about opposition to the French threat. As early as November 1752 and May 1753, Dinwiddie wrote about French forts on the Mississippi River and additional activity in the Ohio Valley. He requested both military aid from South Carolina and assistance in influencing the Catawbas, Cherokees, and even the Creeks to assist the British.[68] Glen stated that he thought South Carolina was in greater danger, and he was unwilling to provide aid until he got instructions from the Crown. He also added that his Council had advised him not "to promise any great Assistance from this Province in its present Situation."[69] Dinwiddie persisted and appealed again for assistance with the Catawbas and Cherokees, as well as with the Creeks and Chickasaws in early 1754. He moved vigorously ahead to invite several tribes to Winchester, Virginia, in May 1754 in order to receive presents from the King. Invitations went directly to the Catawbas and Cherokees by Abraham Smith, an Indian trader. Glen was angered at this move, for he considered himself "the proper Channell of . . . Correspondence" to these two tribes. His Council itself, in November 1753, had stated that the Catawbas and Cherokees "have always been under the Direction and Influence of this Province," and we "would naturally expect to have that Overture communicated to them by us."[70] Dinwiddie asserted the urgency of the situation and explained that the Winchester meeting was not a "New Treaty" but a friendly meeting "to concert the common Welfare."[71]

While minimizing the French threat in the Ohio Valley, Glen did recognize the potential of French encroachment and advocated "an Union or Association" of the American colonies for "mutual Defence." He wrote to Dinwiddie on March 13, 1754: "Massachusets, New York, Pensilvania, Maryland, Virginia, North Carolina, South Carolina. They will keep all the Power of France in this Part of the World at a Distance at least from their own Territories, but they must be determined to stand and fall together, to feel when any of them is hurt, and in general to act upon every Occasion like the Members of the same Body."[72] A few days later Glen reiterated the proposal for a joint meeting of colonies in June and suggested Virginia as most appropriate for such a meeting, but the following month Dinwiddie countered that this was a "very improper Time" for a conference with the French "on their March." Furthermore, he thought his proposed meeting at Winchester would interfere with his participation.[73] Glen had his own proposal for meetings with all Indians in alliance with Britain as he had earlier advocated to Governor Clinton of New York; and he, no doubt, thought his ability to conduct a successful conference was superior to Dinwiddie's, as, indeed, it was. He complained to Secretary of State Thomas Robinson:

The Government of Virginia knows little of our Indians and can have no great Knowledge in any Indian Affairs. They have nevertheless busied themselves for these three or four Years past with all the Indians contiguous to and in Alliance with this Province, which has been Matter of great Concern to every Member [of] this Community as they are sensible how dangerous it may be when Matters of so great Delicacy are handled by Gentlemen that can have no great Experience in them.[74]

Writing directly to Dinwiddie on June 1, 1754, Glen claimed control over the Cherokees and reiterated that South Carolina was "extremely Jealous of any other Colonies intermingling with our Indians, by long experience we have become acquainted with their nature and Inclinations and have managed them so as to keep them steadily in the British interest."[75]

Instructions from the Earl of Holderness, successor to Thomas Robinson as Secretary of State for the Southern Department, forced Glen to send one of the independent companies of regulars in South Carolina to Virginia during 1754 and 1755. Glen unsuccessfully requested its return as early as June of 1754.[76] Further instructions urged support for the planned expedition of Major General Edward Braddock in 1755 after the defeat of Colonel George Washington and his forced evacuation of Fort Necessity on July 5, 1754. After considerable delay about financial assistance, caused partly by controversy with the Assembly, Glen was able to send an appropriation of £4,000 for aid to Braddock's expedition in May 1755, to be paid in bills of exchange, with the potential of an additional £2,000.[77]

Glen, however, gave no assistance to Dinwiddie in recruiting Indian warriors for Braddock. Dinwiddie's appeals at Winchester had been ineffective, with few representatives present. Through direct contacts with the Cherokees and Catawbas, Dinwiddie stated that they had promised to send 800 to 1,000 warriors against the French. Communications with the Cherokees, however, were complicated by the conflict between the trader-messenger, Richard Pearis, and the more reliable Nathaniel Gist, son of Christopher Gist of the Ohio Company.[78] The results of all these efforts failed as General Braddock marched off in the spring of 1755 toward the Forks of the Ohio River without enough Indians to serve even as scouts. The defeat of his forces on July 9 is a well-known and controversial story. The French with a force of around 850, over 600 of whom were Indians, inflicted a total of 977 casualties on the English contingent of 1,459, which at the time of the Monongahela crossing had only eight Indians.[79]

Failure to recruit Indian allies cannot be attributed to any one person. Braddock himself had little experience with Indians, and his leadership efforts discouraged the few natives available. One Pennsylvania chief complained that "he never appeared pleased with us; and that was the reason that a great many of our warriors left him and would not be under his command."[80] Dinwiddie was also inexperienced as Glen lamented on several occasions. At the same time, the Cherokees not only listened to Dinwiddie and Glen's competing requests, but they were also still threatened by northern Indians under French influence and tended to pull back toward a position of neutrality. Glen was still interested in providing the fort requested by the Overhill Cherokees to ward off threats from northern Indians and to negotiate another treaty that would yield large areas of Cherokee territory as well as bring them under the more direct influence of the British. Consequently, he persisted in arranging for a meeting with Old Hop, the Fire King, to conclude these arrangements. This conference occurred in June of 1755 at Saluda at the same time that Braddock was on the march.

The governor had been interested in a fort for the Overhill Cherokees for many years. In his 1746 meeting with Cherokees at Saluda Old Town, he had been able to renew friendship with them, but the Overhill leaders were not enthusiastic about an English fort because of French influence among them. After two emissaries from South Carolina representing both Glen and the Assembly visited the following year, the Cherokees became more receptive to a fort. Consequently, the executive and legislative branches of South Carolina considered numerous proposals during 1747 and 1748 for financing the fort, but without approval partly over questions of prerogative and responsibility for expenses. When the Assembly did finally authorize expenditures, Glen, as previously described, chose in 1753 to build first at Keowee among the Lower Towns as a counter to the aggressive and sometimes uncooperative attitude of the Chota Overhills in their determination to dominate Cherokee affairs.

In 1754, as the French threat on the frontier became more evident and as Glen realized the ascension of Chota leadership of Old Hop and the Little Carpenter over the ineffective Ammonscossitte of the Hiwassee-Tellico connection, renewed efforts were forthcoming to provide at least one Overhill fort, if not more. Glen proposed to Secretary of State Robinson that two forts be built at the confluence of the Tennessee, Ohio, and Wabash rivers to cut off traffic between the French in Canada and Louisiana. He also hoped the construction could be built at imperial expense. But if it fell to the colonies to finance, he suggested a shared formula for a total expense of £12,000: for Virginia, £3,000; Pennsylvania, £3,000; South Carolina, only £2,000; New York, £2,000; North Carolina, £1,000; and Maryland, £1,000.[81] Such a formula was simply Glen's idea.

Time and circumstances did not permit such complicated schemes to work their way through both colonial and imperial channels.   Glen, therefore, proceeded on his own to promote a meeting with Overhill leaders to arrange for a fort and to seek agreement for an English protectorate over the Cherokees which several agents had been urging. Glen invited Old Hop, the Little Carpenter, and other Cherokee leaders to Charles Town. Old Hop declined to make the long trip, pleading his health. The Little Carpenter, Oconostata, and a few Lower Town leaders did confer with Glen and the Council in Charles Town in May 1755. At their meeting, they directed more attention to the improvement of trade in the absence of Old Hop, who was identified as the appropriate official for such diplomatic affairs as a fort.[82] Upon suggestion from the Little Carpenter and urging by both the Council and a committee of the Commons House, Glen agreed to meet Old Hop in June. Old Hop vowed to meet him halfway and to make the difficult trip to Saluda even on the backs of his people.

The agreement on the site of the conference away from Charles Town has ramifications beyond the obvious practical considerations as one recent study of "Dividing Paths" has suggested.[83] Old Hop's declining health was a factor, as well as the past experience of illnesses (some fatal) for Cherokees on their treks to the colonial capital. On more than one occasion, they apparently suffered from impure water, different diets, or possibly the fevers of the Low Country.

These concerns were at times secondary to the assertion of equal status for the Indian by agreeing to a neutral locale for treaty conferences. From the Indian point of view, arrangement for an intermediate site undergirded the logical claim for negotiation of powers of equal status consistent with the population and strength of the Cherokee nation at this point in time.

Once agreement on the place of the conference was reached, the scenario was set for a memorable meeting in an impressive forest surrounding Saluda Old Town on the south side of the Saluda River and about ten miles north of present-day Saluda. The governor started out with a relatively small entourage but learned en route near the Congarees that the Cherokees were coming with a delegation of over 500. Ever mindful of making the correct impression in Indian negotiations, Glen recruited between 400 and 500 armed colonists to accompany him. The conference lasted a week, and its dramatic climax occurred on the sixth day, July 2, 1755. The governor and Old Hop sat under an arbor with nearly 500 Carolina gentlemen and a variety of military personnel behind them, while in front over 500 headmen and warriors sat in a crescent extending under the trees. Old Hop, because of age and fatigue, declined to be the major speaker for the Indians, so the natives elected the Little Carpenter as their representative. He delivered an oration of such dignity and grace that some contemporaries, probably with some exaggeration, compared him to a Roman or Greek orator. Holding a bow in one hand and a shaft of arrows in the other, the Little Carpenter declared that the Cherokees were now "Brothers with the People of Carolina" and their children were the children of King George. He even had a little child brought forth and presented to Governor Glen with assurance that the child could be a witness to this agreement for the next generation.

The Little Carpenter continued by opening a small leather bag with earth and presenting a parcel of dirt to be sent to the King to signal the transfer of territory. He then opened another small bag with a similar donation of parched corn flour as evidence of submission of all to the King. Next he presented his bow and arrow as a token of obedience but with the appeal to have better English arms and ammunition to supplement the limited weapons the Indians were able to create. Strings of wampum were added near the end of the Indian presentation. One final request was to have the agreements of the conference written down, read to the Indians, and then finalized by their signatures.[84] The treaty was completed with the signatures first of Old Hop and other Cherokee headmen and then the governor with witnesses of twenty-four Carolinians in attendance. During negotiations, Glen promised increased trade for the Cherokees and renewed the commitment to build a fort in the Overhills near Chota as security against the French and other hostiles. While it is not certain exactly what the Indians meant by their territorial cession,[85] future events of the Cherokee War of 1760 and the Proclamation Line of 1763 following the French and Indian War resulted in the English not preempting the land on the basis of the Saluda treaty. It did temporarily cement closer relations between

South Carolina and the Cherokees, but it increased tension with Virginia over the need to obtain Indians allies for General Braddock's campaign.

Governor Dinwiddie incorrectly asserted that the territory had been previously purchased from the Cherokees and pointed an accusing finger at Glen in his letter of September 25, 1755: "five of th[a]t Nat'n were lately in here and declar'd their Intent'n of com'g with a great No. to our Assistance, but . . . the G'r of So. Carolina had so frequently and earnestly desir'd a Meet'g with their Great Men th[a]t on their determining to meet him put a Stop to their intended March to our aid."[86]

Governor Arthur Dobbs of North Carolina joined Dinwiddie in criticizing Glen. The South Carolina governor chose the very time the Cherokees were wanted "to appoint a meeting" for a treaty, Dobbs declared, and thus he has "regarded himself and not the Public Service."[87] Dobbs's views, however, were not unbiased, for he was a fellow member of the Ohio Land Company with Dinwiddie and had also had bitter disputes with Glen over the controversial boundary line between North and South Carolina.

General Braddock directed his major criticism at Dinwiddie for not providing the promised Indian allies. While initially commending him in March of 1755 for his zeal in public service, he lashed out two months later at "the folly of Mr. Dinwiddie and the roguery of the assembly." When Indian allies from the Cherokees and Catawbas failed to join his expedition, Braddock naively inquired why coordination had not been made with the Carolinas since these Indians were their "natural allies."[88]

Glen modified his position after Braddock's defeat and the criticism that followed by encouraging the Catawbas to send warriors to Virginia, but he strongly maintained until the end of his administration in 1756 that he and the colony of South Carolina should be the intermediary for the Cherokees. Nevertheless, Dinwiddie continued his efforts for assistance directly with both tribes. Osteneco, Second Warrior of the Overhill Cherokees and a rival of the Little Carpenter, sought favor with Virginia and led about 100 Cherokees along with a few Catawbas in an expedition under Major Andrew Lewis against the Shawnee town of Scioto on the Ohio River. This winter campaign in February of 1756 was unsuccessful with bad weather and flooding rains that caused heavy loss of supplies.[89] In the same month, Dinwiddie pressed on with negotiations with both the Cherokees and Catawbas by sending out Peter Randolph and William Byrd III, both Virginia Council members and county lieutenants. They concluded separate treaties with the Catawbas at Catawba Town in February and a ten-article agreement with the Cherokees in March at Broad River, North Carolina.[90] The Catawbas promised forty or more warriors within forty days, but the Cherokees procrastinated and agreed to send 400 warriors only after a fort was completed among the Overhills. In fact, the Little Carpenter as the spokesperson for the Cherokees was extremely critical of Governor Glen for not completing the fort that again had been promised at the Saluda conference. "We do not find that that Governor has yet made the least Preparations," he exclaimed; "we don't much rely on him" for he "has forfeited his Word. "[91] Randolph and Byrd, frustrated at their lack of success with the Cherokees, returned home by way of Charles Town and informed Governor Glen of their failure.   Stung by the Indians' criticism and very sensitive to Virginia's continued approaches to the Cherokees, Glen again attempted to proceed with the promised fort.

Glen's frequent recommendations to imperial officials for the need of a fort for the Overhill Cherokees had helped convince the Board of Trade and the Secretary of State for the Southern Department of its validity.   Consequently, Secretary of State Thomas Robinson in July 1754 had noted Crown approval for the expenditure of £10,000 for American colonial defense.[92]   Unaware or unconcerned about how best to get intercolonial cooperation, he had made Governor Dinwiddie the administrator of the fund, with instructions to cooperate with Glen in building the Cherokee fort.   Upon Dinwiddie's request for an estimate of expenses for the project, Glen sent an elaborate design for the fort with the price tag of £7,000, explaining later that he wanted more than "a few Palisadoes or Puncheons put together."[93]   Shocked by this extensive request, Dinwiddie allocated only £1,000 and urged Glen to seek additional funds from his Assembly and to constrict his plans.[94]

Glen made other unsuccessful proposals to Dinwiddie and then turned to his own Assembly in efforts to proceed with the project.   At first the Assembly objected and contended that the fort was beyond the bounds of the colony and would serve the security of several colonies who should either share the cost or have the Crown finance it.   The Assembly did finally agree to make two loans of £1,000 each on the assumption that the Crown would repay the full amount.[95]   Delays resulted even in making these funds available from quibbling in the Assembly over a tax bill, so interested citizens loaned £2,000 to the Assembly and Glen was able to proceed.[96]

The governor set out from Charles Town on May 19 with an expedition of 300, made up of Captain Raymond Demeré's Independent Company of 90 and 210 Carolina provincials.   The controversial engineer, William Gerard De Brahm, accompanied the group as well as the botanical expert, Dr. Alexander Garden.   Glen proceeded for the fort with renewed determination following the many frustrating delays, but he had gone no farther than Ninety-Six when he received not only word of the arrival of his gubernatorial successor, William Henry Lyttelton, but also orders to disband the expedition.[97]

Governor Lyttelton reorganized the expedition and placed the new force of over 200 provincial troops and regulars from independent companies under the command of Captain Demeré.   Governor Dinwiddie had sent a smaller Virginia expedition of about sixty workers under Major Andrew Lewis with the intention that the two groups would cooperate in building one Overhill fort.   The clever and resourceful Cherokees seized the opportunity to have two forts built along the Little Tennessee River—one on the south side to protect the western approaches and the other on the north side to ward off possible attacks from the

French and their supporters in the Ohio Valley. Major Lewis completed the flimsy Virginia fort on the north side one mile from Chota in July of 1756, hoping to recruit Cherokee warriors for Virginia campaigns. By the spring of 1757, Demeré constructed a more substantial fortification on the south side, despite the erratic behavior of De Brahm who eventually abandoned the scene on Christmas night of 1756. The Carolina fort was named Fort Loudoun in honor of the new commander of British forces in America, John Campbell, fourth Earl of Loudoun.[98]

What appraisal, then, can be made of the role of the two governors in this controversy over Indian affairs and intercolonial cooperation? Glen was undoubtedly more skillful in Indian negotiations and had the opportunity to gain much wider influence and experience with the southern Indians, particularly the Catawbas and Cherokees. In fact, Glen ranks well among colonial officials who attempted to guard the rights and welfare of the Indian and to satisfy the persistent demand for more land for western expansion of colonial settlers.

Both governors were expansionists or imperialists and were in agreement with members of the English ministry such as Lord Halifax, who favored extension of the colonies beyond the Appalachian Mountains rather than restriction of settlements east of the mountains. Some mercantilists, however, preferred restriction and argued that the colonies would most safely remain as producers of staples and raw materials rather than develop as competing manufacturers. Both Glen and Dinwiddie provided for forts to the west that would protect friendly natives as well as colonial settlers and that also would serve as a wedge for territorial expansion. Dinwiddie displayed a more universal view of British interests and was more zealous in efforts to solicit intercolonial cooperation in challenging the French threat to British expansion. On the other hand, Dinwiddie faced one of the major French threats appearing in the Ohio Valley, which was more contiguous to Virginia than to South Carolina, and he was a member of the Ohio Company with land claims in the contested area. Glen's warning about serious threats to the Tennessee Valley never materialized, and his estimation of the enemy situation was less sound than that of Dinwiddie. While not engaged in land speculation as was Dinwiddie, he did have economic interests in the Indian trade. Glen's particularistic emphasis on South Carolina's prerogatives with the Indians and his interest only in South Carolina's expansion modified his imperialism to the point that in a sense it became provincialism.

Both governors must share responsibility for the lack of closer cooperation between the colonies. Glen was guilty of frustrating the various proposals for better cooperation in Indian affairs, and Dinwiddie suffered from lack of experience in Indian negotiations. The results for the overall English effort were that the Indians could not only play the English off against the French, but they could also frequently play one English colony against another. The resulting chaos contributed to the decision to establish superintendents as imperial officials. They addressed not only the matter of Indian allies but also the related problems of regulation of Indian trade for both diplomatic and economic purposes and the negotiations that continued to obtain title to Indian lands. Sir William Johnson had already been appointed superintendent for the North in 1755. By 1756 Edmond Atkin, who had provided the extensive report on Indians in the Southeast and was an old foe of Glen, received the appointment as superintendent for the South as Glen's term as governor came to a close.[99]

Governor Lyttelton began his administration free of the tension between Governor Glen and the South Carolina Assembly of recent years and at a time when England had officially declared war on France in May 1756, in what was known as the Seven Years' War (1756-1763). Its counterpart in America, identified as the French and Indian War, had begun, as previously noted, in 1754. Lyttelton was, therefore, able to persuade the Assembly not only to change the loans of £2,000 for the Overhill expedition to direct appropriations, but also to add the amount of £7,000.[100] His lack of experience and standing with the Cherokees, however, resulted in inept decisions that contributed to the outbreak of the devastating Cherokee War of 1760-1761. When a Cherokee delegation led by Oconostata appeared in Charles Town for peace talks with Lyttelton, he declined negotiations because of questions about its official status. Upon mixed advice from his Council on a four to four split, Lyttelton proceeded with a military expedition eventually totaling 1,700 men to Fort Prince George in October and took the Indian delegation with him. In negotiations, he demanded twenty-four Cherokees (later reduced to twenty-two) for execution to atone for recent murders, in compliance with the treaty of 1730. He then decided to hold this number as hostages, awaiting fulfillment of the treaty provisions to which six Cherokee headmen including the Little Carpenter had reluctantly agreed. The governor returned to Charles Town on January 8, 1760, with his expedition weakened by measles and smallpox and with a false sense of accomplishment which became very evident with increased violence and bloodshed. After a fatal ambush of Lieutenant Richard Coytmore as commander of Fort Prince George in February 1760, all Indian hostages were murdered. Later in August the starving garrison of white soldiers at Fort Loudoun were forced to capitulate. Promised safe conduct from the Indian country, the retreating garrison was attacked by a mass of Cherokees, and all were killed or taken captive save John Stuart, later superintendent of Indian affairs in the South after Atkin. He was the only white restored to freedom by the assistance of his friend, the Little Carpenter.[101] Fort Loudoun, designed to protect the Cherokees from their enemies, had proved to be a trap for white contingents deep in Indian country when war erupted. By this time, Governor Lyttelton had been given a new assignment of royal governor of Jamaica, and imperial forces were left to chastise the errant Cherokees. It is inconceivable that the more experienced Glen, whatever the advice of Councilors, would have followed the dangerous course of holding a peace delegation as hostages—one of the serious mistakes leading to disruption of the longtime peaceful relations with the Cherokees, whom Glen frequently called the "Key to Carolina."

7

Years of Transition

*We beg leave to lay at your Royal feet the tribute of our humblest Thanks for
. . . your Majestys appointment and long continuance of his Excellency James
Glen Esqr., our present Governour, who by his Vigilance contributed to our safety
during a long War and by his Diligence endeavored to promote our prosperity in
Peace and both in Peace and War having made the Happiness of the People his
peculiar care, has thereby shewn himself to be truly your Majestys Representative.*

Commons House, 1755

The changing currents of British politics at midcentury became more threatening
to Governor Glen's position in Carolina as well as to other contemporary
appointees as royal governors in the colonies. Glen had been appointed in 1738
during the long administration of Sir Robert Walpole as prime minister with
Lord Wilmington as his major patron. Walpole was forced to resign in 1742
after inadequate support in the elections of 1741. Lord Wilmington, president
of the Privy Council and nominal head of the government with Lord Carteret
succeeding Walpole as prime minister, died in 1743. The Pelhams then
emerged as powerful leaders as King George II continued in office. Henry
Pelham became prime minister in 1744 and held that position until his death in
1754. His brother, Thomas Pelham-Hobbes, the Duke of Newcastle, served as
Secretary of State for the Southern Department from 1724 to 1748, then as
Secretary of State for the Northern Department in 1748, and finally as First
Lord of the Treasury and prime minister from 1754 to 1756, succeeding his
brother upon the latter's death. The Southern Department was responsible for
diplomatic negotiations with countries of southern Europe and management of
colonial affairs, whereas the Northern Department had responsibilities for
northern Europe.[1]

After Newcastle left the Southern Department in 1748, his successor, the

Duke of Bedford, appointed the Earl of Halifax as the new president of the moribund Board of Trade.   Halifax and other reformers on the Board, as previously noted, adopted a more diligent approach to administration of the American colonies and became increasingly concerned about further encroachments on the royal prerogative in the colonies.   Their principal approach was through admonitions to royal governors to adhere to their many instructions that had been evaded over the years, especially in South Carolina with the aggressive Commons House of the Assembly.   Governor Glen had attempted to follow a middle course by working with the Assembly and at the same time to reestablish the guidelines of his instructions as urged by the Board of Trade.

Glen was almost replaced as early as 1754 when the Earl of Halifax had to yield some of the prerogatives of the Board of Trade's control over the colonies to domestic politics as instigated by Prime Minister Henry Pelham. The prime minister worked out a political arrangement with Thomas Pitt whereby, in exchange for his support to the government in several areas including Old Sarum, he would become governor of South Carolina at the salary of £2,400, a figure much larger than Glen and his predecessors had received. Halifax yielded to Pelham's plan and had already drawn up a letter for Glen's recall at the time of Pelham's death. Pitt finally preferred an annual contribution of £1,000 from the government, thus temporarily saving Glen's position.[2] The governor, however, learned of this plan and consequently was aware of the uncertainty of his office during the remainder of his tenure to 1756. Along with Glen, two other prominent appointees of the Walpole-Wilmington era were also terminated with criticisms, including failure to uphold the royal prerogative: Governor George Clinton of New York in 1753 and Governor William Shirley of Massachusetts in 1756, the latter also accused of incompetent military leadership.[3]

During Glen's last two years in office, he was placed in the role of compromiser as the Commons turned its aggressive campaign for more power against the Council rather than its previous challenges to the governor. The major focus of the argument was on selecting the colonial agent in London. As previously noted, James Crokatt had succeeded Peregrine Fury in 1749 without an enthusiastic endorsement of this change from Glen.   The Commons influenced Crokatt through its preponderance of members on the Assembly committee of correspondence. Crokatt, however, had followed an independent course at times in failing to heed the Commons' desire to advocate an increase of paper money and in supporting Charles McNaire's claims following the Choctaw revolt partly because of McNaire's financial obligations to him.

The crisis between Commons and Council developed when Crokatt stated his intention to resign in his letter of July 1753. The Council as Upper House quickly accepted the resignation and maintained that his ordinance of appointment had expired in opposition to the Commons' contention that he could and should continue as agent. The Upper House insisted that the agent should have the approval of both houses of the Assembly, but the Commons continued to consider Crokatt as the colonial agent.[4] Governor Glen and the Upper House preferred Charles Pinckney who was then residing in England and turned to him to present an urgent request for imperial support for a fort among the Overhill Cherokees.   Pinckney had the support of Speaker Andrew Rutledge of the Commons and of Crokatt himself, and Governor and Mrs. Glen were renting his house in Charles Town during his stay in London.   Two agents, one representing the Commons and the other the governor and Council, created an awkward and unsatisfactory situation. Both houses of the Assembly introduced their own statutory appointment for a new agent, each of which was rejected by the other.[5] The Commons' attempt to obtain appointment by resolution of both houses also failed. The crisis continued.

The conflict between the two houses then moved to a tax bill that involved broader issues of constitutional powers and resulted in heated exchanges, with the governor attempting to reduce tensions. Even though the Upper House had accepted Crokatt's resignation, the Commons ingeniously included his salary in its tax bill of March 1755, with the intention of controlling the position by its prerogative of creating money bills. But the Upper House detected the ploy and first made amendments to payments to Crokatt to exclude salary as a public officer. It then demanded records of the "Account of his Disbursements" before it would give approval.[6] The Commons flatly refused and proceeded to question the assertion that the precedents of Parliament assured the Upper House a role in appointing an agent. Furthermore, the Commons continued, "the Agent being a Person appointed for solliciting the Affairs of this Province, we conceive the Province should be understood to be the People, and as the People only are to pay for his services it seems just and reasonable that the Representatives of the People should have the nomination of their Agent, notwithstanding such Agent cannot be appointed by Law but with the Assent of the Governour and the advice and consent of His Majestys Council."[7]   An oxymoron, to be sure!

The Upper House objected to this conception of the province as the people and termed it "both new and extraordinary." "Is it not a Sollecism," the Upper House contended, "to say that any Branch of the Legislature is represented by any other Branch of it? And to what purpose are the Governour and Council to assent and consent to a Law appointing an Agent if they are to be the only Persons precluded from freely judging of his services?"[8]

The Commons rejected the amendments of the Upper House but attempted to satisfy it by sending Crokatt's letters without the accounts requested, but the Upper House refused to read them. Then "upon the most cool, dispassionate and mature deliberation," it again rejected the tax bill.[9]

The governor at this point intervened to prorogue the Assembly on April 12 until April 28 with the exhortation that members return to "meet with Mildness" and that "Heats" be "cooled" during the recess.[10] As the Assembly reconvened in late April, Glen added that "the Happiness of the Province depended upon the

Harmony of the several Branches of the Legislature" and that this harmony was "the Cement of the Society and the Bond of Peace."[11]   During the first half of May, the two houses continued to jockey back and forth over the tax bill. The Commons consistently voted to leave out of Crokatt's appropriation the phrase "*for services and Disbursements*," which was again desired by the Upper House to deny salary as a public officer.[12]   The Upper House suggested that the governor again prorogue the Assembly, but on May 19 it finally yielded by passing the tax bill to provide defense for the colony. At the same time, it still protested that its original position was part of the British constitution and the "Parliamentary Rights we are invested with."[13]

In a separate action that very day of May 19, the Commons took a new tack by offering a gratuitous tribute to both the Crown and Governor Glen:

Most Gracious Sovereign
We your Majestys most Dutiful and Loyal Subjects the Commons House of Assembly of this your Province of South Carolina met in General Assembly, sensible that your Auspicious Reign is the source of all Blessings to all your People, never fail to put up the most fervent prayers to almighty God for the preservation of your precious Life; and that the British Scepter may never cease to be swayed by one of your Royal House that our Nation may ever continue a free People.

We beg leave to lay at your Royal feet the tribute of our humblest Thanks for the many Tokens of your Royal Bounty to this Colony and particularly for your Majestys appointment and long continuance of his Excellency James Glen Esqr., our present Governour, who by his Vigilance contributed to our safety during a long War and by his Diligence endeavoured to promote our prosperity in Peace and both in Peace and War having made the Happiness of the People his peculiar care, has thereby shewn himself to be truly your Majestys Representative.

Permit us, Sir, to approach the Throne then, and in Gratitude for the Blessings of his Excellency mild and good Administration to beg leave to express our Sentiments of his services and humbly to submit the same to your Royal consideration.[14]

Such a glowing tribute would appeal to anyone but particularly to Governor Glen, who frequently sought approval of his administration and who was constantly being criticized by the Board of Trade which was considering his replacement.

The Council, still resenting having to yield as the Upper House to the tax bill, attempted to clarify its status by requesting in the fall of 1755 that a committee be appointed to determine whether it was constitutionally a Council of State to advise the governor about assent to bills of the Assembly, or whether, "consistently with the Charter of this Province," it was to be considered an Upper House with legislative capacity similar to the British House of Peers. The Commons postponed any such action on the basis of the extensive research needed but agreed to continue the usage of the past without considering it a precedent until the matter could be resolved at a later date.[15]

As the conflict between the two houses continued, the Council, though mired in the question of basic rights and failing to provide funds for a fort among the

Overhill Cherokees, unwisely criticized Governor Glen in February 1756 for not proceeding with the project and requested detailed plans and estimated expenses for the fort. When Glen did not immediately reply, the Council had its request published in the *Gazette* on March 11, which was apparently designed to embarrass him. The article stated that the Council was "unwilling that the Public should suffer Detriment or Inconvenience by any Delay" and gave the impression that the Crown had provided £10,000 for the fort when Governor Dinwiddie had only allotted £1,000 from the larger amount.[16] Glen resented the Council's request and the public expression which he later termed unnecessary. Such inept moves by the Council did not serve it well in subsequent conflicts with the Commons.

The two contending houses temporarily eased tensions by excluding former candidates and agreeing in March of 1756 on a new agent, William Middleton, who was then residing in England and represented a prominent South Carolina family.[17] But before the month was out, a new tax bill renewed the feud over payment for Crokatt's past services. In early April, the Commons still stubbornly refused to submit accounts to the Upper House. The dispute dragged on toward Easter Week as Glen became more and more disturbed over the Assembly's failure to pass even the loan needed for him to proceed with building the Cherokee fort. While it was customary for the Assembly not to meet during Passion Week, Glen opposed adjournment and urged a mutual yielding and compromise as "A Work of Peace & Love" in this holy week.[18] The Commons, however, remained steadfast and still refused to send the requested accounts to the Upper House, contending that it had no knowledge of the House of Peers in Britain exercising this right.[19] Following Easter, the governor, stating that he might be near the end of his administration, still felt obligated to intervene. He called the Commons' attention to his thirteenth instruction that assemblies that "have taken upon them the sole framing of money-bills refusing to let the Council alter or amend the same" was an encroachment on the royal prerogative. The instruction repeated that "It is also our further pleasure that the Council have the like power of framing Money-Bills as the Assembly." Glen added that he considered the dispute over accounts "not about Essentials" and urged the Commons to yield them without damaging "the rights of the People."[20] Passing over the governor's long message, the Commons denied that the question of accounts was "a trivial Matter" and again refused to comply with the request of the Upper House.[21] Both the Upper House and the Commons seemed willing to let the common good of society suffer while quibbling over institutional prerogatives.

The Commons then went on the offensive with the completion of its "Humble Remonstrance" to the governor on April 29, 1756. The remonstrance reviewed in detail the rejection of three tax bills by the Council acting as the Upper House and enumerated the dangers therein, including the delay of the Cherokee fort. The business of the province, the Commons contended, "cannot be transacted with Men whose Actions demonstrate that their sole Views are the advancement of their own Power beyond it's due Limits, and an abridgment of the inherent & most valuable Rights & Privileges of the People." Then the appeal continued its earlier praise of the governor by stating "There is no one in this Government who knows the British Constitution better than your Excellency." Consequently, the Commons urged Glen, if he felt their body was at fault, to dissolve the Assembly; but if Council members were in the wrong, he should suspend the guilty members and appoint others.[22]

The Upper House drew up its own representation for the governor on May 1. It reviewed the history of legislative procedures since the time of the proprietors and noted the first challenges to the Upper House's role in money bills in 1735 and 1739. It commended the governor for agreeing that the Commons should have presented the accounts of Agent Crokatt for inspection by the Upper House. But it attempted to justify its own role in obstruction of tax bills and excoriated the Commons for denying the Upper House its "very existence as a Branch of the Legislature."[23]

Two days later, Governor Glen responded to the remonstrance of the Commons House. He bemoaned the disruption of harmony in the Assembly and stated that the Upper House was wrong in opposing the tax bills at a time that "seems to be no Juncture for disputing Questions about Rights and Privileges." Yet he was critical of both houses for the impasse by stating that the Commons should have sent the accounts and that the Upper House should have approved the tax bills without them. He did "assert the Council's Right of rejecting Bills" but declined either to dissolve the Assembly or to suspend any members of the Council.[24] The Commons was apparently satisfied with Glen's blame on the Council as Upper House and had both its "Humble Remonstrance" and the governor's answer printed in the *Gazette* on May 6.[25] The Council's representation never appeared in newsprint.

One week later a more overt public assault on the Council as the Upper House was printed in the *Gazette* under the authorship of T——s W——t, identified later as Thomas Wright, son of a former chief justice, member of the Commons House, and vice chair of the committee of the Commons to explore the status of the Council as a Council of State or an Upper House of the legislature. Reviewing early charters, the rule of the proprietors, and the transition to royal government, Wright maintained that the province had only two estates—the lords proprietors and the people. If the King were to appoint a Council to sit as an Upper House or House of Peers, this action would destroy the old balance and be "contrary to the usage of our mother-country." Denying the Council's right to serve as the Upper House of the Assembly, he asserted that it existed only by the instructions of the governor, that its members had no "commission or patent for their places,"[26] and he doubted that they have an "instrument of writing, by which they claim their privileges of an upper house." Even if the Crown were by instructions to create an Upper House, Wright argued, this would "lessen the rights of assembly, or totally take away all their privileges." Furthermore, the Council was also very different from the House of Peers in England, for its members were not hereditary and they voted in elections of the Assembly.[27]

In view of this constant barrage of criticism and this constitutional challenge to exist as an Upper House, the Council appointed a committee of five members on May 5 to present its own vindication. The members of the committee were James Kinloch, William Bull, Jr., William Wragg, James Michie, and Othniel Beale.[28] The committee's detailed report then appeared in three issues of the *Gazette* of May 22, May 29, and June 5. The report attempted to shift the blame for the delay of the tax bill to the Commons, and it again criticized the governor for not proceeding with the Cherokee fort. It even attempted, in paradoxical statements, to assure the public that blocking tax bills in the past had not produced dire results.[29] Most unusual, however, in the final issue on June 5 was the constitutional argument that the Crown was the source of all authority: "This province, and the legislation of it, is entirely subordinate and dependent. Its powers are *derivative*, and not *original*." Instructions to governors were the implementation of the Crown's authority that provided for three estates in government, not just two as previously argued. In conclusion, the reports stated that "We look upon the British Constitution to be the *best* that ever was established," and you cannot imitate Great Britain without acknowledging the "power in the Council as A FIRST PRINCIPLE." The reports, however, declined to respond to Glen's answer to the remonstrance of the Commons but suggested this might be done later at a more opportune time with more light on the subject.[30]

The Council never returned to the task of responding to Glen, for as previously noted, he departed to build the Cherokee fort with private loans of £2,000 but was recalled upon the arrival of Governor Lyttelton as his successor. Under Lyttelton, the Council as Upper House finally yielded on the tax bill only for the sake of expediency. The Council's decline continued as several protests by William Wragg to Lyttelton's policies and the actions of the Commons led the governor to suspend him from the Council. The Board of Trade and the Privy Council approved the suspension following a distorted criticism from Lyttelton. In one letter he denounced Wragg as "an insolent and litigious spirit" and the "Chief Incendiary" of distracting contests to public business. While a "zealous stickler for the rights & priviledges" of the Council, Lyttelton continued, "I have allways observ'd where those rights were not concern'd, that he eagerly objected to every thing which seem'd to favour the Prerogative." A few months later he was still denouncing Wragg as "a man of a most assuming nature and of the hottest spirit I ever knew."[31] Thus, Glen's successor delivered the final *coup de grace* to the effectiveness of the Council as Upper House as the Commons gained even more power and prestige over the Council than it had obtained over royal governors. The Council's decline as Upper House inevitably diminished its role as executive to the governor. The status of the Council, therefore, continued to fall with the appointment of several placemen and with an unprecedented number of refusals by native South

Carolinians to serve.[32]

During his last two years in office, Governor Glen faced an unexpected problem from the arrival of Acadians from Canada. The Treaty of Utrecht ending the War of Spanish Succession (Queen Anne's War in America) in 1713 had yielded Acadia from France to Great Britain, which then became Nova Scotia (New Scotland) with uncertain boundaries. Its simple and illiterate peasantry had been under the influence of French missionaries and was slow to take the oath of allegiance to the British Crown. After Anglo-French hostilities again erupted in the French and Indian War in 1754, Governor Charles Lawrence of Canada became alarmed at their continued presence and their continued refusal to take an unqualified oath of British allegiance. He, therefore, initiated a policy, also supported by Governor Shirley of Massachusetts, to deport the Acadians and distribute them, by force if necessary, among the English colonies.[33]

South Carolina received its first group in November 1755, with several hundred soon added so that by mid-January of 1756 Glen counted a total of 993.[34] What was to be done with these unexpected immigrants who refused to take an oath of allegiance? They were still Catholic with rights of free exercise of religion under the Treaty of Utrecht as provided under British laws, but the colony of South Carolina had prohibited Roman Catholics within its bounds by a law of 1697.[35] The Commons, finding the supposed threat to security and the burden of providing for these refugees intolerable, urged that they be shipped out of the province. The Council also endorsed this action.[36] Glen at first responded by providing signed blank certificates for the commissary general to use in exporting the new arrivals to England or other ports. Yet the governor was convinced that the criticism of the Acadian threat was exaggerated and that such stories as that of the French deserter-spy with a map of Charles Town had "been extremely wrong." He urged humanitarian consideration for these "poor People . . . in the depth of distress."[37] By February 1756, he concluded that shipping out the Acadians was illegal. He contended that for several presumed criminals this would be in violation of his fifty-fourth instruction that forbade sending them to England without convincing proof of their crimes. He confirmed his doubts by conferring with the Crown's attorney general and the chief justice of the colony, Peter Leigh. This consultation brought confirmation that such action would not only be a violation of Magna Carta but would also subject him to the penalties of the British Habeas Corpus Act, which could not be alleviated by the power of pardon of the King.[38]

Other schemes to meet the crises were tried. The colony of Georgia aided the Acadians in obtaining boats to return northward and provided passes for them to enter South Carolina. Glen eventually ordered scout boats to restrict this migration, but upon the Council's advice the governor endorsed the passes from Georgia Governor John Reynolds and encouraged them to move on. Glen made further arrangements to expedite the departure of some of the Acadians[39] but not as vigorously as both the Council and the Commons thought desirable.

These two houses even stopped feuding over such issues as the tax bill to agree on criticizing the governor for not exporting several Acadians in jail. If "disappointed in these our reasonable Expectations," the Upper House communicated to the Commons, "our Conscience informs us that we have discharged our Duty to the Public."[40] Glen agreed that the Acadians would be less of a threat in more populous colonies to the north and passed the initiative back to the Commons to conduct "this whole Affair," but the Acadians' demands for pilots to accompany them thwarted the project.[41]

The problem of the Acadians remained unsolved as Governor Lyttelton succeeded Glen in June of 1756. Lyttelton arrived with instructions from the Secretary of State that the Acadians were to remain in the province and not be sent to England. By July, the new governor and the Assembly completed legislation mandating the dispersal of Acadians throughout the colony; four-fifths were to be removed from Charles Town, and some adults and children were to be forced into contracts of indenture, sometimes ruthlessly.[42]

Still another problem confronted Governor Glen during his last two years in office. This was the controversy over the boundary line with North Carolina which had plagued former governors and would continue even into statehood during the nineteenth and twentieth centuries. Originally identified as one province in the proprietary grant of 1663, Carolina had developed along separate lines and by 1712 Edward Hyde became governor of North Carolina. At that time, only general boundaries were designated as the area lying north and east of the Cape Fear River. Confusion resulted in the undefined areas between the two colonies.[43] The Board of Trade had attempted to settle the problem in the transition from proprietary to royal governments through the cooperation of the two proprietary governors who received royal appointments: Colonel Robert Johnson for South Carolina in December 1729, and Captain George Burrington for North Carolina in January 1730. The King sent the following instruction to the two governors:

And, in order to prevent any disturbances that may arise about the [southern, northern] boundaries of the province under your government, we are graciously pleased to signify our pleasure that a line shall be run by commissioners appointed by each province beginning at the sea thirty miles distant from the mouth of Cape Fear River on the southwest thereof, keeping the same distance from the said river as the course thereof runs, to the main source or head thereof, and from thence the said boundary line shall be continued due west as far as the South Seas; but if Waggamaw River runs within thirty miles of Cape Fear River, then that river to be the boundary from the sea to the head thereof, and from thence to keep the distance of thirty miles parallel from Cape Fear River to the head thereof, and from thence, a due West Course, to the South Seas.[44]

The two governors, however, disagreed in implementing these instructions, employing different interpretations in relating the Waccamaw River to the Cape Fear. Governor Burrington advocated the Pee Dee River as the boundary that would be more favorable to North Carolina. It was not until Gabriel Johnston succeeded Burrington that the two governors, Johnston of North Carolina and Johnson of South Carolina, appointed commissioners to survey the boundary line. The commissioners, with Governor Johnston of North Carolina serving as mediator, agreed on the survey line of 1735. The boundary was to begin at the ocean thirty miles from the west side of the mouth of the Cape Fear River, run northwest to the thirty-fifth parallel of north latitude, and then due west to the South Seas. If the northwest line came within five miles of the Pee Dee River before reaching the thirty-fifth parallel, then the line was to proceed five miles from the Pee Dee River, provided the line did not come closer than thirty miles to the Cape Fear River. If the line were to include any part of the Catawba or Cherokee Indian lands, they were to be "set off" to remain within South Carolina.[45] Even this agreement was modified as the commissioners sought a more direct line rather than paralleling the Cape Fear River, a line that was later contested by South Carolina. Further extension of the boundary resulted in 1737 when the commissioners believed, erroneously, that they had reached the thirty-fifth parallel.[46]

Governor Glen's general instructions from the Crown issued in 1739 simply repeated the same directions given earlier to Governors Johnson and Burrington in 1730.[47] Little was done about the boundary until additional conflicts arose with western settlements on lands claimed by the new governor of North Carolina, Arthur Dobbs. He had become a land speculator when in 1745 he obtained a grant of some 400,000 acres with Colonel John Selwyn for part of the area issued earlier to Henry McCulloh.[48] Anson County was organized in North Carolina in 1750, and settlers continued to move into the controversial area to the west in the Waxhaws. When Dobbs became governor of North Carolina in 1754, he sought to develop his lands with additional immigrants but found the confusion over jurisdiction a major obstacle to peaceful settlements. Furthermore, revenue was being lost as settlers ignored responsibility to the government of either colony. Writing to the Board of Trade in August of 1755, Dobbs reiterated these points and was critical of South Carolina and of Glen in assuming the right to issue warrants to the lands in dispute and in urging King Hagler of the Catawbas not to let Englishmen settle within thirty miles of his nation.[49]

The Board of Trade's inefficient action in formulating instructions to Governor Dobbs added fuel to the intercolonial conflict. The Board left out the instructions to earlier governors about settling the boundary conflict—similar to those to Governor Glen—and directed Dobbs, without informing Glen and South Carolina, to review the situation and make recommendations for correcting possible violations of instructions and removing "inconveniencies" for North Carolina settlers.[50] Governor Dobbs and the North Carolina Council prepared a report that reviewed the history of the conflict and recommended to the Board that the line be moved much farther south to benefit North Carolina by having the boundary along Winyaw Bay and the Pee Dee River from the sea to 34° 20'.

This would facilitate trade for North Carolina. It also was justified, the report stated, because of the large grant in North Carolina that had been made to Lord Granville to satisfy his proprietary claim and the additional restriction on North Carolina boundaries to the west by the creation of the colony of Georgia. The Catawba Indian lands would also fall within the North Carolina bounds.[51] Even though these detailed changes were not sent to Governor Glen, he and the South Carolina Assembly were attempting to arrange a satisfactory boundary on the basis of Glen's instructions.[52] In these efforts, Glen did digress to protest again the Commons' encroachment on the royal prerogative, as its communication to him named George Hunter and John Pearson as the surveyors who should be appointed to work with North Carolina commissioners. Glen asked: "Is this, Gentlemen, the Language of the Constitution? I mean of the British Constitution."[53]

Glen delivered his strongest invective against Governor Dobbs, with support of the Commons, for Dobbs's proposing a new boundary line that would be more favorable to North Carolina on the basis of instructions unknown to South Carolina. When Dobbs described his new instruction from the Board of Trade in his letter to the South Carolina governor, Glen found it incredible, responding that he thought "it some Memorandum or minute copied from your Copy book, for it has more the air of the advice of a friend, or of a verbal direction from some private Person than of a written Instruction from his Majesty to one of his Governors." Glen doubted that the statement by Dobbs was the complete instruction, and he asked for the "entire Instruction or instructions." Glen also wanted to have a copy of Dobbs's letter to the Board of Trade relative to boundary proposals.[54]

Governor Dobbs retorted with equal invective. Dobbs stated to Glen that his letter

is wrote in a very extraordinary style, I may say dictatorial, not as one Governor to another having equal powers from his Majesty, and independant of each other, but as if I was dependant upon you, and obliged to give you an account of my behavior in the transacting Affairs of this Government, taxing me with sending you scraps of my instruction about the Boundary line and concealing the remainder of it, alledging that my instruction was the advice of a friend, or some verbal direction from some private person, which you are rather inclined to believe.[55]

Conflict over the disputed boundary area continued beyond Glen's tenure. Violent actions erupted in both colonies to protect their grantees, and the hostility between governors became even more bitter. In response to North Carolina's eviction of two South Carolina grantees in 1762, Governor Thomas Boone with the support of his South Carolina Council excoriated Dobbs for his action and exclaimed: "I have ordered the persons concerned to treat the Ejectment with the contempt it deserves and in no respect to acknowledge the Jurisdiction of North Carolina. I was in great hopes Sir that you would have been Contented to have waited the decision of our Superiors upon a Subject which you and I are neither competent or impartial Judges of, But if you have too much impetuosity to wait this determination, I have too little Tameness to submit to yours." Boone concluded with a denouncement of Dobbs's "manifest indifference" toward harmony between the colonies "because a few paultry Acres of your own are in Question."[56]

Some progress was made in extending the boundary line in 1764 with the appointment of Lieutenant Governor William Tryon of North Carolina, with still another extension in 1772. Yet controversy persisted, with North Carolina protesting the 1772 line on the basis of the Bill of Rights in its state constitution.[57] In 1800, Governor John Drayton of South Carolina, in one of the most bitter letters of the conflict, threatened to use force in repelling North Carolina commissioners if they "enter the Territory of this State" to run a line.[58] Stabilizing the line and rerunning it for clarification continued even into the twentieth century, and authorizations for new surveys were made as late as 1915 and 1919. Permanent marking of the boundary was not finally achieved until 1928.[59]

Governor Glen's last two years in office placed him more in the role of compromiser between the Commons and the Council as Upper House. The Commons stepped up its persistent drive for more power by now directing its assault more toward the Upper House than toward the governor. This change became evident in such issues as the selection of colonial agents and the provisions of tax bills. In fact, the Commons initiated a bitter constitutional debate by attempting to deny the Council's role as Upper House. Through flattery, it was partially successful in obtaining Govrnor Glen's assistance in criticizing the Upper House, although the governor did remind the Commons of the royal provisions for the appropriate role of the Council in legislative matters. It was Glen's successor, Governor Lyttelton, who rendered the telling blow to the Council by suspending William Wragg, an action eventually approved by imperial officials. This incident diminished the status of the Council both as Upper House and as executive advisor to the governor. This was a paradoxical result for the royal prerogative since the Council had only recently demonstrated its support of the prerogative, having made a very strong statement in support of the Crown as the source of political authority and the implementation of this power through royal instructions to governors. During his last two years as governor, Glen also faced the problems of the Acadians and the boundary controversy with North Carolina. Although he showed compassion for the displaced Acadians, he was aware of legal restrictions, and so he left the final solution to his successor and the Assembly, with new instructions from the Crown. The boundary dispute had engaged the attention of previous governors and continued to confront subsequent officials in the nineteenth and twentieth centuries. Several governors engaged in bitter conflicts and heated exchanges, but Glen's criticisms were directed primarily at Governor Dobbs of North Carolina.

8

The Twilight Years

He found them in ashes and left them fair, fortified and flourishing.[1]

Casket copper plate, 1777

After Governor William Lyttelton succeeded James Glen as royal governor of South Carolina, the Commons House proposed a resolution on July 6, 1756, to pay Glen £500 for his passage to Great Britain and for any services and claims he may have against the public except for an account from John McQueen for presents that Glen had given to the Indians.[2] Upon returning from the interrupted efforts to build a fort among the Cherokees, Glen decided to remain in the colony and actually stayed on until 1761.

William Pitt emerged in England as nominal head of the ministry despite his unpopularity with King George II, although he was not officially prime minister. This led to reorganization of the failed efforts of the English against the French in the French and Indian War. Pitt assumed primary responsibility for English campaigns, recalled many of the officers then in command, and designated Major General James Abercromby as successor to Lord Loudoun as commander-in-chief of British forces in North America. By 1758, these impressive efforts began to turn the tide of victory toward the English, with the fall of Louisburg in July and the surrender of Fort Frontenac on Lake Ontario in August.

Meanwhile, Brigadier General John Forbes had been appointed to direct military operations in the southern province, and Lieutenant Colonel Henry Bouquet was second in command for the campaign directed against Fort Duquesne at the forks of the Ohio River. A native of Scotland, Forbes had received training in medicine but turned to a military career instead and joined the Royal Scots Greys Regiment. Following service in the War of the Austrian Succession and in the bloody battle of Culloden against the Jacobites in his native Scotland of 1746, he became deputy quartermaster general and then adjutant general in the army before being elevated to the rank of brigadier general to command the Fort Duquesne expedition in 1758.[3]   Bouquet descended from French Huguenots who migrated to Switzerland, and he became a soldier of fortune early in his career. After military service in Europe, he came to America in 1756 and rose to regimental commander of the new Royal American Regiment before being called upon by William Pitt to serve with Forbes.[4]

Glen was a cousin of his fellow Scotsman, Forbes, and had cordial relations with both commanders of the new expedition. He came to Philadelphia from South Carolina with Colonel Archibald Montgomery's regiment of Scottish Highlanders to visit Forbes in June of 1758.[5]   When he learned of the difficulties of retaining the Cherokee warriors for the campaign, he volunteered to go along to assist in this effort. He proceeded ahead of Forbes from Philadelphia to Carlisle, Pennsylvania, and on June 21 moved on to Winchester, Virginia, with Jamie St. Claire as "his Companion and Conductor."[6] Forbes continued to be solicitous of Glen's welfare on the expedition and thanked Colonel Bouquet in July for taking care of the former governor. He also passed along entertaining messages by way of Bouquet, telling Glen "not to turn Indian" and not to despair of the delays in the progress of the expedition. He also thought that Glen may be weary of military life by August but was pleased to learn that he remained "so jocular" and still had "leggs left" while Forbes admitted his limited mobility because of the extreme illness he suffered on the campaign. Forbes promised to bring or send Glen both port and claret.[7]

As Glen moved on to Fort Cumberland by July 5, his correspondence reflected the difficulties of frontier campaigns. Writing to Colonel Bouquet, he stated that "I write by the light of a farthing candle, uneasily seated" with "thousand bells rattling. I cannot say ringing around me."[8] In a letter a week later to General Forbes, he noted that "I write this late at night with broken glasses. I can hardly see but I must acknowledge your letter."[9]

Glen visited the camp of Colonel George Washington who was then in command of nearly 600 men, including five companies of the First Virginia Regiment that had arrived only three days earlier. He had a pleasant visit with Washington but eventually had to oppose his choice of routes for the expedition. The crux of the issue was a choice between the former route of General Braddock in his ill-fated campaign of 1755 by way of Fort Cumberland and the dangerous crossings of the Youghiogheny and Monogahela rivers, or to proceed more directly by cutting a new route through central Pennsylvania from Carlisle to Raystown and west over the mountains to the forks of the Ohio. Both Washington and Colonel William Byrd III, commander of the Second Virginia Regiment, favored the Braddock route. They maintained that, even though a little longer in distance, it would take a shorter time to cover than cutting a new route, all of which would make it easier to reach their destination before winter set in and to retain the impatient Indian allies that had reached over 600. Incidentally, it would also better serve Virginia economically if this route prevailed as the major corridor to the west. Others, however, argued that the central Pennsylvania route would be more direct in distance and would provide a better source of horses and wagons for the necessary means of transportation. Furthermore, it would eliminate the treacherous river crossings of the Braddock route. Glen was not the first to advocate the Pennsylvania route, for John St. Clair apparently had supported it earlier.[10] Writing on July 26 to Forbes, Glen submitted his arguments for the route from Raystown. He expressed concern about the lack of adequate pasturage by the Braddock trail, the threat of mountain passes, the greater distance, and again the number of potentially dangerous river crossings. In conclusion, he stated: "Weigh all these circumstances and you will find nothing in Braddocks scale. This must preponderate with every disinterested person."[11] Glen added one intriguing caveat for his cousin: "You are to consider that the Provencial part of your Army is divided up this point [i.e., which route to take to Fort Duquesne] and tho' Washington is a cool sensible modest young man and should you meet with any difficulties in your March on any other Path it will be said why did you not take the wellknown tried and beaten road."[12]

Forbes and Bouquet chose the Pennsylvania route much to Washington's disappointment. He exclaimed: "All is lost by Heavens!—Our Enterprize Ruind; & We stopd at the Laurel Hill for this Winter—not to gather laurels by the by . . . The Southern Indians turn against Us—and these Colonies become desolate by such an Acquisition to the Enemy's Strength."[13] Forbes was suspicious of the Virginians' motives, but Washington maintained convincingly that he was "uninfluenced by Prejudice—having no hope or fears but for the General Good." Yet the economic motive was a potential for many Virginians.

Even in military service, Washington continued to be concerned about the "General Good" and decided to be a candidate again for the Virginia House of Burgesses from Frederick County in the Valley. Having been unsuccessful in 1755, he was eager to succeed in 1758. Yet his military responsibilities conflicted with the need to be in Winchester to campaign in person. Many of his most trusted advisors in Virginia urged him to return to Frederick on election day on July 24. Writing on July 19, Glen was of the same opinion as stated in his letter to "Col. Washington and Col. [William] Byrd or either of them":

I wish Col. Washington could be prevail'd upon to think with me that his presence is more necessary at Winchester, for one day at least, than in Camp Cumberland, had I the pleasure of being better acquainted I would press it, had I any authority I would command it, I hope he will permit me to pray it. A propos I was at public prayers this morning before four O'clock.[14]

Washington actually requested permission from Colonel Bouquet to be absent for a few days and received, as one friend reported, a "very handsome and polite" response. Yet the friend added the confidential observation that Washington would still be responsible for activities at Camp Cumberland during his absence.

Washington finally decided to remain on duty and let others manage his campaign on polling day. He was, indeed, successful as he led the ticket among four candidates for the two seats in the House of Burgesses, aided, no doubt, by the free drinks dispensed by his friends. He ended up with a bill for £39 6s for 160 gallons of rum, beer, wine, and other drinks estimated at about a quart and a half for each of the over 390 voters, plus a dinner of appreciation for his supporters.[15]

As preparations for the Fort Duquesne expedition continued, Glen learned more about the problem with the Cherokee warriors who were expected to provide the major Indian allies for the English. Forbes estimated that 800 Cherokees had assembled in May, but the delay in organization and the limited forces that were evident led them to return home. Only 100 to 200 remained in June and July, with the number further reduced to 80 in early September.[16] Glen dispatched a message to the Cherokees by Joseph Langdon, an Indian trader, reminding them of the warm friendship while he was governor and urging the Little Carpenter to assist the English against their long-standing enemy, the French. Glen's message also came to Christopher Gist, assistant to Edmond Atkin who had been appointed superintendent of Indian affairs in the South in 1756.[17] Forbes was later very critical of Atkin for being a thousand miles away when needed to assure Indian support for his campaign.[18] By this time serious trouble had broken out on the Virginia frontier near Bedford as returning Cherokees had engaged in horse stealing and looting of frontier homes. Frontiersmen retaliated with attacks and killed several Cherokees. This action evoked a spirit of clan revenge throughout the Cherokee nation, particularly among the Lower Cherokees, and eventually contributed to the outbreak of the Cherokee War in 1760.

The Little Carpenter did come to Pennsylvania with Cherokee warriors but with his major mission in behalf of Old Hop to proceed to Virginia to confer with the governor about the violence between his people and Virginia frontiersmen. General Forbes and Glen persuaded him to continue on the expedition toward Fort Duquesne. As they moved westward, the Little Carpenter dispatched a messenger to the Shawnees along the Ohio River even though they were former enemies of the Cherokees. He claimed to have urged them not to hurt the English but to let the French fight for themselves. His messenger returned with information that the French were abandoning the fort. The Little Carpenter reported this information to General Forbes who gave little credence to the account. Two days before nearing the forks, the Little Carpenter withdrew to proceed on his way to confer in Williamsburg. Forbes issued orders to have him stopped and to take from him and his followers the presents and horses that had been issued.[19] This unsuccessful effort was done without Glen's knowledge or consent.

The climax of Forbes's campaign led to the abandonment of Fort Duquesne as the French set fire to the buildings before the English arrived. This occurred, in part, because of the news of the fall of Frontenac and the loss of French supplies for the Ohio River, and in part because of the desertion of the Shawnee Indians and other Native American allies of the French. The treaty of Easton, Pennsylvania, in October between the governors of Pennsylvania and New Jersey with the Six Nations of Iroquois and Delawares had temporarily eased the threat of English occupation of the trans-Appalachian lands within the bounds of Pennsylvania.[20] This treaty information to the Shawnees, Delawares, and Mingos over the mountains influenced their decision to forsake their old allies. General Forbes, conveyed on a litter because of illness, concluded the occupation of Fort Duquesne, renamed it Fort Pitt, and returned to Philadelphia.

Forbes's declining health led him to appoint Glen as executor of his estate in his will of February 13, 1759.[21] The proclamation of his last will and testament following his death on March 11 in Philadelphia gave Glen responsibility for settling Forbes's just debts and dividing his remaining real and personal property evenly between his two brothers, Arthur and Hugh Forbes. Glen engaged in the tedious business of payment of bills extending from funeral expenses, including a coffin lined with "fine white flanel" and the "best Silvered Plates" to medical bills and a variety of supplies for horses and chariots. In completing the settlement of the estate, Glen yielded the commission allowed to himself "to give the benefit to the General's Creditors."[22]

On other occasions, Glen did pursue vigorous efforts to obtain payment to himself for expenses in Indian negotiations that he had advanced from private funds for the Saluda Treaty of 1755. This was one factor that influenced him to stay in South Carolina following his tenure as governor. In a memorial to the Commons House in 1756, he suggested a figure of £5,000 that should be paid overall for the expedition, but he voluntarily reduced the amount to a more reasonable figure of £1,084 in 1761, itemized as follows:

Provisions for 1,000 men for six or seven days	300
Presents for the Indians	150
Hiring of wagons	100
Cost of interpreters	100
Payments to individuals en route for	
expenses on the road	250
Other expenses	100
	£1,000

With interest, this figure of 1,000 would increase to 1,500, but Glen requested payment of half this amount for a total of £750.
Additional items enhanced the total:

Purchase of four Frenchmen from Cherokees	
believed to be spies	60
Loss of clothes and other supplies	69
Cost of cannon	55

Other expenses for campaign to build Fort Loudoun
  before being relieved. Cost of 300
  reduced to one-half   <u>150</u>
                                    £1,084

Glen added that he rendered further service to General Forbes on the Fort Duquesne expedition that could be verified by Forbes and Brigadier General John Stanwix, but he claimed no compensation for that.[23] Even though some of these expenditures seemed somewhat vague, the Commons House agreed to pay £500 and urged Glen to seek the remainder from the Crown because of the benefits that were beyond the bound of one colony. In 1762, Glen noted, however, that he had not received the £500 before his departure from South Carolina.[24] Having arrived in England in 1761, he was able to appear before the Board of Trade several times to endorse his claims and to provide supporting documents.[25] Satisfied with the discussion, the Board on May 27, 1762, recommended to the Lords of the Treasury that Glen receive £504 for the services that were "of great Advantage to his Majesty's Interest."[26] It is not certain from the records available that the governor ever received his payments, for as late as 1773 he still had a claim on the government for over £5,000, although at the same time he did identify the unexpected receipt of £700 for salary since returning from South Carolina.[27]

Glen's other financial ventures were varied and differed sharply from those of some royal governors such as Lieutenant Governor Alexander Spotswood of Virginia and Governor Arthur Dobbs of North Carolina. Spotswood amassed over 85,000 acres on Virginia's expanding frontier.[28] Dobbs purchased with Colonel John Selwyn 400,000 acres in North Carolina and promoted settlements by immigrants as well as joining the Ohio Company of 1748 for land speculation, along with leading Virginians, including Governor Robert Dinwiddie.[29] Glen's financial efforts, in addition to his Scottish properties, focused on the Indian trade, prosecution of ships guilty of smuggling, loans in bonds and annuities to individuals, and limited efforts on a small rice plantation near Charles Town.

Glen realized no significant profit from his attempts to monopolize trade in the failed Choctaw revolt of the 1740s in association with Charles McNaire. Nonetheless, he continued to invest in the trade with support to John Elliott and Cornelius Dougherty. Originally committing about 3,000 pounds currency to their short-lived partnership, Glen enhanced his support to Elliott by 1753 to some 8,000 pounds currency and by the last year of his term as governor he backed him with a surety bond of 4,500 pounds.[30] Elliott was a noted trader among the Overhill Cherokees where he met death by being tomahawked as the Cherokee War erupted in 1760. Dougherty was an illiterate trader who dominated traffic among the Valley Cherokees at Hiwassee for over thirty years.[31] Glen's itemization of his income in 1773 identified no income from these investments, whatever small sums may have accrued in the 1750s.

Glen's major effort to use his position as governor to obtain profit from the Dutch ships *Vrow Dorothea* as a prize of war not only failed while he was in Carolina, but it also threatened to haunt him upon his return to England and Scotland. Both the governor and the commander of vessels capturing illegal cargoes were entitled to share in the prize. The long dispute over the Dutch ship, which Chief Justice James Graeme ruled in 1748 was guilty of smuggling, had taken another turn in 1755 after the Dutch appeal on the South Carolina court's lack of jurisdiction resulted in overturning the 1748 decision. The ship had deteriorated in the harbor, and its spoiled contents were sold at auction in January 1756 for the benefit of the owners before Glen left office. This legal reversal raised the specter of a lawsuit for damages against William Hopton who had captured the ship as well as the governor in prosecuting the alleged smuggling offense.[32] In a secret bond agreement Glen provided Hopton with £3,000 to provide defense against a potential suit or to mediate a settlement out of court with the shipowners.[33] This lingering threat may have been another factor in detaining Glen in South Carolina to 1761. John Drayton, writing to Thomas Glen in 1757 from Charles Town, suggested the possibility: "Your brother is here. I really don't believe they will go away some years yet. They seem set down, settled for Life. They never speak of Home. I fear he has some dread of the Dutch ship falling upon him when he goes home. It behooves you to pry into it and if possible get some convincing proof they wont Molest him in that affair."[34]

Over an extended period of time, Glen invested rather heavily in loans to individuals by means of bonds or annuities, for the eighteenth-century going rate of 6 or 8 percent interest. For example, he loaned Benjamin Harvey, a Stono planter and local constable, 2,500 pounds currency in March of 1751. He provided a larger amount of 21,000 currency in August of 1754 to James Bulloch, who had entertained Creeks for the colony, with the stipulation of annual payments of 1,500 currency, a rate between 7 and 8 percent.[35] In 1773, Bulloch was still paying Glen annually this same amount, which was computed in sterling at £210. Glen also had a bond for £536 for which John Lumsdaine was paying interest of £26:16:00 in 1773.[36]

Glen was even more extensively involved with John Drayton of the magnificent Drayton Hall over the years in familial relations as well as complex financial arrangements. Drayton had served in the Commons House during part of the 1740s from St. Andrews and in 1752 had married as his third wife, Margaret Glen, sister of the governor. Glen recommended Drayton for the South Carolina Council as early as 1752, an appointment that finally received imperial approval in 1761.[37] The agreements between the two involved several loans or bonds from Glen as well as business arrangements in the administration of Glen's plantation after his return to Britain. In Glen's informal summary of his financial status in 1773, he noted that John Drayton owed him for one bond of £2,234 an annual interest at 8 percent of £178:13:5 and for another bond of £1,300 at 6 percent an annual payment of £78.[38]

Correspondence between the two upon Glen's return home reveals the limited extent to which Glen participated in Carolina's plantation rice economy. Glen purchased nineteen blacks as slaves in 1756, the year of his termination as governor.[39] Drayton later provided the following report for Glen's income from the planting of rice from 1761 to 1764:

Year	Glen's Share of the Crop	Balance after Expenses
1761	£445:5 for eight hands	£351:5
1762	£529:12 for seven hands	£417:17
1763	£511:1:8 for six hands	£440:11:8
1764	£483:12 for six hands	£413:17

Plantation expenses included wages for the overseer (£36), clothes and shoes for the slaves, blankets, hoes, and axes. Within this period one slave, Bellah, suffered a disorder by fits and later died, while another one had a leg injury that "decayed" and was under doctor's care. Drayton reported that the slave was able to work only in the boat in rice culture.[40] By 1773 Glen stated that his slaves recently brought in £200 each year, but death and desertion along with old age had reduced this figure to approximately £50. One slave, Savannah, had been stolen by a white settler, and Glen paid a constable £15 for the expenses for her return.[41]

Glen assumed a major role in assisting the Drayton family upon his return to Britain. Drayton's second marriage to Charlotta Bull had resulted in two children, William Henry (1742-1779),[42] who was a leading patriot in the American Revolution, and Charles (1743-1820), who was educated as a doctor of medicine. When these two went to England for their education, they were at first supervised and assisted by Charles Pinckney and his wife, Eliza Lucas Pinckney. Glenn and Thomas, the two sons of John Drayton and Margaret Glen, also went abroad for their education. The former governor supervised both Glennie and Tom as well as assisting with William Henry and Charles. The high cost of their education, combined with the children's lack of conscientious attention to their educational requirements, created tension between Glen and Drayton. Writing to Glen soon after his return to Britain in 1761, Drayton suggested that Charles may go to college with his brother, William Henry, "if you approve . . . or he may be directed as you please otherwise, so he comes not out in an awkward, or disagreeable light."[43] William Henry studied at Balliol College, Oxford, for two years and returned to South Carolina. Charles, however, stayed on to complete his medical education. In April 1762, the father expressed to Glen "the greatest uneasiness lest they may be troublesome,"[44] but by 1768, he himself was much harassed by the expense.

Records of accounts between Drayton and Glen reveal the nature and extent of expenses for the sons in Britain. In 1763, for example, the father sent Charles £110 for a year's allowance for his study of medicine, £40 more for clothes as he left Oxford and traveled to Scotland, and £30 for him to pay his professors and for board for one quarter. Glennie received £40 for his year's allowance.[45]

In 1768, John complained both about the continued expenses and Charles's failure to write a "scrap" for two years, an absence of communication that later extended to four years. He opined that if Glen thinks "all I can do will not, nor cannot make him shine in the Profession [medicine] in which he has chosen—I think then the sooner I am quit and rid of that Expense is the better."[46] The next year he was even more disturbed by the information that, despite the expense of Charles's education, "he is not able to go through the least part of his Examination at the College." Drayton exclaimed: "Charles little knows the many hot summers day I have been out in the field broiling my Head, while he is spending with ease & pleasure what I so hard fatigued for." Had he returned to South Carolina earlier, John continued, he could have married a girl of "good fortune" but there was not one in the market now.[47]

Glen was supportive of Charles and reminded his father that part of the expense for him in Britain came from the work of his own slaves. Having close contact with Charles for the ten years between 1761 and 1771, Glen gave a positive endorsement of the son: "Never young man left a country with a better character than he has done in Scotland . . . his fellow students, his acquaintances, men and women all join in his praise." Known as a "Physician" and an "accomplished gentleman," Glen continued, "He has cost you money, but there is not a shilling misspent . . . never was money better laid out."[48] Charles did graduate with his medical degree from the University of Edinburgh in 1770. After returning to Carolina, he also pursued other interests, making notable achievements in botany; eventually, he became a planter and squire of Drayton Hall, perpetuating its leading position among the plantation homes of Charles Town.

William Henry made a return visit to Britain in 1770 before Charles came home. While in Scotland, Glen as his step-uncle had him confirmed as a "Burgess and Build Brother of the Burg of Linlithgow." In England, according to his son, he was received at the court of King George III and had the opportunity to mingle with members of British nobility, including Lord Sandwich.[49]

Young Glennie was also abroad and attended St. Andrews University in Scotland from 1769 to 1771, when he abruptly had to terminate his affiliation, possibly because of the accusation that he had fathered an illegitimate child. Described as "wild & ungovernable," father John lamented that "I am unhappy in two of my Sons & I fear as I have been told I shall be unhappy in a third very soon."[50] He reiterated: "Oh, hard is my fate to live and see my sons turn out all bad & extravagant to the last degree."[51] Glennie did indeed prove to be the greatest disappointment of the four sons.

The fourth son, Tom, also journeyed to England for his education, but initially he was not under Glen's direction, for his mother, Margaret, had moved to England to improve her health. Father John was still defensive about criticism of support for the education of his sons. Writing to Glen in 1773, he complained: "Had you Sir four sons and you to furnish them so liberally as you seem to want me to furnish my sons, give me leave to tell you those four sons will leave you not a penny to spend."[52]   By this time he did ask Glen to determine whether or not Tom should study Latin; Tom had displayed great temper in resisting the subject because he thought it of little value for his plans to be a planter.

Glen also assumed a protective role in the relationship of his sister, Margaret, as the wife of John Drayton. He had been a participant in the marriage settlement agreement in 1752 between John and Margaret, and he provided the dowry payment in her behalf of 5,000 pounds Carolina currency. In return for this investment, John agreed to an annuity that would provide Margaret with £200 annually for her support, which would also continue if she survived John. There was also a provision from John's estate for the children to get equal portions, including those from previous marriages. The following amounts were stipulated: £1,000 for sons and daughters. If there were no additional sons but one daughter, the amount would be increased to £2,000; if two daughters, £1,200 each; and if three daughters, £1,000 each. However, if the children after the age of twelve behaved poorly, the amount for that child could be cut in half and distributed among others.[53]

Glen's concern increased after Margaret suffered such health problems that she first visited in Britain and upon her brother's urging, she decided to reside in England despite John's hesitation to agree to this separation in 1769. Glen had paid John £1,200 for the annuity to the doctor for Margaret's treatment in Carolina.[54] Her health continued to deteriorate until her death in 1772. Glen's implied criticism of inadequate care evoked from John a review of the money provided her and the angry retort in 1773 that "an actual consumption to the amount of £80:14:9 & £593:3:3 in hard money besides, in her possession for her own personal expenses, ought in common justice to me, to have preserved me from the very cruel imputation, of not having made a necessary provision for her."[55]

Tension between Glen and John increased even further when John's investments in land and slaves along with the decline of commercial contacts between Britain and the colonies on the eve of the Revolution prevented him from meeting payments on schedule. "Our courts are all shut up, no money can be recovered,"[56] John explained.   Glen had borrowed money with the expectation of remitting payments from income from Drayton.   When this income was not forthcoming in full, he complained in May 1775 that John had "ruined my Credit" in both England and Scotland. Both men protested the declining friendship between them.[57] John lamented in 1774 that Glen was "on the point of forgetting an alliance which I shall always remember with sincere affection.[58] A year later Glen complained to John: "Why you should take such pains to get rid of the best friend you ever had, I cannot conceive, but I am determined it shall not be in your power, for I will still wish for your wellfare, still pray for the prosperity of your family, and promote it when in my power."[59]

A series of events drove an even deeper wedge between the two former friends. The death of Margaret Glen, the return of the four Drayton sons from Britain, and John's fourth marriage at age fifty-nine to young Rebecca Perry at age seventeen contributed to changing attitudes. Two daughters and another son by the fourth marriage not only seemed to make John less conscientious in payments to Glen but also strained his relationship with the children of his earlier marriages. Glen was concerned that John was still investing in additional real estate rather than meeting his financial obligations. As late as 1777, John did sell part of his Stono lands and his Jerico plantation, but before the year was out he purchased a 1,500 acre plantation on the Wateree River for £19,687.[60]

Glen turned to John's relatives to attempt to rectify the financial shortcomings, even though John in 1774 had warned Glen that "your making a legal demand upon me cannot but be *very* injurious in its consequences to your nephews."[61] William Drayton, nephew of John and chief justice of Florida, apologized for his uncle's delay in payment. Glen also wrote John's son, William Henry, enclosing a statement in 1776 of the delinquent accounts and deploring John's failure to respond. He stated that "this cruel and unjust treatment has put a final period to all future correspondence between him and me."[62] William Henry acknowledged the obligation and attempted in 1777 to correct an error in the computation of his father's debt to Glen.[63] The death of Glen in 1777 and of John in 1779 left the tedious settlement of these obligations to their estates.

Upon returning to Britain in 1761, the former governor divided his time between Scotland and England. In Scotland he devoted attention to the maintenance and improvement of the estates inherited from his father in the area of Linlithgow. Extant records note the expenditure in the late 1760s of £115:13:8 for enclosing by fence his lands between the High Road and the Loch Milne and an additional expense of £28 for the same purpose at the West Port requiring 163 chains and links. Glen also purchased young ash and elm trees in 1768, and in the same year he provided for the weeding of hedges at the West Port and for repair of the Loch Milne Road. Part of the work was done by women who were employed both for weeding the hedges and for gathering stones for road improvement.[64] Glen continued collections and payments for bonds and annuities, and he even added minor land acquisitions as is evident from his purchase of an acre of ground from the incorporation of coopers in Linlithgow for 550 merks Scots.[65]

Glen compiled an informal summary of his income and debits in 1773 reflecting his assets but also the problem of a consistent cash flow. He estimated an annual income of £1,400, including £600 from his Linlithgow estates, £131 from Linlithgow Palace rent, £256 interest from John Drayton, £100 from an annuity of William Drayton of Florida, and £210 from an annuity of James Bulloch. Other obligations that were due from previous years expanded his annual income to £2,348:17:0. Among these overdue items were £530 from John Drayton, £105 from Bulloch, and £200 from William Drayton. Beyond this, Glen still had a claim of £5,684 against the British government which he maintained was "justly due" him, but which he may well have reasoned would be difficult to collect. On the debit side he tallied his "constant yearly unavoidable expenses" at a total over £500. Among these were £76 as a factor for the palace, £120 for a house in London, £50 for travel to London and to Bath, £50 for servant wages, and payments to relatives. This last item included £100 to his brother, Dr. Thomas Glen, for an annuity on a heritable bond and £25 to him as interest on a personal bond that his brother agreed not to collect "during life." He also provided his sister, Mrs. James Gordon (Elizabeth), £30 for an annuity bond when she insisted that she had as much right to receive money as her sister, Mrs. David Bruce (Agnes). Mrs. Bruce had been the recipient of earlier contributions from Glen after her husband's death around 1750. Beyond these "unavoidable expenses," Glen maintained that he owed "no mortal but as above."[66]

By the mid-1770s, Glen's wife was apparently no longer surviving, and he spent much of his time in London living at Golden Square in the parish of Saint James's Liberty of Westminster and County of Middlesex. His diary for 1775 reveals an active social life and a wide acquaintance of both male and female companions. While he dined occasionally with organized groups such as the Sussex Club at St. Albans Tavern and sometimes separately at the Smyrna, he more often either entertained at home or dined with friends. He employed a cook for his home and an attendant or valet to assist in hospitality, including generous amounts of claret, madeira, and port wines. His guest list at various dates in 1775 included Lord Dalhousie, Lord Panmure (related to the Dalhousies), Lord Advocate David Kenedy, Sir Alexander Gilmore, Sir Lawrence Dundas, Lord Mount Stuart and his brother, and the Polish envoy, Francis Bukaty. He also dined with various women, most often with Mrs. Grimston, Mrs. Ingoldsby, Mrs. Stanhope, and Lady Baird. His success at playing cards varied as he won at cards several times, but he also noted losses in cards, including over £4 in debits in the first week of June.[67]

Glen continued his residence in Golden Square where he completed his last will and testament on February 18, 1777. He named as his executrix his niece, Elizabeth, daughter of Andrew Glen, and by then the Countess of Dalhousie through her marriage to George, the Eighth Earl of Dalhousie in 1767. Glen reviewed in his will the various obligations from bonds and annuities to him from James Bulloch and Isaac Nichols, William Drayton, and most extensively from his brother-in-law, John Drayton. He estimated the value of these assets and other effects in America at £6,000. He specified separate legacies after debts were paid from his estate. These included £700 to his godson, Glen Drayton, whose education he had supervised in Britain, and £500 more to his sister, Mrs. Bruce, although he had previously assisted her after the loss of her husband. Since he had not made comparable donations to another sister, Mrs.

Gordon, he provided an alternate grant to her son, Captain James Gordon, of either £1,000 in money or an annuity of £100 annually during his natural life, which if selected, could begin six months after Glen's death. The governor acknowledged that his brother, Dr. Thomas Glen, had needed no financial assistance from him, but he wanted him to accept £100 "for the purpose of Mourning." He left the remainder of his estate to his niece and also placed under her care the two children in Linlithgow of his black deceased servant, Jacob.[68]

Before the year was out, Glen died on July 18 and was buried at St. Michael's Church adjacent to Linlithgow Palace in West Lothian, Scotland. His grave can no longer be located, for all of the tombstones at St. Michael's identify only nineteenth-century Scots except for four or five from the last decade of the eighteenth century. A copper plate from the grave identifying Glen as governor of South Carolina with the date of his death now hangs on the wall of the Capitol in Columbia, South Carolina, having been presented to the state in 1901 by John B. Cleveland. The background frame for the plate identifies Glen as governor from 1738 to 1755 rather than the correct 1756 and includes the quotation: "He found them in ashes and left them fair, fortified and flourishing."[69]

Glen's will was filed for administration on September 10, 1777, with John Seton Esquire serving as the attorney for the Countess of Dalhousie as executrix. The Scottish Record Office in Edinburgh contains fifteen pages of detailed legible accounts of settlements of obligations of Glen's estate in account with David Erskine as clerk of the signet. They were signed both by the clerk and by Lord Dalhousie in behalf of his wife. These records embrace a variety of legal expenses, a summation of income to Glen, and expenditures by the estate to balance out the total of £1,939:19:11.[70] The transmission of Glen's real property to his niece followed similar procedures of inheritance by which Glen as the eldest son had been declared heir to his father.

9

Retrospect: Summation and Evaluation

James Glen . . . began his administration of almost thirteen years, the longest in South Carolina history and one of the best. . . . He was the most progressive and active of any of our royal governors.[1]

David Duncan Wallace

In domestic affairs, by reason of his considerable ability and wide range of information, his essential integrity and sincere devotion to the public service, he made an excellent record. But in his chosen role of imperialist his success was indifferent.[2]

Robert L. Meriwether

James Glen descended from a long line of local government administrators in Scotland and continued this tradition by his service as provost of Linlithgow. In preparation for his career as a public servant, he joined hundreds of other Scots in journeying to the University of Leiden in the Netherlands in order to study Roman law, which was more applicable to the legal traditions in Scotland than the common law of England. He gained limited experience for imperial duties by his administrative work as provost, and he had an introduction to national politics by participating along with other municipal leaders in selecting members of Parliament in London. He experienced the rough-and-tumble tactics of local politics in the election of members of the town council of his royal burgh. He was guilty of one of his two greatest indiscretions in permitting the use of force and violence as armed guild members supporting Glen entered the town Counil house in unsuccessful attempts to get a seat on the council for his favorite, John Bucknay.

Governor Glen's royal appointment as governor in 1738 as a lawyer contrasted with past years when a predominant number of military officials were appointed. His experience in electing members of Parliament from Scotland and his recommendations from Scottish political leaders contributed to his selection as governor, but the most influential support came from Lord Wilmington, Lord President of the Privy Council, whose illegitimate (natural) daughter, according to Lord Egmont, married Glen and one of Glen's sisters became a new mistress to the prime minister, Sir Robert Walpole, at age sixty-four. Glen, however, delayed in coming to Carolina until 1743, primarily because of protracted negotiations over salary. The £1,000 from the Crown paid to previous governors as commander-in-chief of military forces in the colony was substantially reduced because General Oglethorpe had earlier been appointed to the joint command of forces in Georgia and South Carolina.

When Glen did finally arrive, he "found the whole frame of Government unhinged." The royal prerogative of the Crown had been significantly diminished by the aggressive action particularly of the Commons House of the Assembly in control over appointments and money bills. Past governors had yielded to this erosion of royal authority, and the Council as Upper House of the Assembly had excluded the governor from debate on its legislative agenda. The governor also found the defense of the colony and its fire protection in poor condition indeed. Characteristic of his energetic approach to the challenges of his office, Glen even joined the bucket brigade of firefighters in extinguishing flames in Charles Town.

The three-way contest for power among the governor, Council, and Commons House was a persistent theme throughout Glen's administration. Glen as governor never achieved the influence over the Council as executive advisor that would have provided a more compatible relationship. Some of his recommendations for members of the Council were implemented by imperial officials, but other appointments resulted from favorite connections in England. Some long-established members of the Council such as Edmond Atkin also featured themselves and the Council as the prime protector of the royal prerogative and challenged the governor on actions with which they disagreed. Glen initially tended to support the Council as Upper House in its contests with the Commons, despite his being excluded at times from its legislative deliberations. Mindful of his many directives both in his royal appointment and the over 100 instructions issued from the Crown, he attempted to mediate such conflicts between the two houses over tax bills and the selection of agents of the colony in England. The governor had his own disagreements, particularly with the Commons over such issues as the term of legislative bodies, requirements for a quorum, the nature of jury selection, control over fortifications, and jurisdiction over appointments in religion. He attempted to get along with the Commons despite its aggressive encroachment on the royal prerogative, but he refused to follow its suggestion to approve legislation without consent of the Upper House. He did yield to its flattery near the end of his tenure in its contest with the Upper House over a tax bill. The Council as Upper House unwisely criticized the governor in the press for not proceeding with the construction of a fort among the Overhill Cherokees, even though it had failed to approve financial expenditures for the project in its quarrel with the Commons over financial legislation. Both the Council and the Commons House were at times guilty of letting the welfare of the colony suffer while disputing institutional prerogatives.

The struggle over the jurisdiction of each branch of government was indeed complex. Governor Glen used his power of veto over legislation and of proroguing the Assembly in exerting his influence. He also increased his political support by the 1750s when he in pragmatic fashion made peace with the Bull family and worked more closely with other leading families, including the Draytons through the marriage of his sister in 1752 to John Drayton of Drayton Hall. Yet he was at a distinct disadvantage, as were other royal governors who had part of their salary and provisions for housing dependent on the local Assembly. Even though Glen had a limited income from his Scottish property, he was vulnerable to the Commons' threats to cancel appropriations either for salary or housing if he refused to agree with its policies. In the struggle for power, both the Council and the Commons turned to the press to criticize the governor and at times threatened to send protests to imperial officials. The tension increased further when Glen was admonished by the reform-minded Board of Trade to adhere to his instructions and protect the royal prerogative that had already seriously eroded under past governors. These pressures on Glen were most acute after Lord Halifax became president of the Board of Trade in 1748 and joined other reformers on the Board to supervise colonial administration more closely and at times to harass Glen. Insistent demands were made to have a contingency clause in legislation pending approval by imperial officials, to include in paper money bills provisions for withdrawal or redemption on a specific schedule, and numerous directions for the administration of Indian affairs when the Board in England had much less knowledge and less experience in handling these frontier policies.

Indian affairs were the most dominant issue of Governor Glen's administration. Devoting unlimited energy to these challenges, he was successful in many negotiations for the benefit of South Carolina and the British Empire, although he experienced some failures. He not only traveled to more distant parts of the colony to visit white settlements than any previous governor, but he was also willing to journey to the frontier for direct negotiations with Indian leaders—to the Congarees, to Fort Moore on the Savannah River, and to Saluda Old Town near Ninety-Six. While initially critical of Native American culture in ethnocentric terms, he came to appreciate the Indians' vital role in the international struggle for North America and to advocate policies more sympathetic to them than the Assembly was always willing to follow.

The governor's hands-on approach to Indian affairs involved a variety of experiences. He persuaded the Catawbas to ignore the traditional law of blood revenge for the Natchez murder of members of their tribe by influencing the

Natchez to yield the guilty attacker's heads which in turn were pickled and turned over to the Catawbas. He entertained Indian leaders in elaborate fashion while on visits to Charles Town, and he even on occasion had them spend the night in his own home. He supervised in person the building of Fort Prince George among the Lower Cherokees in 1753. He also advocated a fort among the Overhill Cherokees, which was eventually built by his successor as Fort Loudoun, but it proved to be a trap for white soldiers with the outbreak of the Cherokee War in 1760. At times he advanced money from his own personal resources for projects for the Indians when the Assembly either disagreed with their purpose or failed to act because of disputes with the governor or the Council as Upper House over institutional prerogatives. Glen also exposed himself physically to hazards of the frontier, such as during his trek to Ninety-Six in 1746 and the hurried expedition with supporting military personnel in 1753 to assure safe passage from the colony for Malatchi and his Creek party after suffering an ambush by northern Indians near Dorchester.

Yet it was Indian affairs that also resulted in one of his greatest failures and the second of his most serious indiscretions of his career. He put too much faith in the possibility of winning over the large Choctaw nation from French influence with the revolt led by Red Shoes in the late 1740s. Furthermore, he attempted to profiteer from the Indian trade by investing in a secret company and granting it a monopoly of the Choctaw traffic. Even worse, upon the company's failure to win over the Choctaws, he engaged in a coverup of his role in the venture and distorted information to defeat the expense claims of Charles McNaire and James Adair and at the same time to minimize criticism from both colonial and imperial officials for this failure.

Glen displayed a more commendable character in his conscientious and intelligent responses to the multitude of inquiries from the Board of Trade and other imperial officials. In his serious approach to these requests, he completed extensive research and composed replies reflecting his legal training and a fluent use of Latin that was characteristic of well-educated leaders of this period. When responding to what some governors considered a routine bureaucratic inquiry in 1749, Glen wrote his *Description of South Carolina*, which was later printed. It remains the most valuable comprehensive contemporary commentary on colonial South Carolina and one that compares favorably with any other contemporary account of American colonies.

Governor Glen displayed great admiration for South Carolina in this report, and his love for the colony increased with the passing years. Upon completion of his tenure as governor in 1756, he stayed on in Carolina until 1761 and made a modest investment in slaves and a rice plantation near Charles Town. John Drayton noted in 1757 that Governor and Mrs. Glen "seem set down, settled for Life. They never speak of home."[3] As late as the early 1770s after returning to Scotland and England, Glen was still interested in information from Drayton about possible government appointments in South Carolina.[4] Extant records do not reveal Glen's overt views on the conflict between the colonies and the mother country in the American Revolution, but there are hints from his love of South Carolina that he understood and perhaps sympathized with the protests of the American patriots until his death in 1777.

The governor vigorously championed the role of South Carolina in intercolonial relations and worked successfully with New York in mediating conflicts between northern and southern Indians. He was adamant in upholding South Carolina's priority in both the Indian trade and Indian diplomacy in bitter conflicts with both Virginia and Georgia. Like other governors before and after him, he persistently pressed South Carolina's interests in the perennial boundary dispute with North Carolina.

As Robert L. Meriwether concluded, Governor Glen's success in his role as imperialist was "indifferent." He submitted plans to imperial officials in 1745 and again in 1748 which had some merit for attacks on the Spanish in Florida, the French in Mobile and New Orleans, and the use of different Indian tribes in the international conflict. He failed, however, to assess correctly the potential for Choctaw assistance. As the French and Indian War began, he also underestimated the French threat in the Ohio Valley and exaggerated a danger to the Tennessee Valley that never materialized. Nonetheless, his persistent efforts to promote peaceful relations among tribes friendly to the British and to obtain assistance from them in the international conflict were in large part successful, despite the difficulty of long-standing feuds among some of these tribes and their determination to pursue their own agenda in diplomatic commitments.

Glen was more extrovert than introvert in personality, for he relished association with others and reveled in formal ceremonies on both diplomatic and military occasions. He was prolix in correspondence particularly to imperial officials, and he frequently sought approval of his role as governor. However, this was not always forthcoming with the early years of a moribund Board of Trade, which later became hypercritical of his actions at a time when his patron supporters were no longer around to defend him. As the eldest son he had a keen sense of family responsibility and frequently provided assistance to his sisters. He took an enthusiastic interest in assisting the sons of John Drayton while they were in England and Scotland for their education, although father John thought Glen much too indulgent of their desires while he labored on his plantations to support them. Glen was also a man of great compassion that was displayed, for example, in his sympathy for the distress of the displaced Acadians.

In the final analysis, Governor Glen found himself at the center of conflicting crossroads of theories and philosophies of empire as related to colonial administration. By the mid-eighteenth century, the role of colonial assemblies was well established as legitimate in asserting the voice of the governed in political and administrative issues. This was as prevalent in South Carolina as in any other mainland colony, if not most evident there. In contrast to this view, imperial officials still clung to the theory of colonial dependency whereby administration of the colonies was exercised through imperial bureaucracy. Glen was faced with the efforts of imperial officials (the Board of Trade, Privy Council, Secretary of State for the Southern Department, and the King) to exercise control by commissions and instructions to governors, not only currently to protect the royal prerogative but also to recover those powers that had seriously eroded over past years. Governors were expected to uphold the royal perogative while left dependent in part on local assemblies for financial support of salary and housing. This was an impossible situation despite Glen's legal training and his extensive knowledge of the British constitution. His experience, then, was a prime example of the failure of British imperial officials to reassert the theory of colonial dependency by use of instructions to governors. The sequel to this dilemma was the turn to another road of imperial reform by parliamentary legislation. This approach resulted in efforts to extract colonial revenue and impose control by such measures as the Stamp Act of 1765 and the Townshend Duties of 1767. This eventually led to the American patriots' assertion of the legal fiction that the colonials were responsible only to the King, not to the Parliament. And even this recognition was abandoned by 1776 with the Declaration of Independence and the decision to persist in the fight for separation from the empire.

Notes

Introduction

1. Mary Pilkington, *Biography for Girls: or, Moral and Instructive Examples for Young Ladies* (London, 1799).

2. John A. Garraty, *The Nature of Biography* (New York, 1964), 49.

3. Paul Murray Kendall, *The Art of Biography* (London, 1965), 39.

4. Ibid., 40-41.

5. William Roper's life of Sir Thomas More was originally published in 1626 under the title, *The mirrour of vertue in worldly greatnes.*

6. Leon Edel, *Literary Biography: The Alexander Lectures, 1955-56* (London, 1957), 17.

7. Sir Sidney Lee, *Principles of Biography: The Leslie Stephen Lecture* (Cambridge, England, 1911), 46.

8. Ronald Steel, "On Writing about Walter Lippman," *Michigan Quarterly Review*, 23 (1984), 543.

9. Thomas Carlyle, *On Heroes, Hero-Worship and the Heroic in History* (London, 1841), 29.

10. Ralph Waldo Emerson, *Essays. First Series, Being Volume II of Emerson's Complete Works* (Boston, 1898), 15.

11. Walt Whitman, as cited in *The Complete Poetry and Prose of Walt Whitman . . . with an Introduction by Malcolm Cowley*, 2 vols. (New York, 1954), 1:47.

12. Edward Mendelson, "Authorized Biography and Its Discontents," in Daniel Aron, ed., *Studies in Biography, Harvard English Studies*, 8 (Cambridge, Mass. and London, 1978), 10.

13. Quoted in Ira Nadel, *Biography: Fiction, Fact, and Form* (London, 1984), 178.

14. See, for example, William E. Woodward's *George Washington, the Image and the Man* (New York, 1926).

15. Garraty, *Nature of Biography*, 123.

16. Deirdre Bair, "Samuel Beckett," in Jeffrey Meyers, ed., *The Craft of Literary Biography* (London, 1985), 214.

17. Art Berman, *From the New Criticism to Deconstruction: The Reception of Structuralism and Post-Structuralism* (Urbana, Ill., 1988).

18. Sharon O'Brien, "Feminist Theory and Literary Biography," in William Epstein, ed., *Contesting the Subject* (West Lafayette, Ind., 1991), 123-33.

19. Jean-Francios Lyotard, *The Postmodern Condition* (Manchester, 1984), 27-37, 71-82; Linda Hutcheon, *A Poetics of Postmodernism: History, Theory, Fiction* (New York, 1988) 9-10, 16, 60, 79-80, 118-19, 173-74, 224; Brian McHale, *Postmodernist Fiction* (New York and London, 1987), 197-202.

20. David Bromwich, "The Uses of Biography," *Yale Review*, 73 (1984), 161.

21. Frederick R. Karl, "Joseph Conrad," in Myers, *Craft of Literary Biography*, 70.

22. Nadel, *Biography*, 170-71.

23. Quoted in ibid., 153.

24. James William Anderson, "The Methodology of Psychological Biography," *Journal of Interdisciplinary History*, 11 (1981), 455-75.

25. Jesse Lemisch, "The American Revolution Seen from the Bottom Up," in Barton J. Bernstein, ed., *Towards a New Past: Dissenting Essays in American History* (New York, 1968).

26. Leon Edel, "Biography and the Science of Man," in Anthony M. Friedson, ed., *New Directions in Biography* (Honolulu, 1981), 9.

27. Frank E. Vandiver, "Biography as an Agent of Humanism," in James F. Veninga, ed., *The Biographer's Gift: Life Histories and Humanism* (College Station, Tex., 1983), 6.

Chapter 1

1. John Ferguson, *Linlithgow Palace: Its History and Traditions* (Edinburgh and London, 1910), 3-4; William F. Hendrie, *Linlithgow: Six Hundred Years A Royal Burgh* (Edinburgh, 1989), 5-6; George Waldie, *A History of the Town and Palace of Linlithgow*, 3rd ed. (Linlithgow, 1879), 9-19; *Linlithgow Marches: An Illustrated History with Poems & Songs* (Linlithgow, 1981); and Mark N. Powell, *Linlithgow: A Brief Architectural and Historical Guide* 2nd ed. (Linlithgow, 1990), 11-15.

2. Rosalind Mitchison, *A History of Scotland* (London, 1970), 38-49.

3. W. E. Lunt, *History of England*, 3rd ed. (New York and London, 1945), 262-64.

4. C 3/18/folio 227, Register of the Great Seal (*Registrum Magni Sigilli*), Scottish Record Office, Edinburgh, hereafter cited as SRO.

5. Joseph G.B. Bulloch, *A History of the Glen Family of South Carolina and Georgia* (Washington, D.C., 1923), 8, 19-20; Charles Rogers, *Memorial of the Scottish Family of Glen* (Edinburgh, 188), 12-14; C 2/80/ff. 51-52 and C 2/87/f. 27, Register of the Great Seal, SRO.

6. J. Ferguson, *Linlithgow Palace*, 298.

7. The writings on Jacobitism are extensive as demonstrated in Dorothy A. Guthrie and Clyde L. Grose, "Forty Years of Jacobite Bibliography," *Journal of Modern History*, 11 (1939), 49-60. Recent studies include Bruce Lenman, *The Jacobite Risings in Britain, 1689-1746* (London, 1980) and David Daiches, *The Last Stuart: The Life and Times of Bonnie Prince Charlie* (New York, 1973).

8. C 22/58/ff. 470-71, SRO.

9. The Will of James Glen, formerly in Somerset House, London, is now in the Public Record Office of Great Britain, Chancery Lane, London, 11/1034. An incomplete copy is in GD 45/16/f. 2647, SRO.

10. Bulloch, *Glen Family*, 8-10, 12, 20.

11. For further information, see James Bruce, *Travels to Discover the Source of the Nile, in the Years 1768, 1769, 1770, 1771, 1772 and 1773* (Edinburgh, 1790); Francis B. Head, *The Life and Adventures of Bruce, the African Traveller* (New York, 1841); and James M. Reid, *Traveller Extraordinary: The Life of James Bruce of Kinnaird* (New York, 1968).

12. *South-Carolina Gazette*, March 2, 1752.

13. William Ferguson, *Scotland: 1689 to the Present*, vol. 4 of *The Edinburgh History of Scotland* (Edinburgh, 1968), 46-53; Alexander Murdoch, '*The People Above*': *Politics and Administration in Mid-Eighteenth-Century Scotland* (Edinburgh, 1980), 1-5.

14. Murdoch, '*The People Above*,' 4-20; David M. Walker, *The Scottish Legal System: An Introduction to the Study of Scots Law*, 4th ed. (Edinburgh, 1976), 126-34.

15. There were sixty-six burghs in Scotland in 1707 with populations extending from 40,000 in Edinburgh to only a few hundred in the smallest burghs.

16. C 3/18/f. 227, Register of the Great Seal, SRO.

17. RH 2/4/f. 450, ibid.; J. Ferguson, *Linlithgow Palace*, 299.

18. W. Otterspeer, Academisch Historisch Museum, Rijksuniversiteit, Leiden, to the author, January 14, 1991.

19. Richard H. Scott, "The Politics and Administration of Scotland, 1725-1748," Ph.D. diss., University of Edinburgh, 1982, 11; Margaret S. Bricke, "Administration and Management of Scotland, 1707-1765," Ph.D. diss., University of Kansas, 1972, 109-13.

20. W. Ferguson, *Scotland*, 143.

21. Ibid., 135.

22. The freeholder franchise consisted of land held from the Crown valued at 40 shillings under the antiquated system of assessing the second estate, or 400 pounds Scots under the valuation of the eighteenth century.

23. James Glen's service as provost may be followed in the Minute Book, Linlithgow Town Council, 1724-1736, B 48/9/7-9, SRO.

24. B 48/9/7, ibid.

25. B 48/9/9, ibid.

26. Town minutes for January, March, and July 1733, ibid.

27. Summons of the Court of Session, CH 4403, ms room, National Library of Scotland, Edinburgh.

28. Town minutes for September 11, 1725, B 48/9/8, SRO.

29. Town minutes for September 18 and 23, 1725, ibid.

30. Town minutes for October 4, 1725, ibid.

31. Town minutes for September 10, 1726, ibid.

32. Town minutes for November 16, 1728, B 48/9/9, SRO.

33. Town minutes for October 5, 1730 and October 4, 1736, B 48/9/9, ibid.

34. Town minutes for July 22, 1727, B 48/9/9, ibid.

35. Town minutes for January 20, 1728, B 48/9/8, SRO.

36. Town minutes for September 18, 1736, B 48/9/9, SRO.

37. Murdoch, '*The People Above*,' 7-8; Scott, "Politics and Administration," 11; John M. Simpson, "Who steered the Gravy Train, 1707-1766?" in N. T. Phillipson and Rosalind Mitchison, eds., *Scotland in the Age of Improvement* (Edinburgh, 1970).

38. John Bucknay to Andrew Fletcher, Lord Milton, February 13, 20, 21, and March 3, 17, 1738, Saltoun Papers, ms. room, National Library, Edinburgh.

39. William, Sixth Earl of Dalhousie, was a colonel in the army and assisted Glen until his death on December 8, 1739.

40. *Dictionary of National Biography*, 4:906-907.

41. Horace Walpole, *Memoirs of the Reign of King George the Second*, 3 vols. (New York, 1970), 1:178n.

42. Letter of Glen, June 28, 1739, Airth Papers, ms room, National Library, Edinburgh.

43. Glen to Lord Wilmington, April 29, 1740, *The Manuscripts of the Marquess Townshend*, Historical Manuscripts Commission, Eleventh Report (London, 1887), 264-65.

44. See, for example, *The Letterbook of Eliza Lucas Pinckney, 1739-1762*, edited by Elise Pinckney with the editorial assistance of Marvin R. Zahniser (Chapel Hill, N.C., 1972), 76-77, 76n.

45. Sir Bernard Burke, *A Genealogical and Heraldic Dictionary of the Peerage and Baronetage, Together with Memoirs of the Privy Councillors and Knights* (London, 1899), 1547.

46. R. A. Roberts, ed., *Manuscripts of the Earl of Egmont: Diary of Viscount Percival, Afterwards First Earl of Egmont*, Historical Manuscripts Commission, 3 vols. (London, 1920-1923), 3:49.

47. Ibid., 3:248.   Mary, the natural daughter of Sir Robert Walpole and his mistress, Maria Skerrett (later Lady Walpole), became Lady Maria Walpole and in 1746 married Charles Churchill, son of Lieutenant General Charles Churchill and Anne Oldfield, an actress. Sir Robert Walpole arranged for the patent declaring her legitimate and proclaiming her as the Earl's daughter on February 8, 1742. *The Yale Edition of Horace Walpole's Correspondence*, edited by W. S. Lewis et al., 42 vols. (New Haven, Conn., 1937-1980), 28:389-90, 389n.

48. The designation of captain general was substituted for lieutenant general in Glen's commission. *Acts of the Privy Council of England, Colonial Series, 1613-1783*, edited by William Grant, James Munro, and A. W. Fitzroy, 6 vols. (London, 1908-1912), 3:621-22.

49. Letter of Glen, June 28, 1739, Airth Papers, ms. room, National Library, Edinburgh.

50. Scott, "Politics and Administration," 20-23, 50-52, 61-62, 76.

51. Glen's financial summary, 1773, James Glen Papers, South Caroliniana Library, Columbia.

52. *Egmont Diary*, 3:149.

53. Richard P. Sherman in his biography, *Robert Johnson: Proprietary & Royal Governor of South Carolina* (Columbia, S.C. , 1966), 82, describes Governor Johnson's salary as £500 plus a present of £500 and £114 for the rent of his residence.

54. Glen to Lord Wilmington, April 29, 1740, *Townshend Manuscripts*, 264-65.

55. Petition of Glen to Sir Robert Walpole and Lords Commissioners of the Treasury, n.d., ibid. 265-66.

56. Leonard W. Labaree, *Royal Government in America: A Study of the British Colonial System before 1783* (New Haven, Conn., 1930), 330.

57. Board of Trade Journal in the manuscript collection identified as Records in the British Public Record Office Relating to South Carolina, 1663-1782, 36 vols., in South Carolina Department of Archives and History, Columbia, South Carolina, and available in microfilm, hereafter cited as S.C. Pub. Recs., 20:309-10.

58. Labaree, *Royal Government*, 330-31.

59. Instruction no. 26. Glen's instructions were never printed in full but are available in the Colonial Office Papers of the British Public Record Office, London, hereafter cited as C.O., PRO. These instructions are in C.O. 5:198, PRO, pp. 101-58. No. 26 is on p. 114.

60. Glen's commission may also be found in C.O. 5:198, PRO, pp. 77-96; S.C. Pub. Recs., 19:299-318; and Leonard W. Labaree, ed., *Royal Instructions to British Colonial Governors, 1670-1776*, 2 vols. (New York and London, 1935), 2:816-25.

61. *Acts of the Privy Council*, 3:622-23.

62. Ibid., 3:622-23; C.O. 5:198, PRO, p. 114.

63. *Acts of the Privy Council*, 3:553.

64. See below, pp. 79-80.

65. S.C. Pub. Recs., 20:12-13.

66. *Journals of the Commissioners for Trade and Plantations preserved in the Public Record Office, 1704-1775*, 13 vols. (London, 1920-1937), hereafter cited as *Board of Trade Journals*, 7 (1734/5-41), 398 and 8 (1741/2-49), 4-5; *Acts of the Privy Council*, 3:572-73, 699-700.

67. Allen D. Candler, ed., *Journal of the Earl of Egmont, First President of the Board of Trustees*, in *The Colonial Records of Georgia*, 26 vols. (Atlanta, Ga., 1904-1916), 5:546-48.

68. Memorial of Sir Archibald Gant, 1742, SRO.

69. Walter B. Edgar, ed., *The Letterbook of Robert Pringle*, 2 vols. (Columbia, S.C. , 1972), 2:468.

70. Ibid., 1:170, 289-90.

71. Letter of Traders to South Carolina, S.C. Pub. Recs., 20:201-202.

72. Harold Orel, "Scottish Stereotypes," in *The Scottish World: History and Culture of Scotland*, edited by Harold Orel et al. (New York, 1981), 21.

73. W. Ferguson, *Scotland*, 153.

Chapter 2

1. The present sword of state of the South Carolina Senate is a replica of the original sword that was stolen in the 1940s.

2. December 17, 1743, Council Journal, South Carolina Department of Archives and History, Columbia.

3. Glen to Board of Trade, March 1751, S.C. Pub. Recs., 24:314.

4. For a discussion of possible contributions, see Peter H. Wood, *Black Majority: Negroes in Colonial South Carolina, From 1670 through the Stono Rebellion* (New York, 1974), 56, 59-62.

5. For views on Eliza Lucas Pinckney and the introduction of indigo, see H. Roy Merrens, ed., *The Colonial South Carolina Scene: Contemporary Views, 1697-1774* (Columbia, S.C. , 1977), 144-63; David L. Coon, "Eliza Jucas Pinckney and the Reintroduction of Indigo Culture in South Carolina," *Journal of Southern History*, 42 (1976), 61-76; John J. Winberry, "Reputation of Carolina Indigo," *South Carolina Historical Magazine*, 80 (1979), 242-50.

6. David Duncan Wallace wrote *The Life of Henry Laurens* (New York and London, 1915), and the South Carolina Historical Society is sponsoring the publication of *The Papers of Henry Laurens*, edited by Philip M. Hamer et al. (Columbia, S.C. , 1968-).

7. January 11, 1744, *The Journal of the Commons House of Assembly*, Series 1 of

The Colonial Records of South Carolina, edited by J. H. Eastrby et al. (Columbia, S.C., 1951—   ), *1742-1744*, 513-15; hereafter cited as *Commons Journal*, Glen's message was also printed in the *S.C. Gazette*, January 16, 1744.

8. January 12, 1744, *Commons Journal, 1742-1744*, 516-17.

9. Glen to Board of Trade, February 6, 1744, S.C. Pub. Recs., 21:235-41.

10. James Glen, *A Description of South Carolina*, in *Colonial South Carolina: Two Contemporary Descriptions*, edited by Chapman J. Milling (Columbia, S.C. , 1951), 34.

11. Glen to Board of Trade, February 6, 1744, S.C. Pub. Recs., 21:236.

12. Benjamin Whitaker to Duke of Newcastle, July 12, 1733, S.C. Pub. Recs., 22:410-13; M. Eugene Sirmans, *Colonial South Carolina: A Political History, 1663-1763* (Chapel Hill, N.C., 1966), 138-40, 234-35. For other changes in the transition from proprietary control, see John Alexander Moore, "Royalizing South Carolina: The Revolution of 1719 and the Evolution of Early South Carolina Government (Royalization)," Ph.D. diss., University of South Carolina, 1991.

13. Glen to Board of Trade, February 6, 1744, S.C. Pub. Recs., 21:236-37.

14. Ibid., 21:237-39.

15. For more detailed discussion of the Spanish, see Charles Gibson, *Spain in America* (New York, 1966), 91-95; John T. Lanning, *The Diplomatic History of Georgia: A Study of the Epoch of Jenkins' Ear* (Chapel Hill, N.C., 1936), 178; Max Savelle, *The Origins of American Diplomacy: The International History of Angloamerica, 1492-1763* (New York, 1967), 323-25, 348-50; W. Stitt Robinson, *The Southern Colonial Frontier, 1607-1763* (Albuquerque, N.M., 1979), 185-90.

16. Quoted in J. Leitch Wright Jr., *Anglo-Spanish Rivalry in North America* (Athens, Ga., 1971), 87.

17. Lanning, *Diplomatic History of Georgia*, 199-219, 223-24; Wright, *Anglo-Spanish Rivalry*, 89, 90-92, 94; Trevor R. Reese, *Colonial Georgia: A Study in British Imperial Policy in the Eighteenth Century* (Athens, Ga., 1963), 78-80. For documentary sources on the St. Augustine campaign, see John T. Lanning, ed., *The St. Augustine Expedition of 1740: A Report to the South Carolina General Assembly* (Columbia, 1954); *Letters to Montiano, Siege of St. Augustine*, Collections of the Georgia Historical Society, vol. 7, pt. 1 (Savannah, Ga., 1909).

18. Wallace, *History of South Carolina*, 1:440; Edward McCrady, *The History of South Carolina under the Royal Government, 1719-1776* (New York, 1899), 224-29.

19. The edition by Lanning in note 17 reproduces the report included in *Commons Journal*, 1741-1742, 78-247.

20. *Egmont Journal, Ga. Col. Recs.*, 5:572; *Commons Journal, 1744-1745*, 133-34, 153.

21. *Egmont Journal, Ga. Col. Recs.*, 5:499.

22. Wright, *Anglo-Spanish Rivalry*, 95-97; see also *The Spanish Official Account of the Attack on the Colony of Georgia, in America, and of Its Defeat on St. Simons Island by General James Oglethorpe*, Collections of the Georgia Historical Society, vol. 7, pt. 3 (Savannah, Ga., 1913).

23. Quoted in John P. Corry, *Indian Affairs in Georgia, 1732-1756* (Philadelphia, 1936), 127n.

24. Glen to Duke of Newcastle, July 2, 1744, S.C. Pub. Recs., 21:378-82.

25. Ibid., 21:382; Glen to Board of Trade, March 12, 1744, S.C. Pub. Recs., 21:245-50.

26. February 24, 1744, Council Journal.

27. September 8, 1744, ibid.

28. September 5, 1744, ibid.

29. January 25, 26, 1744, ibid.

30. October 5, 1744, ibid.

31. October 5, 1744, *Commons Journal, 1744-1745*, 246-48; December 7, 1744, Council Journal.

32. Thomas Cooper and David J. McCord, eds., *The Statutes at Large of South Carolina*, 10 vols. (Columbia, S.C. , 1836-41), 3:633-37.

33. Sirmans, *Colonial South Carolina*, 221-22.

34. Richard Waterhouse, "South Carolina's Colonial Elite: A Study in the Social Structure and Political Culture of a Southern Colony, 1670-1760" Ph.D. diss., Johns Hopkins University, 1973 and University Microfilms International (Ann Arbor, Mich., 1989), 289.

35. Ibid., 283.

36. M. Eugene Sirmans, "The South Carolina Royal Council, 1720-1763," *William and Mary Quarterly*, 3rd ser., 18 (1961), 377-78.

37. Glen to Board of Trade, May 28, 1745, S.C. Pub. Recs., 22:100.

38. *S.C. Gazette*, June 11 and July 4, 1744.

39. May 28, 1744, *Commons Journal, 1744-1745*, 198-99. Isaac Holmes was one of the wealthiest merchants with his estate worth a total of £14,427 with twenty-four slaves and 2,210 acres of land. Sirmans, "S.C. Royal Council," 376.

40. May 29, 1744, *Commons Journal, 1744-1745*, 200, 202.

41. Edgar, *Pringle Letterbook*, 2:636, 745.

42. May 22, 1745, *Commons Journal, 1744-1745*, 533.

43. This action was later reported by William Bull, Jr., to Earl of Dartmouth, September 18, 1773, S.C. Pub. Recs., 33:306.

44. Glen to Board of Trade, May 28, 1745, S. C. Pub. Recs., 22:102.

45. Labaree, *Royal Instructions*, 1:218-19.

46. Jack P. Greene, *The Quest for Power: The Lower House of Assembly in the Southern Royal Colonies, 1689-1776* (Chapel Hill, N.C., 1963), 113-14.

47. C.O. 5:198, PRO, pp. 148-49.

48. May 17, 1744, Council Journal.

49. Board of Trade to Glen, October. 26, 1748, S.C. Pub. Recs., 23:250-52.

50. Cooper and McCord, *Statutes*, 3:656-58.

51. March 2 and 7, *Commons Journal, 1744-1745*, 40, 48. For further reaction to the Great Awakening, see David T. Morgan, "The Great Awakening in South Carolina, 1740-1775," *South Atlantic Quarterly*, 70 (1971), 595-606.

52. April 30, 1745, *Commons Journal*, 1744-1745, 456.

53. Cooper and McCord, *Statutes*, 3:657.

54. Ibid., 3:656-58, 692-93.

55. Ibid., 2:690, 3:54.

56. Glen to Duke of Bedford, October 10, 1748, S.C. Pub. Recs., 23:232-45; Glen to Board of Trade, October 10, 1748, C.O. 5:372, PRO, ff. 80-87; quotation is on ff. 86-87.

57. Glen to Duke of Bedford, October 10, 1748, S.C. Pub. Recs., 23:240.

58. The full report is recorded for May 7, 1745, Upper House Journal, South Carolina Department of Archives and History, Columbia, S.C. , 118-74.

59. Ibid., 137-38, 153-54, 171; quotation is on 171.

60. C.O. 5:198, PRO, pp. 79, 103.

61. Glen to Board of Trade, October 4, 1746, S.C. Pub. Recs. 22:205-08.

62. Sirmans, *Colonial South Carolina*, 264; Glen to the Board of Trade, October 4, 1746, S.C. Pub. Recs., 22:205-08. The Chancery Court complaint is on 206.

63. A review of the Upper House Journal reveals numerous times when only three or even two members were present. For example, in 1748, there were only three members present for May 17, June 8, 11, 16, 28, and 29. On June 15, only two members were in attendance with the lieutenant governor. A random sample of the Council Journals for 1746 and 1748 also shows limited attendance on many occasions: there were only three members present along with the governor for February 17, 18, March 20, 28, and October 24, 29 in 1746. For 1748, the same limited attendance prevailed for January 13, 27, April 16, May 10, 14, 18, 19, June 6, 8, 9, 13, 14, 20, 27, 29, 30, July 12, 18. This is hardly regular attendance and is overall a poor efficiency rating for attendance from a body of twelve members.

64. Glen to Board of Trade, October 4, 1746, S.C. Pub Recs., 22:205-08; Sirmans, "S.C. Royal Council," 390, 392.

65. Glen to Duke of Bedford, October 10, 1748, S.C. Pub. Recs., 23-232-43; Glen to Board of Trade, October 10, 1748, C.O. 5:372, PRO, ff. 80-87.

66. Glen to Duke of Bedford, October 10, 1748, S.C. Pub. Recs., 23:234-36; Glen to Board of Trade, October 10, 1748, C.O. 5:372, PRO, f. 82.

67. Glen to Duke of Bedford, October 10, 1748, S.C. Pub. Recs., 23:236-37; Glen to Board of Trade, October 10, 1748, C.O. 5:372, PRO, ff. 82-83.

68. Greene, *Quest for Power*, 223-25.

69. Cooper and McCord, *Statutes*, 2:305-306, 656.

70. Quoted in Greene, *Quest for Power*, 225.

71. Cooper and McCord, *Statutes*, 3:148-49.

72. September 13-15, 1721, Commons Journal, C.O. 5:426, PRO, pp. 121-31.

73. Labaree, *Royal Instructions*, 2:821.

74. C.O. 5:198, PRO, p. 136.

75. Cooper and McCord, *Statutes*, 2:239-40.

76. E.B. O'Callaghan and B. Fernow, eds., *Documents Relative to the Colonial history of New York*, 15 vols. (Albany, N.Y., 1856-1887), 4:146.

77. Arthur H. Basye, *The Lords Commissioners of Trade and Plantations Commonly Known as the Board of Trade, 1747-1787* (New Haven, Conn., 1925),

Chapter 3

1. Savelle, *Origins of American Diplomacy*, 376-77.

2. Letter of Glen, February 6, 1744, S.C. Pub Recs., 21:242-43.

3. Glen to Duke of Newcastle, February 3, 1748, C.O. 5:389, PRO, ff. 42-46. There is confusion in numbering of these manuscripts. The stamped folio numbers are used in these citations.

4. Atkin's *Report* has been published in Wilbur R. Jacobs, ed., *Indians of the Southern Colonial Frontier: The Edmond Atkin Report and Plan of 1755* (Columbia, S.C., 1954), 1-74, hereafter cited as Atkin, *Report*.

5. Estimates of Indian population have varied extensively because of the lack of sufficient ethnohistorical data, inadequate archaeological artifacts and skeletal remains, and recent variations in demographic studies. Several studies have suggested the increase of ten to twelve times or more for traditional estimates, based primarily on formulas

devised from studies of Central and South America. See, for example, works of Sherburne F. Cook, Woodrow Borah, and Henry F. Dobyns's "Estimating Aboriginal American Population: An Appraisal of Techniques with a New Hemispheric Estimate," *Current Anthropology*, 7 (1966), 395-449 and his *Their Number Become Thinned: Native American Population Dynamics in Eastern North America* (Knoxville, Tenn., 1983). See also Peter Wood, "The Changing Population of the Colonial South: An Overview by Race and Region, 1685-1790," in *Powhatan's Mantle: Indians in the Colonial Southeast*, ed. by Wood et al. (Lincoln and London, 1989).

6. Glen to Duke of Newcastle, February 3, 1748, C.O. 5:389, PRO, f. 43.

7. Atkin, *Report*, 42.

8. James H. Merrell, *The Indians' New World: Catawbas and Their Neighbors from European Contact Through the Era of Removal* (Chapel Hill, N.C., 1989), 92-95; 118-19; Charles M. Hudson, *The Catawba Nation*, University of Georgia Monographs, no. 18 (Athens, Ga., 1970), 28.

9. Frederick W. Hodge, ed., *Handbook of American Indians North of Mexico*, Bureau of American Ethnology, Bulletin 30, 2 vols. (Washington, D.C., 1907-1910), 1:234, 247.

10. James Adair, *The History of the American Indians* (London, 1775), 232; there is a useful subsequent edition by Samuel Cole Williams, ed. (Johnson City, Tenn., 1930).

11. Glen to Duke of Newcastle, February 3, 1748, C.O. 5:389, PRO, f. 43.

12. Atkin, *Report*, 42.

13. Glen to Duke of Newcastle, February 3, 1748, C.O. 5:389, PRO, f. 43.

14. Atkin, *Report*, 43.

15. Glen to Duke of Newcastle, February 3, 1748, C.O. 5:389, PRO, ff. 43-44.

16. Atkin, *Report*, 42.

17. John R. Swanton, *The Indians of the Southeastern United States*, Bureau of American Ethnology, Bulletin 137 (Washington, D.C., 1946), 123.

18. Glen to Board of Trade, April 28, 1747, S.C. Pub. Recs., 22:278.

19. Atkin, *Report*, 43-44.

20. For a discussion of the Virginia experience, see W. Stitt Robinson, "Tributary Indians in Colonial Virginia," *Virginia Magazine of History and Biography*, 67 (1959), 49-64.

21. Langdon Cheves, ed., *The Shaftsbury Papers and Other Records relating to Carolina*, Collections of the South Carolina Historical Society, 5 (Charleston, S.C., 1897), 338.

22. March 2, 1744, Council Journal.

23. Walter B. Edgar, ed., *Biographical Directory of the South Carolina House of Representatives*, 2 vols. (Columbia, S.C., 1974-1977), 2:244-45.

24. Representation of John Fenwick to Board of Trade, n.d., C.O. 5:371, PRO, ff 61-65. Received by Board of Trade, April 9 and read, April 23, 1745.

25. *Dictionary of National Biography*, 11:292-95.

26. Ibid., 19:1101-1102.

27. Glen to Duke of Newcastle, February 3, 1748, C.O. 5:389, PRO, ff. 44-46.

28. Edgar, *Biographical Directory*, 2:685-86.

29. Glen to Board of Trade, September 22, 1744, S.C. Pub. Recs., 21:401-402; Merrell, *Indians' New World*, 155-56.

30. William H. Gilbert, Jr., "The Eastern Cherokee," *Anthropological Papers*,

Bureau of American Ethnology, Bulletin 133 (Washington, D.C., 1943), 321, 363; Fred Gearing, *Priests and Warriors: Social Structure for Cherokee Politics in the 18th Century*, Memoir 93, *American Anthropologist*, 62, no. 5, part 2 (1962), 5-6, 85-87. The theories of Indian government set forth by these writers are challenged in John P. Reid, *A Law of Blood: The Primitive Law of the Cherokee Nation* (New York, 1970), 18-27. See also Theda Perdue, *Slavery and the Evolution of Cherokee Society, 1540-1866* (Knoxville, Tenn., 1979), 32.

31. Sir Alexander Cuming, "Georgia and the Cherokees," Edward E. Ayer Collection, Newberry Library, Chicago, 22, 47-48.

32. The treaty may be consulted in William L. Saunders, ed., *Colonial Records of North Carolina*, 10 vols. (Raleigh, N.C., 1886-1890), 3:129-33.

33. David H. Corkan, *The Cherokee Frontier: Conflict and Survival, 1740-62* (Norman, Okla., 1962), 16-17; Reid, *Law of Blood*, 12.

34. Emperor of Cherokees to Glen, October 10, 1744, S.C. Pub. Recs., 22:25-27.

35. Glen to Duke of Newcastle, February 11, 1746, S.C. Pub. Recs., 22:134-35.

36. Ibid., 22:137-38.

37. April 14, 16 and June 4, 1746, *Commons Journal, 1745-1746*, 188, 197-98, 200-201.

38. Glen to Board of Trade, September 29, 1746, S.C. Pub. Recs., 22:199-204; Glen to Board of Trade, April 23, 1748, S.C. Pub. Recs., 23:116-17; Glen to Duke of Newcastle, May 2, 1746, C.O. 5:388, part 2, PRO, ff. 158-60.

39. Cooper and McCord, *Statutes*, 2:309-16.

40. Ibid., 2:357-59; *Acts of the Privy Council*, 2:610-14.

41. For further discussion of this conflict, see Robinson, *Southern Colonial Frontier*, 128-29.

42. Cooper and McCord, *Statutes*, 2:677-80.

43. Ibid., 3:86-96.

44. Greene, *Quest for Power*, 311-13.

45. Patricia K. Galloway, "Choctaw Factionalism and Civil War, 1746-1750," in Carolyn Keller Reeves, ed., *The Choctaw before Removal* (Jackson, Miss., 1985), 121-26; Jesse O. McKee and Jon A. Schlenker, *The Choctaws: Cultural Evolution of a Native American Tribe* (Jackson, Miss., 1980), 16-17, 27-28; Angie Debo, *The Rise and Fall of the Choctaw Republic* (Norman, Okla., 1934), 15, 27-28; Michael James Foret includes a chapter on the Choctaw revolt in "On the Marchlands of Empire: Trade, Diplomacy, and War on the Southeastern Frontier, 1733-1763," Ph.D. diss., College of William and Mary, 1990 and University Microfilms International (Ann Arbor, Mich., 1992), 170-208.

46. Edmond Atkin, "Historical Account of the Revolt of the Chactaw Indians . . . ," London, January 20, 1753, Landsdowne ms. (British Museum, London), 809, p. 2, hereafter cited as Atkin, "Choctaw Revolt"; September 12, 1738 and January 17, 1739, *Commons Journal, 1736-1739*, 575, 590.

47. Galloway, "Choctaw Factionalism," 133-34.

48. Adair, *History of the American Indians*, 314.

49. Glen to "Honble Gentlmen & Gentlemen" of the Assembly, c. 1750, 31 pp., Glen Papers, Caroliniana, Columbia, hereafter cited as Glen, "Choctaw Revolt."

50. Ibid., 5-6.

51. Galloway, "Choctaw Factionalism," 134.

52. Charles William Paape, "The Choctaw Revolt: A Chapter in the Intercolonial

Rivalry in the Old Southwest," Ph.D. diss., University of Illinois, Urbana-Champaign, 1946, 91.

53. Vaudreuil to Maurepas, April 1, 1746, *Mississippi Provincial Archives, French Dominion, 1729-1763*, edited by Dunbar Rowland, A.G. Sanders, and Patricia Kay Galloway, vols. 4 and 5 (Baton Rouge La., and London, 1984), 4:264-65.

54. Atkin, "Choctaw Revolt," 2-3; Paape, "Choctaw Revolt," 93.

55. Galloway, "Choctaw Factionalism," 142.

56. Atkin, "Choctaw Revolt," 2-3.

57. April 15, 1747, *Commons Journal, 1746-1747*, 221.

58. April 14, 1747, ibid., 215; Atkin, "Choctaw Revolt," 3-4.

59. Atkin, "Choctaw Revolt," 3-5.

60. November 13, 1747, Council Journal; Atkin, "Choctaw Revolt," 6-7.

61. Galloway, "Choctaw Factionalism," 143.

62. Atkin, "Choctaw Revolt," 7.

63. Adair, *History*, 305, 314, 321, 324, 329-30.

64. Atkin, "Choctaw Revolt," 12-14.

65. Adair, *History*, 321.

66. Atkin, "Choctaw Revolt," 15-16.

67. Adair, *History*, 324, 328.

68. Atkin, "Choctaw Revolt," 31-33—quotation is on 31; Galloway, "Choctaw Factionalism," 149.

69. Vaudreuil to Rouillé, January 28, 1752, *Mississippi Archives*, 5:109-10.

70. May 12, 1749, Upper House Journal; May 16 and 23, 1749, *Commons Journal, 1749-1750*, 96, 179.

71. *Commons Journal, 1750-1751*, 6 and 6n.

72. May 23 and 27, 1749, ibid., *1749-1750*, 179, 183-84, 221.

73. Glen, "Choctaw Revolt," two pages unnumbered following 4.

74. *S.C. Gazette*, February 26 and March 12, 1750.

75. March 17, 1750, *Commons Journal, 1749-1750*, 484.

76. *S.C. Gazette*, April 9, 1750.

77. May 7, 1750, Council Journal.

78. May 3, 1750, Upper House Journal.

79. May 10 and 11, *Commons Journal, 1750-1751*, 98, 100.

80. Atkin, "Choctaw Revolt," 40-41.

81. Glen, "Choctaw Revolt"; see note 49, this chapter.

82. Atkin, "Choctaw Revolt," 41-42.

83. May 14, Upper House Journal; May 16, 1750, *Commons Journal, 1750-1751*, 9, 108-09.

84. *Commons Journal, 1750-1751*, 8-9.

85. May 17, 1750, ibid., 9-10, 113.

86. Ibid., 10-11.

87. May 31, 1750, ibid., 11-12, 176-79, 183.

88. Ibid., 12.

89. November 22, 1750, ibid., 188.

90. November 23, 1750, ibid., 191.

91. James A. Henretta, *"Salutary Neglect": Colonial Administration Under the Duke of Newcastle* (Princeton, N.J., 1972), 283-87, 308.

92. Board of Trade to Glen, December 20, 1748, S.C. Pub. Recs., 23:276-80;

quotation is on 278.

93. Glen to Board of Trade, December 23, 1749, C.O. 5:389, PRO, ff. 160-62.

94. Board of Trade to Glen, November 15, 1750, S.C. Pub. Recs., 24:148-56.

Chapter 4

1. *Commons Journal, 1748*, xi.

2. January 22, 23, 27, March 3, 1748, ibid., 14, 18, 26, 97-99, 100.

3. March 12, 1748, ibid., 168-69. In his message to the Commons House, Glen stated relative to the act for sloops that "I shall consider of it." This was tantamount to imposing his veto.

4. May 11, 1748, ibid., 235-36.

5. May 13, 1748, ibid., 249-50.

6. June 29, 1748, ibid., 400-02; quotation is on 400.

7. The relationship of proclamation money to colonial currency, as indicated here, was one to five, while during the same period the ratio between colonial currency and British sterling was one to seven.

8. June 11 and 13, 1748, *Commons Journal, 1748*, 305-306, 311.

9. March 4 and 5, 1748, ibid., 110-11, 118-19; March 5, 1748, Upper House Journal.

10. June 27 and 28, 1748, *Commons Journal, 1748*, 368, 374.

11. June 29, 1748, ibid., 396-97.

12. Henry A. M. Smith, "Charleston and Charleston Neck: The Original Grantees and the Settlements along the Ashley and Cooper Rivers," *South Carolina Historical and Genealogical Magazine*, 19 (1918), 23-25. The specific description in 1721 stated that the plantation was "on Oyster Point *alias* Charles Town neck bounding North on Doctr Charles Burnham East on a marsh of Cooper river South part on marsh and part on Gillson Clapp and West on the Highway or Broadpath."

13. June 29, 1748, *Commons Journal*, 402-403.

14. *S.C. Gazette*, July 9, 1748.

15. Hennig Cohen, *The South Carolina Gazette, 1732-1775* (Columbia, S.C., 1953), 3-5, 241-43.

16. Edgar, *Biographical Directory*, 2:672-75.

17. *S.C. Gazette*, July 29 and August 8, 1748.

18. May 23, 1749, *Commons Journal, 1749-1750*, 173-77.

19. April 4 and May 15, ibid., 31, 93.

20. May 16, ibid., 109-10.

21. Ibid., 111.

22. May 24, ibid., 185.

23. May 25, ibid., 191.

24. Greene, *Quest for Power*, 266-67.

25. See earlier, p. 23.

26. May 19, 1749, *Commons Journal, 1749-1750*, 142.

27. June 1, 1749, ibid., 276; June 1, 1749, Upper House Journal.

28. See below, pp. 108-10, 111.

29. Edgar, *Biographical Directory*, 2:279-80.

30. Ibid., 2:289-90.

31. Glen to Duke of Bedford, July 27, 1748, C.O. 5:389, PRO, p. 70.

32. Sirmans, *Colonial South Carolina*, 238.

33. Glen to Board of Trade, January 29, 1752 and August 26, 1754, S.C. Pub. Recs., 25:3-4 and 26:115; Edgar, *Biographical Directory*, 2:201-202.

34. William L. McDowell, Jr., ed., *Documents relating to Indian Affairs, May 21, 1750-August 7, 1754, Colonial Records of South Carolina* (Columbia, S.C., 1958), 33-35, 92-99, 105-107, 110-12, 138-46, 202-204, 354-58.

35. *S.C. Gazette*, April 3, 1755.

36. Board of Trade to Glen, December 20, 1748, S.C. Pub. Recs., 23:280.

37. Board of Trade to Glen, November 15, 1750, ibid., 24:168.

38. The statute of 1731 with similar provisions was still in effect at this time, Cooper and McCord, *Statutes*, 3:274-87. See p. 275 for the reference to the drawing by a child.

39. Glen to Duke of Bedford, October 10, 1748, S.C. Pub. Recs., 23:241.

40. April 24, 1751, *Commons Journal, 1750-1751*, 344-45.

41. May 4, 1751, ibid., 397-98.

42. April 24, 1751, ibid., 346-47.

43. April 24, 1751, ibid., 348-49.

44. Cooper and McCord, *Statutes*, 2:239-40, 287-88.

45. April 24, 1751, *Commons Journal, 1750-1751*, 347-49.

46. *S.C. Gazette*, April 29, 1751.

47. The communication from the Assembly for the agent, James Crokatt, with reasons for Crown assent to the St. Philip's bill under date of April 27, 1751, is reproduced from the journals of the Upper House in *Commons Journal, 1750-1751*, 543-46.

48. May 4, 1751, ibid., 400.

49. May 4 and 9, 1751, ibid., 399, 408-10.

50. May 7, 1751, ibid., 402-403.

51. May 8, 1751, ibid., 404-405.

52. May 10, 1751, ibid., 429.

53. May 9, 1751, ibid., 414.

54. May 18, 1751, ibid., 464.

55. June 6 and 14, 1751, ibid., 467-68, 515-16; quotation is on 516.

56. Glen to Board of Trade, January 29, 1752, S.C. Pub. Recs., 25:3-4.

57. Greene, *Quest for Power*, 255-56.

58. January 21, 1744, *Commons Journal, 1742-1744*, 543-44.

59. Labaree, *Royal Instructions*, 2:822.

60. January 22, 1752, *Commons Journal, 1751-1752*, 77-78.

61. March 11 and April 29, 1752, ibid., 142-43, 258.

62. May 5, 1752, ibid., 278-81; quotations are on 280 and 281.

63. May 14, 1752, ibid., 354-56; quotations are on 355 and 356.

64. September 27, 1752, ibid., 376-77, 376n.

65. December 7, 1752, ibid., *1752-1754*, 41.

66. September 27, 1752, *ibid.*, *1751-1752*, 376-77, 376n.

67. December 7 and 13, 1752, *ibid.*, *1752-1754*, 42, 60.

68. November 25, 1752, ibid., 15.

69. December 7, 1752, ibid., 41-45; quotation is on 44.

70. December 13, 1752, ibid., xiv, 54-57.

71. December 12, 1752, ibid., 52-53.

72. Ibid., 1752-1754, xiv-xv.

73. W. Roy Smith, *South Carolina as a Royal Province, 1719-1776* (New York, 1903), 206-207; Greene, *Quest for Power*, 258-59.

74. This paragraph is based on the excellent article by Robert M. Weir, "'The Harmony We Were Famous For': An Interpretation of Pre-Revolutionary South Carolina Politics," *William and Mary Quarterly*, 3rd ser., 26 (1969), 473-501.

75. Ibid., 474.

76. Ibid., 484.

77. Ibid., 500.

Chapter 5

1. See, for example, the report of Governor Edmund Andros of Virginia in 1697, W. Noel Sainsbury et al., *Calendar of State Papers, Colonial Series, America and West Indies* (London, 1860-   ), *1696-1697*, 455-56.

2.   The queries are recorded in the Council Journal for May 3, 1749, pp. 327-28 with the answers on pp. 329-59, and also in the Upper House Journal for May 31, 1749, pp. 82-83 with the answers on pp. 83-107.

3. Glen to Board of Trade, July 19, 1749, S.C. Pub. Recs., 23:336-83.

4. London, 1761.

5. In addition to the 1761 publication, Glen's report has been reproduced in the following: B. R. Carroll, comp., *Historical Collections of South Carolina: Embracing Many Rare and Valuable Pamphlets and Other Documents Relating to the History of that State . . . to . . . 1776*, 2 vols. (New York, 1836), 2: 193-272; Plowden Charles Jennett Weston, ed., *Documents Connected with the History of South Carolina* (London, 1856), 61-99; and Chapman J. Milling, ed., *Colonial South Carolina: Two Contemporary Descriptions* (Columbia, S.C., 1951), 1-104.

6. Glen to Board of Trade, July 19, 1749, S.C. Pub. Recs., 23:336.

7. May 5 and 6, 1749, *Commons Journal, 1749-1750*, 54, 56-58.

8. May 8 and 10, 1749, ibid., 59, 64, 76-77.

9. May 16, 1749, ibid., 97-105, 109-12, 115-16.

10. June 1, 1749, ibid., 271.

11. May 16 and June 1, 1749, ibid., 98, 271-72.

12. June 1, 1749, ibid., 272-73.

13. Glen to Board of Trade, July 19, 1749, S.C. Pub. Recs., 23:341, 356-57. This report includes the original pagination of the printed version of 1761 and different numbers for this edited publication of 1951. The pagination for the 1951 edition is used in these notes.

14. Glen to Board of Trade, July 19, 1749, S.C. Pub. Recs., 23:373; Milling, *Colonial S.C.*, 67.

15. Glen to Board of Trade, July 19, 1749, S.C. Pub. Recs., 23:360; Milling, *Colonial S.C.*, 52.

16. Milling, *Colonial S.C.*, xvi-xvii.

17. Ibid., 53.

18. David Duncan Wallace, *South Carolina: A Short History, 1520-1948* (Chapel Hill, N.C., 1951), 48-49.

19. Milling, *Colonial S.C.*, 9-13.

20. Wallace, *Short History*, 23; Samuel E. Morison, *The European Discovery of America: The Northern Voyages, A.D. 500-1600* (New York, 1971), 157, 191.

21. Milling, *Colonial S.C.* , 16; John J. McCusker and Russell R. Menard, *The*

Economy of British America, 1607-1789 (Chapel Hill, N.C., and London, 1985), 181.

22. Milling, *Colonial S.C.*, 13-19.

23. Glen to Board of Trade, July 19, 1749, S.C. Pub. Recs., 23:349.

24. Milling, *Colonial S.C.*, 19-37.

25. Ibid., 38-39.

26. Ibid., 39-42; quotations are on 40.

27. Ibid., 42-44; quotation is on 42-43.

28. The classic modern study of mercantilism is Eli F. Heckscher, *Mercantilism*, 2 vols., 2nd ed. (London, New York, 1955); for more direct attention to the American colonies, see Michael Kammen, *Empire and Interest: The American Colonies and the Politics of Mercantilism* (Philadelphia, New York, Toronto, 1970).

29. Milling, *Colonial S.C.*, 51.

30. Ibid., 48-49, 53-55.

31. Ibid., 51.

32. Ibid., 58-63.

33. Wallace, *Short History*, 189-90.

34. Milling, *Colonial S.C.*, 63-66.

35. For comparison of these figures, see pp. 38-39 of this text, and Atkin, *Report*, 42-45.

36. Milling, *Colonial S.C.*, 67-73; quotations are on 69 and 73.

37. Glen to Board of Trade, July 15, 1750, S.C. Pub. Recs., 24: 64-65.

38. Glen to Board of Trade, February 1751, S.C. Pub. Recs., 24:268.

39. Ibid., 24:268-94.

40. Ibid., 24:270-77.

41. Ibid., 24:277.

42. Latin translation: As if the placing of feet was superseded by the establishment of dwellings.

43. Latin translation: "that which previously has belonged to no one, by natural doctrine is conceded to him who occupies it."

44. Glen to Board of Trade, February 1751, S.C. Pub. Recs., 24:277-81.

45. Glen to Board of Trade, Mar., 1751, S.C. Pub. Recs., 24:303-30; quotation is on 304.

46. Ibid., 24:315-17; quotation at end of paragraph is on 317.

47. Ibid., 24:314-15.

48. Ibid., 24:318-19.

49. Robert M. Weir, *Colonial South Carolina: A History* (Millwood, N.Y., 1983), 214-16.

50. Ibid., 24:312-13.

51. Ibid., 24:323-27.

52. McCusker and Menard, *British Economy*, 145.

53. Labaree, *Royal Instructions*, 2:836-37.

54. Glen to Board of Trade, March, 1753, S.C. Pub. Recs., 25:174; Labaree, *Royal Instructions*, 2:885. Quotations of Glen about his general and trade instructions in this and subsequent citations in this chapter are from the Labaree edition.

55. Glen to Board of Trade, April, 1753, S.C. Pub. Recs., 25:218; Labaree, *Royal Instructions*, 2:880-81.

56. Labaree, *Royal Instructions*, 1:60-62.

57. Glen to Board of Trade, April, 1753, S.C. Pub. Recs., 25:219-20; Labaree,

Royal Instructions, 2:881.

58. Labaree, *Royal Instructions*, 2:881n, note 9.

59. Glen to Board of Trade, April, 1753, S.C. Pub. Recs., 25:221-222; Labaree, *Royal Instructions*, 2:882-83.

60. Instructions to Governor Lyttelton in S.C. Pub. Recs., 26:265-344; Labaree, *Royal Instructions*, 2:883n, note 15.

61. Glen to Board of Trade, April, 1753, S.C. Pub. Recs., 25:222-223; Labaree, *Royal Instructions*, 2:883.

62. Labaree, *Royal Instructions*, 2:883n, note 21.

63. Glen to Board of Trade, April, 1753, S.C. Pub. Recs., 25:224; Labaree, *Royal Instructions*, 2:883-84, 883n, note 17, 884n, notes 26, 33, 34.

64. These instructions of September 7, 1739, may be found in C.O. 5:198, PRO, pp. 163-91.

65. Glen to Board of Trade, March., 1753, S.C. Pub. Recs., 25:175-76; Labaree, *Royal Instructions*, 2:886.

66. Glen to Board of Trade, March, 1753, S.C. Pub. Recs., 25:176-80; Labaree, *Royal Instructions*, 2:886-88.

67. Glen to Board of Trade, March 1753, S.C. Pub. Recs., 25:182-88; Labaree, *Royal Instructions*, 2:889-92.

68. Labaree, *Royal Instructions*, 2:892n, note 8.

69. Glen to Board of Trade, March, 1753, S.C. Pub. Recs., 25:188; Labaree, *Royal Instructions*, 2:892 and 892n, note 11.

70. Glen to Board of Trade, March, 1753, S.C. Pub. Recs., 25:192-94; Labaree, *Royal Instructions*, 2:894-95.

71. Danby Pickering, ed., *The Statutes at Large from the Magna charta, to the end of the eleventh Parliament of Great Britain* (Cambridge, England, 1763), 8:160-67.

72. Glen to Board of Trade, March, 1753, S.C. Pub. Recs., 25:196-201; Labaree, *Royal Instructions*, 2:896-98; quotation is on 201 and 898.

73. Glen to Board of Trade, March, 1753, S.C. Pub. Recs., 25:201-04; Labaree, *Royal Instructions*, 2:898-900.

Chapter 6

1. Savelle, *Origins of American Diplomacy*, 442.

2. Lawrence H. Gipson, *Zones of International Friction: North America, South of the Great Lakes Region, 1748-1754*, vol. 4 of *The British Empire Before the American Revolution* (New York, 1939), 11-12.

3. Ibid., 16.

4. Ibid., 107n; Glen to Duke of Newcastle, February 3, 1748, C.O. 5:389, PRO, ff. 45-46.

5. Quoted in Wallace, *History of South Carolina*, 1:213.

6. William Bull, Sr., to Board of Trade, June 15, 1742, S.C. Pub. Recs., 20:570.

7. Glen to Board of Trade, February 3, 1748, S.C. Pub. Recs., 23:74.

8. Atkin, *Report*, 47.

9. For a recent analysis of the challenges to the Catawbas, see Merrell, *Indians' New World*, chap. 4, "Modern Indian Politics: Catawba Diplomacy."

10. McDowell, *Documents . . . Indian Affairs, 1750-1754*, 9, 84-86.

11. Ibid., 166-67.

12. Ibid., 92-99.

13. For the treaty proceedings, see ibid., 138-46.

14. Ibid., 167-68, 205-06, 213-14.

15. Ibid., 357-58.

16. David H. Corkran, *The Creek Frontier, 1540-1783* (Norman, Okla., 1967), 4-5; for further information on the Creeks, see John R. Swanton, *Early History of the Creeks and Their Neighbors* (Washington, D.C., 1922).

17. December 13 and 14, 1743, *Commons Journal, 1742-1744*, 492, 494-95.

18. July 3-4, 1744, Upper House Journal.

19. Corkran, *Creek Frontier*, 121-22.

20. For further information, see Doris Behrman Fisher, "Mary Musgrove: Creek Englishwoman," Ph.D. diss. Emory University, 1990; E. Merton Coulter, "Mary Musgrove, 'Queen of the Creeks': A Chapter of Early Georgia Troubles," *Georgia Historical Quarterly*, 11 (1927), 1-30.

21. April 7 and 8, *Commons Journal, 1748*, 170, 174, 176.

22. Corkran, *Cherokee Frontier*, 21-22.

23. McDowell, *Documents . . . Indian Affairs, 1750-1754*, 399.

24. Corkran, *Creek Frontier*, 128-30.

25. Corkran, *Cherokee Frontier*, 22-23.

26. June 14, 1751, *Commons Journal, 1750-1751*, 505-506.

27. H. R. McIlwaine et al., eds., *Executive Journals of the Council of Colonial Virginia*, 6 vols. (1925-1966), hereafter cited as *Virginia Council Journals*, 5:349-52.

28. *Virginia Gazette*, August 16 and October 31, 1751.

29. McDowell, *Documents . . . Indian Affairs, 1750-1754*, 173-74, 185.

30. Corkran, *Cherokee Frontier*, 30.

31. Ibid., 32.

32. McDowell, *Documents . . . Indian Affairs, 1750-1754*, 156-69; quotation is on 158.

33. Ibid., 164.

34. Ibid., 187-96.

35. Ibid., 186, 191, 195.

36. Ibid., 197-98.

37. April 29, 1752, *Commons Journal, 1751-1752*, 260-62.

38. McDowell, *Documents . . . Indian Affairs, 1750-1754*, 249-50, 271-72.

39. Ibid., 224-27, 228-31.

40. Ibid., 210-11, 392; quotation is on 392.

41. Ibid., 279-80.

42. Ibid., 334.

43. Ibid., 410-11.

44. Ibid., 402.

45. A partial record of this extensive meeting with the Upper and Lower Creeks is in ibid., 387-414; quotation is on 392.

46. Ibid., 393.

47. Ibid., 407.

48. Ibid., 413.

49. *S.C. Gazette*, June 12, 1753.

50. McDowell, *Documents . . . Indian Affairs, 1750-1754*, 233-34.

51. *Ibid.*, 253-54, 258-59.

52. *Virginia Gazette*, November 17, 1752; *William and Mary College Quarterly*, 1st

ser., 13 (1904), 13-14.

53. *Virginia Council Journals*, 5:415.

54. Ibid., 5:413-15.

55. Corkran, *Cherokee Frontier*, 41.

56. A record of the meeting with the Cherokees from July 3 to 7, 1753, is in McDowell, *Documents . . . Indian Affairs, 1750-1754*, 431-54.

57. Ibid., 434-35; quotation is on 435.

58. Ibid., 452.

59. Ibid., 448-49.

60. May 14, 1752, *Commons Journal, 1751-1752*, 357-58.

61. May 10 and 11, ibid., *1752-1754*, 531, 537.

62. Glen to Board of Trade, August 26, 1754, S.C. Pub. Recs., 26:106-15; quotation is on 106.

63. The deed for the Fort Prince George tract may be found in McDowell, *Documents . . . Indian Affairs, 1750-1754*, 519-21.

64. Discussion of the extent of the Cherokee cession of 1753 is in Wallace, *Henry Laurens*, 503-10.

65. Glen to Board of Trade, August 26, 1754, S.C. Pub. Recs., 26:108-109.

66. *S.C. Gazette*, December 17, 1753.

67. McDowell, *Documents . . . Indian Affairs, 1750-1754*, 537.

68. Ibid., 360-61, 414-16.

69. Ibid., 430-31, 525-26; quotation is on 430.

70. Ibid., 467.

71. Ibid., 472-74; also in R. A. Brock, ed., *The Official Records of Robert Dinwiddie, Lieutenant-Governor of the Colony of Virginia, 1751-1758*, 2 vols., Collections of the Virginia Historical Society, vols. 3-4, New Series (Richmond, 1883-1884), hereafter cited as *Dinwiddie Records*, 1:89.

72. McDowell, *Documents . . . Indian Affairs, 1750-1754*, 477-79; quotation is on 478.

73. Ibid., 522-24.

74. Ibid., 535.

75. Glen to Dinwiddie, June 1, 1754, C.O. 5:14, PRO.

76. McDowell, *Documents . . . Indian Affairs, 1750-1754*, 528.

77. Captain Robert Orme stated in his journal that these bills were the only money contributed by the colonies that "passed through" Braddock's hands, Winthrop Sargent, ed., *The History of an Expedition Against Fort Du Quesne, in 1755* (Philadelphia, 1855), 325.

78. Corkran, *Cherokee Frontier*, 52, 54-56.

79. For a discussion of the conflicting reports on the total strength and casualties of each force, see Douglas Southall Freeman, *George Washington: A Biography*, 7 vols. (New York, 1948-1957), 2:68n, 86; Sargent, *Expedition*, 310. For further examinations of Braddock's campaign, see also Stanley M. Pargellis, "Braddock's Defeat," *American Historical Review*, 41 (1936), 253-69; Lee McCardell, *Ill-Starred General: Braddock of the Coldstream Guards* (Pittsburgh, 1958), 135-272; and Paul E. Kopperman, *Braddock at the Monongahela* (Pittsburgh, 1977).

80. Sargent, *Expedition*, 173.

81. McDowell, *Documents . . . Indian Affairs, 1750-1754*, 538.

82. May 21-22; 1755, Council Journal.

83. Tom Hatley, *The Dividing Paths: Cherokees and South Carolinians Through the Era of Revolution* (New York and Oxford, 1993), 76.

84. *S.C. Gazette*, July 31, 1755.

85. For Glen's concern about the treaty and its relationship to John Mitchell's map of North America, see *Commons Journal, 1754-1755*, xvii, note 19.

86. *Dinwiddle Records*, 2:213.

87. Saunders, *N.C. Col. Recs.*, 5:359-60.

88. Louis K. Koontz, *Robert Dinwiddle: His Career in American Colonial Government and Westward Expansion* (Glendale, Calif., 1941), 322-23, 322n.

89. F. B. Kegley, *Kegley's Virginia Frontier: The Beginning of the Southwest, The Roanoke of Colonial Days, 1740-1783* (Roanoke, Va., 1938), 224-28.

90. A record of the negotiations and the treaties may be found in the *Va. Mag. Hist. Biog.*, 13(1906), 226-64; W. Stitt Robinson, ed., *Virginia Treaties, 1723-1775*, vol. 5 of *Early American Indian Documents: Treaties and Laws, 1607-1789*, Alden T. Vaughan, gen. ed. (Frederick, Md., 1983), 201-22.

91. Robinson, *Virginia Treaties, 1723-1775*, 216.

92. Thomas Robinson to Dinwiddle, July 5, 1754, C.O. PRO, 5:211.

93. Glen suggested the total of £4,000 or £5,000 when appealing to the Commons House. April 9, 1756, *Commons House Journal, 1755-1757*, 207.

94. *Dinwiddie Records*, 2:27-28, 281-82.

95. February 3 and 4, April 9, 1756, *Commons House Journal, 1755-1757*, 78, 79-80, 210-11.

96. Ibid., xxviii.

97. Alden, *John Stuart*, 49-50.

98. Ibid., 58-60.

99. Atkin, *Report*, xvi, 1-95.

100. July 1, 1756, *Commons House Journal, 1755-1757*, 266, 452.

101. Corkran, *Cherokee Frontier*, 195, 218-21.

Chapter 7

1. James A. Henretta, *"Salutary Neglect": Colonial Administration under the Duke of Newcastle* (Princeton, N.J., 1972), *passim*.

2. Ibid., 311.

3. Ibid., 296; *Dictionary of American Biography*, 4:225-26 and 17:120-22.

4. *Commons Journal, 1754-1755*, xii-xiv.

5. January 28, February 6, May 20, 1755, ibid., 79, 110-11, 307-08.

6. March 21, April 9, 1755, ibid., 210, 222n-223n.

7. March 22, 1755, ibid., 212-13.

8. April 8, 1755, Upper House Journal; April 9, 1755, *Commons Journal, 1754-1755*, 220-22, quotation is on 222.

9. April 10 and 12, *Commons Journal, 1754-1755*, 226, 227, 229, 236; quotation is on 236.

10. April 12, 1755, ibid., 241.

11. April 29, 1755, ibid., 242-43.

12. May 1, 2, and 13, ibid., 254-57, 293-94; quotation is on 294.

13. May 19, 1755, ibid., 305.

14. May 19, 1755, ibid., 304.

15. November 25 and 27, 1755, ibid., *1755-1757*, 8, 12-13.

16. *S.C. Gazette*, March 11, 1756.

17. February 12, 18, 21, and March 10, 1756, *Commons Journal, 1755-1757*, 100-101, 109-10, 111, 118-19, 125-26.

18. April 15, 1756, ibid., 217-18.

19. April 15, 1756, ibid., 219-20.

20. April 21, 1756, ibid., 222-25; quotations are on 223-24.

21. April 22, 1756, ibid., 227.

22. April 29, 1756, ibid., 236-40; quotations are on 240.

23. April 29, 1756, ibid., 241-44; quotation is on 242.

24. May 3, 1756, ibid., 249-52; quotations are on 250 and 251.

25. *S.C. Gazette*, May 6, 1756.

26. Ibid., May 13, 1756 Supplement; this document is also reprinted in the Appendix of *Commons Journal, 1755-1757*, 497-502; quotations are on 499 of the *Journal*.

27. Quotations are on 501 and 502 of *Commons Journal, 1755-1757*.

28. *S.C. Gazette*, May 22, 1756; May 5, 1756, Upper House Journal.

29. *S.C. Gazette*, May 22 and 29, 1756.

30. Ibid., June 5; quotations are on 1, 3, and 6.

31. Lyttelton to Board of Trade, December 6, 1756 and June 11, 1757, S.C. Pub. Recs., 27:201-203, 280; *Acts of the Privy Council*, 4:359-60.

32. Sirmans, *Colonial South Carolina*, 313.

33. For further information on the Acadian deportation, see Arthur G. Doughty, *The Acadian Exiles: A Chronicle of the Land of Evangeline* (Toronto, 1916), 88-161; Naomi Griffiths, *The Acadians: Creation of A People* (Toronto, 1973), 52-67; Naomi Griffiths, *The Acadian Deportation: Deliberate Perfidy or Cruel Necessity?* (Toronto, 1969).

34. January 15, 1756, *Commons Journal, 1755-1757*, 31.

35. Cooper and McCord, *Statutes*, 2:131-33.

36. There are numerous discussions of the Acadians. See, for example, January 16, 22, February 4, 1756, *Commons Journal, 1755-1757*, 33, 43-44, 81n.

37. January 27, 1756, ibid., 57-60, also xv; quotations are on 57 and 58.

38. February 21, 1756, ibid., 120-21, also xvii.

39. March 31 and April 28, 1756, ibid., 188, 232, also xviii-xix.

40. April 9, 1756, ibid., 207-208.

41. April 22 and 27, ibid., 225-26, 230.

42. June 22, 29, July 1 and 2, 1756, ibid., 256, 262-63, 266-69, also xviii-xxi.

43. The most extensive examination of this boundary dispute is by Marvin Lucian Skaggs in *North Carolina Boundary Disputes Involving Her Southern Line, The James Sprunt Studies in History and Political Science*, vol. 25, no. 1 (Chapel Hill, N.C., 1941). In highly controversial questions, this study favors North Carolina.

44. Labaree, *Royal Instructions*, 2:704.

45. Skaggs, *N.C. Boundary*, 37-39.

46. Ibid., 43-44.

47. Instruction no. 36, C.O. 5:198, PRO, pp. 119-20.

48. Desmond Clarke, *Arthur Dobbs Esquire, 1689-1765: Surveyor-General of Ireland, Prospector, and Governor of North Carolina* (Chapel Hill, N.C., 1957), 72-73.

49. Saunders, *N.C. Col. Recs.*, 5:358. The full letter of Dobbs extends from 353 to 364.

50. Ibid., 5:1105.

51. Ibid., 5:380-87.

52. January 25, February 6, 7, 27, 1755, *Commons Journal, 1754-1755*, 73, 108, 117, 126-27.

53. March 5, 1755, ibid., 140-43; quotation is on 141.

54. Saunders, *N.C. Col. Recs.*, 5:376-80; quotations are on 377. Glen later decided that these statements were so intemperate that he provided an amended letter for the *S.C. Council Journal* and sent it to Governor Dobbs with a request to ignore the earlier version, *Commons Journal, 1754-1755*, xxn. The letter in *N.C. Col. Recs.* is the original version.

55. Saunders, *N.C. Col. Recs.*, 5:387-93; quotation is on 387-88.

56. Ibid., 6:792-93.

57. Skaggs, *N.C. Boundary*,. 73-75, 87-88, 106.

58. Quoted in ibid., 109n.

59. Ibid., 150-56.

Chapter 8

1. This quotation was a variation of a statement made by Governor Glen in his letter to the Duke of Bedford, October 10, 1748, S.C. Pub. Recs., 23:232: "for I shall reckon it my greatest happiness to be able to say with truth of Charles Town and this Province that I found them in Ashes, Defenceless, Declining. I leave them Fair Fortified and Flourishing."

2. July 6, 1756, *Commons Journal, 1755-1757*, 282.

3. Part of the correspondence of General Forbes has been published in Alfred P. James, ed., *Writings of General John Forbes Relating to his Service in North America* (Menasha, Wis., 1938). A "Biographical Sketch" may be found on pp. ix-xii.

4. Lawrence H. Gipson, *The Great War for the Empire: The Victorious Years, 1758-1760*, vol. 7 of *The British Empire Before the American Revolution* (New York, 1949), 258-59.

5. James, *Writings of Forbes*, 116, 142.

6. Freeman, *Washington*, 2:314; W. W. Abbot et al., eds., *The Papers of George Washington, Colonial Series* (Charlottesville, Va., 1983-   ), hereafter cited as *Papers of Washington*, 5:232n.

7. James, *Writings of Forbes*, 158, 171, 182, 190.

8. Glen to Bouquet, July 5, 1758, Bouquet Papers, British Museum, London, add mss 21643, ff. 137-38.

9. Glen to Forbes, July 13, 1758, GD 45/2/44/4, Forbes Papers, SRO.

10. James, *Writings of Forbes*, 156-58; Gipson, *Great War*, 250-52.

11. *Papers of Washington*, 5:361, note 2.

12. Ibid., 297-98, 298, note 2.

13. Ibid., 360-61.

14. Ibid., 297.

15. Freeman, *Washington*, 2:320-21; *Papers of Washington*, 5:332-34, gives a detailed listing of purchases and 5:334-43 tallies the votes by candidates with a total of 310 for Washington over his nearest opponent at 240.

16. James, *Writings of Forbes*, 119-20; John Richard Alden, *John Stuart and the Southern Colonial Frontier: A Study of Indian Relations, War, Trade, and Land Problems in the Southern Wilderness, 1754-1775* (Ann Arbor, Mich., and London, 1944), 77-78.

17. Gist to Washington, July 10, 1758, GD 45/2/48, Forbes Papers, SRO.

18. Forbes to Lyttelton, August 16, 1758, William Henry Lyttelton Papers, William L. Clements Library, Ann Arbor.

19. April 17, 1759, Council Journal. The manuscript for this date is incorrectly listed as April 7.

20. The treaty of Easton may be found in the *Minutes of the Provincial Council of Pennsylvania, Colonial Records of Pennsylvania*, 16 vols. (Harrisburg, Pa., 1838-53), 8:174-223.

21. Will of Forbes, February 13, 1759, Forbes Papers (film), South Caroliniana Library, Columbia.

22. Glen as executor of the estate of Forbes, March-April, 1759, ibid.

23. Glen's Memorial of April 27, 1761, may be found in J. West to Board of Trade, March 3, 1762, S.C. Pub. Recs., 29:222-27.

24. Glen's expense accounts, Glen Papers, Caroliniana.

25. *Board of Trade Journals*, 11 (1759-1763), 279, 280-81.

26. Ibid., 281.

27. Glen's financial summary, 1773, Glen Papers, Caroliniana.

28. Leonidas Dodson, *Alexander Spotswood, Governor of Colonial Virginia, 1710-1722* (Philadelphia, 1932), 281-82.

29. Clarke, *Arthur Dobbs*, 72, 90-92.

30. Bond of Elliott, December 17, 1753 and David R. Chesnutt, "James Glen: The Perquisites of Power," 13, Glen Papers, Caroliniana.

31. Corkran, *Cherokee Frontier*, 109, 139-40, 192, and *passim*.

32. Draft speech of Glen, c. 1754, Glen Papers, Caroliniana.

33. Articles of Accommodation between Glen and Hopton, May 26, 1757, ibid.

34. John Drayton to Thomas Glen, January 18, 1757, ibid.

35. Chesnutt, "James Glen," 13.

36. Glen's financial summary, 1773, Glen Papers, Caroliniana.

37. Edgar, *Biographical Directory*, 2:201-202; Dorothy G. Griffin, "The Eighteenth Century Draytons of Drayton Hall," Ph.D. diss., Emory University, 1985, 178.

38. Glen's financial summary, 1773, Glen Papers, Caroliniana.

39. Drayton to Glen, October 11, 1761, ibid.

40. Rice account, Glen and Drayton, 1761-1766, and plantation expenses, 1765-1766, ibid.

41. Rice account for 1767-1768 and March 11, 1770, ibid.

42. For further information on William Henry, see William M. Dabney and Marion Dargan, *William Henry Drayton & the American Revolution* (Albuquerque, N.M., 1962).

43. Drayton to Glen, October 11, 1761, Glen Papers, Caroliniana.

44. Drayton to Glen, April 30, 1762, ibid.

45. Accounts current, Drayton and Glen, 1761-1763, ibid.

46. Drayton to Glen, April 30, 1762, ibid.

47. Drayton to Glen, December 24, 1769, ibid.

48. Quoted in Griffin, "Eighteenth Century Draytons," 330-31.

49. Ibid., 267.

50. Drayton to Glen, August 13, 1772, Glen Papers, Caroliniana.

51. Quoted in Griffin, "Eighteenth Century Draytons," 200.

52. Drayton to Glen, February 6, 1773, Glen Papers, Caroliniana.

53. Tripartite indenture, February 27, 1752 and Abstract of Marriage Settlement,

June 15, 1761, ibid.

54. Drayton to Glen, March 1, 1767, ibid.

55. Drayton to Glen, September 10, 1773, ibid.

56. Drayton to Glen, January 19, 1775, ibid.

57. Glen to Drayton, May 1775, ibid.

58. Drayton to Glen, December 8, 1774, ibid.

59. Glen to Drayton, May 1775, ibid.

60. Griffin, "Eighteenth Century Draytons," 316-17.

61. Drayton to Glen, December 8, 1774, Glen Papers, Caroliniana.

62. Glen to William Henry Drayton, c. 1776, ibid.

63. Memorandum of William Henry Drayton, 1775, ibid.

64. GD 45/18/222/44, GD 45/19/222/15, GD 45/19/222/31, GD 45/19/222/36, SRO.

65. GD 45/19/222/9, SRO.

66. Glen's financial summary, 1773, Glen Papers, Caroliniana.

67. Diary of James Glen, 1775, GD 45/16/2643, SRO.

68. Will of James Glen, February 18, 1777, PRO, Chancery Lane, London.

69. See note 1, this chapter.

70. GD 45/16/2653/1-3, SRO.

Chapter 9

1. Wallace, *Short History*, 162-63.

2. Robert L. Meriwether, *The Expansion of South Carolina, 1729-1765* (Kingsport, Tenn., 1940), 211.

3. John Drayton to Thomas Glen, January 18, 1757, Glen Papers, Caroliniana.

4. John Drayton to James Glen, February 3, 1773, ibid.

Bibliographical Essay

MANUSCRIPTS

Central to the study of a person are the records that relate directly to his or her personal and public life with the inclusion of letters and other documents from the subject as well as communications to the individual. A substantial number of such records exist for the study of Governor James Glen, although they are to be found in a variety of depositories and the public documents exceed the personal ones. The Public Record Office of Scotland (SRO) in Edinburgh is a good starting point. The Register of the Great Seal (*Registrum Magni Sigilli*) contains the Latin documents of inheritance of property and of official royal appointments in Scotland. In the absence of county or regional record offices, the SRO in Edinburgh also preserves local town council documents that are valuable for Glen's experience both as provost of Linlithgow and as a member of its council. The Dalhousie Muniments deposited in the SRO by the sixteenth Earl of Dalhousie provide other vital material. These records of Glen came into the Dalhousie family by the marriage of his niece, Elizabeth, to the eighth Earl of Dalhousie and her service as executrix of Glen's estate as stipulated in his will. They include his letter-book as governor and the papers of Brigadier General James Forbes, who as a cousin named Glen as his estate executor following his campaign against Fort Duquesne in 1758. The best portrait of Glen, by the painter Peter Snyers, is now in the possession of the sixteenth Earl of Dalhousie in his private castle in Brechin (frontispiece).

Another very valuable private collection of Glen documents has recently come into the possession of the South Caroliniana Library in Columbia. These 101 manuscripts were obtained in 1974 from Lady Elizabeth Glen Ramsay, a descendant of Glen's niece. They provide information about Glen's financial activities, his economic and familial relations with John Drayton of Drayton Hall, and hitherto unavailable accounts of Glen's experiences with the Indians, particularly the Choctaws.

Two other depositories in Edinburgh have limited references to the governor. The National Library of Scotland has the Letter-Books of Charles Steuart for the period 1751 to 1763, the family papers of the Grahams of Airth, and the papers of the family of Fletcher of Saltoun with Lord Milton's correspondence with Glen.   The University of Edinburgh Library has the Laing Manuscripts extending from 1635 to 1832 collected by David Laing.

More extensive records of Glen's public life are available in the division of the British Public Record Office now located opposite Kew Gardens. I have researched original manuscripts there and also had access to microfilm of the very useful Colonial Office Papers, class 5, vols. 366-403, for his tenure. Class 5, vols. 13-20, include correspondence with colonial officials for the mid-eighteenth century. Class 5, vol. 198, contains the governor's long set of royal instructions at the time of his appointment.

In South Carolina the Division of Archives and History in Columbia has thirty-six volumes identified as Records in the British Public Record Office Relating to South Carolina. They are transcripts covering the period from 1663 to 1782 made under the direction of W. Noel Sainsbury in the late nineteenth century. Vols. 19 through 27 cover the period of Glen's appointment from 1738 to 1756 and include many of the documents from Class 5 of the Colonial Office Papers. Microfilm of these is available.

Indispensable for this study are the legislative and administrative journals of South Carolina. The originals of the journals for the Commons House of the Assembly are in the Department of Archives and History, but fortunately for the period of Glen's tenure, all have been published under the superb editing by J. H. Easterby et al. in Series I of *The Colonial Records of South Carolina*. I have researched the unpublished journals of the Council and the Upper House of the Assembly in the Department of Archives and History and have also had access to the microfilm of these manuscripts identified in William Sumner Jenkins, *A Guide to the Microfilm Collection of Early State Records* (Washington, D.C., 1950).

Other manuscript collections here and abroad have material relating to Glen. The British Museum has the extensive account of the Choctaw revolt by Edmond Atkin entitled the "Historical Account of the Revolt of the Chactaw Indians in the Late War from the French to the British Alliance and of Their Return Since to That of the French," January 20, 1753, in the Lansdowne Manuscripts, vol. 809, ff. 1-32. The William L. Clements Library in Ann Arbor, Michigan, includes Glen correspondence in the George Clinton Papers, the Shelburne Papers, and the records of Brigadier General John Forbes. The William Henry Lyttelton Papers, 1751-1760, also in the Clements, contain numerous references to Glen, often self-serving in criticism of him, as Lyttelton succeeded to the governorship.

OTHER PRIMARY SOURCES

Imperial printed records of value for this study include the *Acts of the Privy*

Council of England, Colonial Series, 6 vols., edited by W. L. Grant, James Munro, and A. W. Fitzroy (London, 1908-1912); *Journals of the Commissioners for Trade and Plantations preserved in the Public Record Office, 1704-1775,* 13 vols. (London, 1920-1937); *Calendar of State Papers, Colonial Series, America and West Indies, 1574—,* edited by W. Noel Sainsbury et al. (London, 1860—); *Calendar of Treasury Books and Papers, 1729-1745,* edited by William A. Shaw, 5 vols. (London, 1897-1903); *The Manuscripts of the Marquess Townshend,* Historical Manuscripts Commission, Eleventh Report (London, 1887); *Manuscripts of the Earl of Egmont: Diary of Viscount Percival, Afterwards First Earl of Egmont, 1730-1747,* Historical Manuscripts Commission, Sixteenth Report, 3 vols. (London, 1920-1923); *The Journal of the Earl of Egmont, 1732-1738,* edited by Robert G. McPherson (Athens, Ga., 1962); and *Royal Instructions to British Colonial Governors, 1670-1776,* edited by Leonard W. Labaree, 2 vols. (New York and London, 1935).

Printed documents for South Carolina include Glen's own *Description of South Carolina* in Chapman J. Milling, ed., *Colonial South Carolina: Two Contemporary Descriptions* (Columbia, S.C., 1951); *The Statutes at Large of South Carolina,* edited by Thomas Cooper and David J. McCord, 10 vols. (Columbia, S.C., 1836-1841); *Records of the Court of Chancery of South Carolina, 1671-1779,* edited by Anne King Gregorie, vol. 6 of *American Legal Records* (Washington, D.C., 1950); *Documents relating to Indian Affairs, May 21, 1750-August 7, 1754* and *Documents relating to Indian Affairs, 1754-1765, The Colonial Records of South Carolina,* edited by Willam L. McDowell, Jr. (Columbia, S.C., 1958, 1970); and *Writings of General John Forbes Relating to His Service in North America,* edited by Alfred P. James (Menasha, Wis., 1938).

SCOTLAND

For the history of Scotland during the time of Glen, one may consult William Ferguson, *Scotland: 1689 to the Present,* vol. 4 of *The Edinburgh History of Scotland* (Edinburgh, 1968); Rosalind Mitchison, *A History of Scotland* (London, 1970); Alexander Murdoch, *'The People Above': Politics and Administration in Mid-Eighteenth-Century Scotland* (Edinburgh, 1980); John M. Simpson, "Who Steered the Gravy Train, 1707-1766?" in N. T. Phillipson and Rosalind Mitchison, eds., *Scotland in the Age of Improvement* (Edinburgh, 1970); Richard M. Scott, "The Politics and Administration of Scotland, 1725-1748," Ph.D. diss., University of Edinburgh, 1982; and Margaret S. Bricke, "Administration and Management of Scotland, 1707-1765," Ph.D. diss. University of Kansas, 1972. Information about Linlithgow and the royal palace is in John Ferguson, *Linlithgow Palace: Its History and Traditions* (Edinburgh and London, 1910); George Waldie, *A History of the Town and Palace of Linlithgow,* 3rd ed. (Linlithgow, 1879); and Mark N. Powell, *Linlithgow: A Brief Architectural and Historical Guide* (Linlithgow, 1974).

BRITISH IMPERIAL STUDIES

There are many publications on British imperial administration and the role of the Board of Trade in the eighteenth century. One of the most valuable is James A. Henretta's *"Salutary Neglect": Colonial Administration under the Duke of Newcastle* (Princeton, N.J., 1972). Also helpful is Leonard W. Labaree's *Royal Government in America: A Study of the British Colonial System before 1783* (New Haven, Conn., 1930). South Carolina is one of the five colonies examined by Marc Egnal in *A Mighty Empire: The Origins of the American Revolution* (Ithaca, N.Y., and London, 1988). Still valuable is the study by Charles M. Andrews of *England's Commercial and Colonial Policy* as vol. 4 of *The Colonial Period of American History* (New Haven, Conn., 1938). Older studies of the Board of Trade worth examining include Arthur Herbert Basye, *The Lords Commissioners of Trade and Plantations: Commonly Known as the Board of Trade, 1748-1782* (New Haven, Conn., 1925) and Oliver M. Dickerson, *American Colonial Government, 1696-1765* (Cleveland, 1912). Colonial agents are evaluated in Ella Lonn, *The Colonial Agents of the Southern Colonies* (Chapel Hill, N.C., 1945) and Michael G. Kammen, *A Rope of Sand: The Colonial Agents, British Politics, and the American Revolution* (Ithaca, N.Y., 1968).

COLONIAL SOUTH CAROLINA

The most valuable recent secondary studies of South Carolina during Glen's administration include M. Eugene Sirmans, *Colonial South Carolina: A Political History 1663-1763* (Chapel Hill, N.C., 1966) which is comprehensive with extensive research but careless in examination of Glen's correspondence; Jack P. Greene, *The Quest for Power: The Lower Houses of Assembly in the Southern Royal Colonies, 1689-1776* (Chapel Hill, N.C., 1963), which depicts clearly the rise of the Commons House of the Assembly and is excellent in providing a historical perspective of major issues; and Robert M. Weir, *Colonial South Carolina: A History* (Millwood, N.Y., 1983), well researched and judicious in analysis. Still very useful and reliable for the mid-eighteenth century are the studies of David Duncan Wallace with 4 vols. of *The History of South Carolina* (New York, 1934-1935) and an excellent condensed version in *South Carolina: A Short History 1520-1948* (Chapel Hill, N.C., 1951); and the more specialized volume of Robert L. Meriwether, *The Expansion of South Carolina, 1729-1765* (Kingsport, Tenn., 1940). Less useful but still worth examining are Edward McCrady, *The History of South Carolina under Royal Government, 1719-1776* (New York, 1899) and William Roy Smith, *South Carolina as a Royal Province, 1719-1776* (New York, 1903).

Other secondary sources of special note include a variety of published and unpublished accounts. M. Eugene Sirmans has a valuable analysis of Council members in "The South Carolina Royal Council, 1720-1763," in *William and Mary Quarterly*, 3rd ed., 18 (1961), 371-91. Richard Waterhouse adds analyses of social structure in "South Carolina's Colonial Elite: A Study in the Social Structure and Political Culture of a Southern Colony, 1670-1760," Ph.D. diss., Johns Hopkins University, 1973 and University Microfilms International (Ann Arbor, Mich., 1989) and his "The Responsible Gentry of Colonial South Carolina: A Study in Local Government, 1670-1770" in Bruce D. Daniels, ed., *Town and Country: Essays on the Structure of Local Government in the American Colonies* (Middletown, Conn., 1978), 160-85. George C. Rogers, Jr., contributes an excellent account of *Charleston in the Age of the Pinckneys* (Norman, Okla., 1969).   Robert M. Weir adds his interpretation of "The Harmony We Were Famous For" in *William and Mary Quarterly*, 3rd ed., 26 (1969), 473-501. Mary F. Carter has the most extensive previous account of the governor in "Governor James Glen of Colonial South Carolina: A Study in British Administrative Policies," Ph.D. diss., University of California, Los Angeles, 1951. Sympathetic to Glen, it includes no information on his Scottish and English experiences and is incomplete in examining the various facets of his career as governor. Other information on the Glen family is available in Joseph G. B. Bulloch, *A History of the Glen Family of South Carolina and Georgia* (Washington, D.C., 1923) and Charles Rogers, *Memorials of the Scottish Family of Glen* (Edinburgh, 1888). Dorothy G. Griffin provides a description of Glen's nephews and the Drayton family in "The Eighteenth Century Draytons of Drayton Hall," Ph.D. diss., Emory University, 1985.   Clarence J. Attig's "William Henry Lyttelton: A Study in Colonial Administration," Ph.D. diss., University of Nebraska, 1958, lacks sufficient critical analysis of Lyttelton's role as governor.   Convenient identifications of political leaders may be found in Walter B. Edgar, ed., *Biographical Directory of the South Carolina House of Representatives*, 2 vols. (Columbia, S.C., 1974-1977).

THE FRONTIER AND INDIAN AFFAIRS

Glen devoted major attention to the frontier and Indian affairs. For an overall view, consult John Richard Alden, *John Stuart and the Southern Colonial Frontier: A Study of Indian Relations, War, Trade, and Land Problems in the Southern Wilderness, 1754-1775* (Ann Arbor, Mich., 1944) and W. Stitt Robinson, *The Southern Colonial Frontier, 1607-1763* (Albuquerque, N.M., 1979). Lawrence H. Gipson presents an imperial view sympathetic to the English in his massive 14 volumes of *The British Empire Before the American Revolution*. Most relevant for this study are vol. 2, *The Southern Plantations* (Caldwell, Idaho, 1936); vol. 4, *Zones of International Frictions: North America, South of The Great Lakes Region* (New York, 1939); and vol. 6, *The Great War for the Empire: The Years of Defeat, 1754-1757* (New York, 1946). The French dimension of the international struggle may be followed in W. J. Eccles, *France in America* (New York, 1972) and Patricia D. Woods, *French-Indian Relations on the Southern Frontier, 1699-1762* (Ann Arbor, Mich., 1980). Spain's role may be examined in J. Leitch Wright, Jr., *Anglo-Spanish Rivalry in North America* (Athens, Ga., 1971). Douglas E. Leach covers the military story in *Arms for Empire: A Military History of the British Colonies in North America, 1607-1763* (New York, 1973).

Valuable descriptions of southern Indians include John R. Swanton, *The Indians of the Southeastern United States*, Bureau of American Ethnology, Bulletin 137 (Washington, D.C., 1946) and *Early History of the Creek Indians and their Neighbors*, Bureau of American Ethnology, Bulletin 73 (Washington, D.C., 1922); David H. Corkran, *The Cherokee Frontier: Conflict and Survival, 1740-62* (Norman, Okla., 1962) and *The Creek Frontier, 1540-1783* (Norman, Okla., 1967); John P. Reid, *A Law of Blood: The Primitive Law of the Cherokee Nation* (New York, 1970) and *A Better Kind of Hatchet: Law, Trade, and Diplomacy in the Cherokee Nation during the Early Years of European Contact* (University Park, Pa., 1965); James Axtell, *The Indian Peoples of Eastern America* (New York, 1981); Theda Perdue, *Slavery and the Evolution of Cherokee Society, 1540-1866* (Knoxville, Tenn., 1979) and "Cherokee Relations with the Iroquois in the Eighteenth Century" in Daniel K. Richter and James H. Merrell, eds., *Beyond the Covenant Chain: The Iroquois and Their Neighbors in Indian North America, 1600-1800* (Syracuse, N.Y., 1987), 135-49; Charles Hudson, *The Southeastern Indians* (Knoxville, Tenn., 1976) and *The Catawba Nation*, University of Georgia Monographs, no. 18 (Athens, Ga., 1970); James H. Merrell, *The Indians' New World: Catawbas and Their Neighbors from European Contact Through the Era of Removal* (Chapel Hill, N.C., 1989) and "'Their Very Bones Shall Fight': The Catawba-Iroquois Wars" in Richter and Merrell, eds., *Beyond the Covenant Chain*, 115-33; Gary B. Nash, *Red, White,and Black: The Peoples of Early North America*, 3rd ed. (Englewood Cliffs, N.J., 1992); and Peter H. Wood, Gregory A Waselkov, and M. Thomas Hatley, eds., *Powhatan's Mantle: Indians in the Colonial Southeast* (Lincoln and London, 1989), including Wood's essay on "The Changing Population of the Colonial South: An Overview by Race and Region, 1685-1790," 35-103. For a recent comparative study of the mutual history of the Cherokees and South Carolinians, see Tom Hatley, *The Dividing Paths: Cherokees and South Carolinians Through the Era of Revolution* (New York and Oxford, 1993).

The controversial Choctaw revolt may be followed in a variety of sources. Two contemporary accounts include manuscripts of Edmond Atkin's "Historical Account of the Revolt of the Chactaw Nation. . . ." previously identified in the British Museum and James Glen's speech to "Honble Gentlemen & Gentlemen" of the Assembly, c. 1750, Glen Papers, Caroliniana. James Adair's *The History of the American Indians* (London, 1775) presents his side of the story with criticism of Governor Glen for excluding him from the Choctaw trade. The most extensive secondary account is by Charles William Paape, "The Choctaw Revolt: A Chapter in the Intercolonial Rivalry in the Old Southwest," Ph.D. diss., University of Illinois, Urbana-Champaign, 1946. Michael James Foret also has a chapter on the Choctaw revolt in "On the Marchlands of Empire: Trade, Diplomacy, and War on the Southeastern Frontier, 1733-1763," Ph.D.

diss., College of William and Mary, 1990 and Univerity Microfilms International (Ann Arbor, Mich., 1992), 170-208. Excellent accounts of the conflicts within Choctaw society are in Patricia K. Galloway, "Choctaw Factionalism and Civil War, 1746-1750" in Carolyn Keller Reeves, ed., *The Choctaw before Removal* (Jackson, Miss., 1980); Angie Debo, *The Rise and Fall of the Choctaw Republic* (Norman, Okla., 1934); and Jesse O. McKee and Jon A. Schlenker, *The Choctaws: Cultural Evolution of a Native American Tribe* (Jackson, Miss., 1980). The role of the French in the conflict may be followed in *Mississippi Provincial Archives, French Dominion, 1729-1763*, edited by Dunbar Rowland, A. G. Sanders, and Patricia Kay Galloway, vols. 4 and 5 (Baton Rouge La., and London, 1984).

NEWSPAPERS

The record of the press is important for this study. *The South-Carolina Gazette* (Charles Town, S.C., 1732-1776) printed many of the governor's speeches and proclamations and is most valuable for the accounts relating to the contest for power among the governor, Council, Upper House, and Commons House. Hennig Cohen provides a history of the paper in *The South Carolina Gazette, 1732-1775* (Columbia, S.C., 1953). *The Virginia Gazette* (Williamsburg, Va., 1736-1780) has commentaries on the conflict with South Carolina over Indian diplomacy and the Indian trade.

NEIGHBORING COLONIES

The following records from neighboring colonies provide information on intercolonial relations with South Carolina: William L. Saunders, ed., *The Colonial Records of North Carolina*, 10 vols. (Raleigh, N.C., 1886-1890); Allen D. Candler et al., eds., *The Colonial Records of the State of Georgia* (1904—); H. R. McIlwaine et al., eds. *Executive Journals of the Council of Colonial Virginia*, 6 vols. (Richmond, Va., 1925-1966); E. B. O'Callaghan and B. Fernow, eds., *Documents Relative to the Colonial History of New York*, 15 vols. (Albany, N.Y., 1856-1887); and R. A. Brock, ed., *The Official Records of Robert Dinwiddie, Lieutenant-Governor of the Colony of Virginia, 1751-1758*, 2 vols., Collections of the Virginia Historical Society, vols. 3-4, New Series (Richmond, Va., 1883-84). Two helpful secondary studies for North Carolina include the biography by Desmond Clarke of *Arthur Dobbs Esquire, 1689-1765: Surveyor-General of Ireland, Prospector, and Governor of North Carolina* (Chapel Hill, N.C., 1957) and Marvin Lucian Skaggs, *North Carolina Boundary Disputes Involving Her Southern Line, The James Sprunt Studies in History and Political Science*, vol. 25, no. 1 (Chapel Hill, N.C., 1941).

Index

About the Author

W. STITT ROBINSON is professor emeritus of history at the University of Kansas. He has received research grants from the Social Science Research Council, American Philosophical Society, National Endowment for the Humanities, and he was a Fellow at the Institute for Advanced Studies in the Humanities at the University of Edinburgh, Scotland. He is the author of *The Southern Colonial Frontier, 1607–1763* in Histories of the American Frontier series (1979). He is the editor of three volumes of Indian treaties in Early American Indian Documents: Treaties and Laws: volume 4, *Virginia Treaties, 1607–1722*, volume 5, *Virginia Treaties, 1723–1775* (1983), and volume 6, *Maryland Treaties, 1632–1775* (1987).

ISBN 0-313-29760-6

9 780313 297601

90000>

EAN

HARDCOVER BAR CODE